PROPHETS OF A NEW AGE

Also by Martin Green

THE MOUNT VERNON STREET WARRENS

NEW YORK 1913

THE TRIUMPH OF PIERROT

CHILDREN OF THE SUN

THE VON RICHTHOFEN SISTERS

TOLSTOY AND GANDHI

PROPHETS
· · · · · · · · · OF · A · · · · · · · · ·
NEW AGE

THE POLITICS OF HOPE FROM THE EIGHTEENTH
THROUGH THE TWENTY-FIRST CENTURIES

■

Martin
Green

CHARLES SCRIBNER'S SONS
New York
MAXWELL MACMILLAN CANADA
Toronto
MAXWELL MACMILLAN INTERNATIONAL
New York • Oxford • Singapore • Sydney

Charles Scribner's Sons   Maxwell Macmillan Canada, Inc.
Macmillan Publishing Company   1200 Eglinton Avenue East
866 Third Avenue   Suite 200
New York, NY 10022   Don Mills, Ontario M3C 3N1

Macmillan Publishing Company is part of the Maxwell Communication Group
of Companies.

Permission acknowledgments appear on page 307.

Library of Congress Cataloging-in-Publication Data
Green, Martin Burgess, 1927–
    Prophets of a new age: the politics of hope from the eighteenth through
the twenty-first centuries / Martin Green.
        p.   cm.
    Includes bibliographical references and index.
    ISBN 0-684-19316-7
    1. New Age movement. 2. Prophecies. 3. Hope. I. Title.
BP605.N48G72   1992
303.49'09—dc20   91-36144
                                                            CIP

Macmillan books are available at special discounts for bulk purchases for sales
promotions, premiums, fund-raising, or educational use. For details, contact:

                    Special Sales Director
                    Macmillan Publishing Company
                    866 Third Avenue
                    New York, NY 10022

10 9 8 7 6 5 4 3 2 1

Printed in the United States of America

To all those who keep the spirit of the New Age alive in the long marches of conformity—at least, to all those who do so without getting silly about it, or sinister.

It is a sign of the times that so many of us should be busy in studying the signs of the times. In no other age since the birth of Christianity has there been manifested the same devouring curiosity about the future, and the same disposition to expect a new earth, if not a new heaven.

A writer in the English
journal *The New Age,* 1911

It was the best of times, it was the worst of times, it was the age of wisdom, it was the age of foolishness, it was the epoch of belief, it was the epoch of incredulity, it was the season of Light, it was the season of Darkness, it was the spring of hope, it was the winter of despair, we had everything before us, we had nothing before us, we were all going direct to Heaven, we were all going direct the other way . . .

The eighteenth-century
New Age, evoked by Charles
Dickens, at the beginning of
A Tale of Two Cities

Contents

PROPHETS OF A NEW AGE

A Declaration of
Provenance and Purpose

Although I strike a quasi-prophetic pose in writing this book, I know no better than anyone else what will happen at the turn of the century and the turn of the millennium. But I can show some striking similarities between our New Agers and their predecessors, between our situation in the 1990s and theirs in 1890 and 1790—defining the New Age type each time as people who see radical degeneration going on around them, but also see the possibility of a radically new life for anyone courageous enough to embrace it.

Moreover, I can show that the 1890s was a crucial decade for the century that followed and that the 1790s was a crucial decade for the nineteenth century. Each century looks back to a New Age as its moral dowry and inheritance. No matter how whimsical or comical that New Age may seem in retrospect, it contains society's store of hope, even after the hope has been defeated as a practical proposition.

How many people today are living on their memories of the 1960s' days of hope! (Even those who revile the sixties still find the topic absorbing.) Some sociologists are saying that it is since 1960 that in advanced industrial societies the post-materialists—those who live by a version of New Age ideas—have grown to be a significant element. My starting point resembles that of those sociologists, though the course of my inquiry is quite different.

If the New Age efforts of the 1790s and the 1890s constituted a source of moral energy transmitted to the nineteenth and the twentieth centuries, then for our twenty-first century, our millennium, we have a need to build a New Age at least as strong as theirs. So a look at historical parallels may help us.

I shall also be declaring my sense of where, within our own New Age, we could profitably invest our energies—in whom we should invest our hope. There are in fact heroes and prophets among us, and even if the current venture in civilization cannot be saved, we can go out in style and in the best of company, if we choose. There is as much courage today, as much wit and will power, as much scope of mind and heart, as ever was to be found in the cultural treasury.

Finally, in thinking about this topic, I found myself distinguishing between three kinds of mind, or temperament, which jointly define my own position. One mind moves always toward power and possession—deals in the lust for gold and blood and guts and grit, to use adventure language: there are politer power-language terms, like "a hundred thousand a year plus expenses" or "briefing the Chiefs of Staff" or "smashing the opposition into a pulp." This is the voice of triumph and authority. We heard that language during the Gulf War (it is always heard in wartime) spoken by, for instance, General Schwartzkopf.

It was always clear to me that I belonged to a different type, with a different voice, whose social refuge is academia (in Christendom's past it was the Church). The mental temperament that flourishes there I call systematic. As far back as one looks there have been educators, priests, or shamans, preserving moral tradition, discriminating between legends, invoking values—systematizing the images and the concepts. They constitute a kind of mind alternative to the authoritarian.

People of this second type find their way to that corner of the field which we call academia, or the clerisy, or the law, if they are lucky. There they mount their constant Cold War against the men of power, and win small battles in the minds of the young. But we (the men of law) wouldn't want to be too much at ease in Zion, too sure that the enemy are lost souls, for they have their own kind of virtue, and our self-complacency needs their challenge.

On another frontier, we meet a different moral challenge from a third type, the naïve and enthusiastic mind that comes to expression in New Ages. People of this type (and we are all of this type part of the time) have a different sense of limits, and try things the others wouldn't dare. They affirm absolutes and realize ideals.

Those of us who belong to the second type must always measure ourselves against both the others, and seek out their virtue, to avoid a stupid pride in difference. Writers of books often belong to the second type. But then, so do most readers of books.

Culture as a whole, and each of us individually, is composed of elements of all three types. We discover this when we meet someone who goes further than we do in our own direction; for then we recoil in dismay, and begin to talk in a voice that is "not our own." Meeting greater enthusiasts for New Age values than themselves, New Agers begin to sound cynical or rationalist; meeting a sterner specimen of their own type, authoritarians begin to assert their right to hope and their need to reason things out.

What can such a book as this hope to do? It attempts to modulate culture's concert of voices by amplifying the New Age voice, which, though quite loud in the event, is feeble in the record, because most historians, being of the second type, diminish it. I remember a conference at Harvard about the run-up to 1914, at which I spoke on the New Agers of Ascona, where afterwards a speaker remarked on the wide range of papers, from someone's very serious topic to my "Loony Tunes characters." This was not an insult to me, and as an insult to my subject it was quite harmless, but as an exclusion from, and a diminishment of, history, it struck me as something I wanted to protest.

I shall of course be asking my readers to adjust their criteria of what they can take seriously, which means to alter their list of the ideas that can be met in the spirit in which they are offered, and the persons who can be met on something like their own terms. A number of the characters I evoke have been denied that status up to now, and so are unknown names. I hope by re-presenting them to draw a somewhat new picture of past and present.

But I shall not be asking you to espouse occult truths or pure idealism or to give up reductive common sense. For instance, the voice I shall recommend as the truest expression of our own New Age is very commonsensical; it employs a Will Rogers drawl to prescribe the values America should cultivate in a better future: "Rational long-view self-interest wouldn't be half bad" (Gary Snyder, "Exhortations for Baby Tigers," Reed College Commencement, May 19, 1991). This New Age is as realistic, in its own way, as the world of power politics and the world of social science.

Invitation to a New Age

> . . . at the end of the century
> Which woke up as if from a heavy slumber
>
> And asked, in stupefaction: "What was that?
> How could we? A conjunction of planets?
> Or spots on the sun?"
>   . . . For History
> Is no more comprehensible. Our species
> Is not ruled by any reasonable law.
> The boundaries of its nature are unknown.
> It is not the same as I, you, a single human.
>
> Czeslaw Milosz, "At Yale" (1990)

It may be hard to say where Milosz draws the line between the comprehensible and the incomprehensible parts of history, but it is easy enough to surmise *some* of the events that have recently provoked his stupefaction. That is easy because most of us had the same reaction. One main group of those events we associate with the name of Mikhail Gorbachev: the end of the Cold War; the invocation of glasnost; the dismantling of the Communist Party in Russia; the change in the regimes of Eastern Europe; the destruction of the Berlin Wall; the reunification of Germany in October 1990; and the election of a playwright-liberal as the president of Czechoslovakia, who professed the "politics of truth and nonviolence"—Gandhi's New Age politics.

Another poet, Gary Snyder, in his commencement address at Reed College in 1991, told his audience that this is a pivotal time in history because of two outstanding challenges, brought by the end of the Cold War and the end of nature. (By the latter he meant of course the end of our traditional way of looking at nature.) It is the first of the two challenges that is more relevant here. For now, Snyder said, capitalism seems to have won the joust with communism, and there is but one superpower on earth, the United States. Naturally, such a suggestion is not a complacent one; it carries a heavy charge of irony and anxiety, not of triumph. Snyder adds, "It is my own crankiness to believe that there is still hope." But that is still a proposition of hope.

The results of these political changes have been manifold as well as profound, and have spread across the world. To take the most striking single case, the regime in South Africa has made concessions to the African National Congress, and allowed Nelson Mandela to act as a political leader, in a way that looked unthinkable until it happened. This change, commentators suggest, has occurred at least partly because of the disappearance of "the Communist threat"; with the changes in Russia and elsewhere, the persuasiveness of maintaining the rigid defensive posture in South Africa was lost. By the same token, the size of the American army, and the budget of the Pentagon, could be reduced.

These events differ in kind, and people have different individual responses to them, but we can put them all together, and ourselves all together, and say like Milosz that "we" are "stupefied" by them. Why that verb in particular? Because they happened so quickly and easily; events that we only dreamed of, or, when we more rationally projected the future, saw as taking decades, moving step by step, and costing treasures of blood and heroism as well as immense efforts of negotiation and propaganda, were changes that in fact followed on each other lightly.

So we could not but feel that they might have happened earlier, during that time when it seemed so clear that they could not happen. Our sense of the possible had been mistaken, our sense of reality had been much too solid, too immovable a wall. We needed and need, it seems, to *hope* much more than we have been doing—or, if that seems too pious a phrase, to redirect our native cynicism against our realistic rather than our idealistic assumptions.

(To make every effort to be clear, here and in what follows, let me stipulate: what constitutes realistic thinking, for anyone, is a function of his/her sense of the real, of "the way things go, despite what we wish"; it is therefore a subjective sense which we can also call "a realism," because it is likely to differ from one person to another.)

That this experience has been disconcerting as well as exhilarating—that we had grown attached to our old sense of reality—was shown by the jocular dismay many of us affected at seeing, when the great change came in Central Europe, the East Germans flooding across the old borders into the West, heading for the famous Berlin stores, to join us in our seven-days-a-week carnival of shopping, our continuous High Mass of consumerism; as if what had held them back before had been nothing more substantial, morally, than brute force. We were dismayed because we wanted to believe that they had—to some degree—acknowledged the value of the Socialist virtuousness forced on them, the drab virtue of asceticism so unlike the life-style of capitalist Germany. We are many of us, after all, uneasy about the capitalist *dolce vita;* we want *someone* to prefer other values. The East Germans had been ascetic on our behalf, we realized—their virtue had been a valued part of *our* world.

This also means that it was part of our sense of reality that good things come into the world only at the price of bad ones—virtue arrives when entailed by tyranny. Now we have to doubt that premise, to think that virtue may be the result of desire and effort. We have to become more naïve. That is not altogether welcome news.

And our sense of reality affects all kinds of things, many of them remote from politics. It controls our sense of the probable and plausible, in novels or nonfiction. It controls our sense of why *we* do what we do, our sense of a good argument, our sense of history, and our sense of a moral action. What should be done, in any situation, is obviously a function of what can be done.

In a moment I will distinguish more fully between the three sorts of mind or temperament: the authoritarian, the systematic, and the naïve. For the time being let me just say that what is realism to the authoritarian mind is black pessimism to the New Ager, and vice versa; what is realism to the New Ager is rose-colored optimism to the other. That is what those words *optimism* and *pessimism* mean. Again, what is realism to the New Ager is hopeless naïveté to the systematic mind, and vice versa; what is realism to the latter is bloodless abstraction to the New Ager. Each person's mind is composed of all three, but the proportions differ between individuals, and also between decades; that is how we come to have New Ages.

Of course there is plenty going on in the world today that confirms our old (pre–New Age) sense of reality: things going on inside Gorbachev's Russia, in South Africa, in the Middle East. But given my focus, the important fact is that some actual events have occurred that challenge the hegemony of the old truths. This suggests that other such events might happen, and thus emits a call to a more energetic, optimistic, idealistic realism.

That sense of the real is part of the mental equipment of most of us most of the time, but in unfavorable epochs, of repression or depression, the exercise of that sense is restricted to fantasy, to idyllic art, or to purely personal relationships. At other times, however, it becomes powerful and enters even political consciousness and inspires political action. Such times are New Ages, which their protagonists sometimes describe in religious terms, such as "spiritual ferment," or "the leaven of the spirit."

We are now being invited to enter such a time of hope, a New Age. But saying this, we should be careful to ask what the term means. "New Age" is too easily associated with cartoon figures, which represent it rather ludicrously. In Gandhi's autobiography he tells us about the "enterprising" lady proprietor of a New Age vegetarian restaurant in Johannesburg, where he met his Nature Cure and Theosophist friends. She was "fond of art and extravagant and ignorant of accounts." Gandhi lent her money that she failed to return, and this got him into trouble, but that need not concern us here. What is to my point is that Gandhi's dry sentence evokes a person lots of us would call "typically New Age." But in fact Gandhi himself (keen on accounts and unenthusiastic about art) was just as much a New Age type, and a much better representative of its strengths.

Today we think first perhaps of candles, crystals, incense, and Tarot cards; or Shirley MacLaine's seminars; or the music labeled New Age; or the current journal with that title. But for me all those are caricatures of the real thing. So what is that real thing, for us today and tomorrow? We must look back into history, to the recurrent phenomena of New Ages, to find guidelines.

A GENERAL THEORY OF NEW AGES

These phenomena often occur at the end of a century—though by no means only then. But those symbolic centenary dates induce an added self-consciousness, first of all in journalists, publicists, and activists, who chant the numbers to charm our attention, and then induce a general questioning of the state of things, a questioning that can interact with other historical stimuli and push into consciousness and even activity the idea that at other times will languish in vagueness. There is good reason to guess that something like that will happen in the 1990s, when not just a century, but a millennium, comes to an end.

William M. Johnston's recent book *Celebrations* studying the cult of anniversaries of events, or of the births and deaths of the great, predicts that the approaching celebrations will be feverish and all-inclusive. But his book is a study of the contrasts and combinations made possible by our plethora of anniversaries, shuffling and redealing the high-culture pack of cards: composers, painters, philosophers, poets. Indeed, Johnston even sees the cult of celebrations as expressing a post-modernist withdrawal from history, since this cult is a nonserious way of remembering the past. The New Age sense of history and culture is more moral and urgent—closer to one kind of religion.

However, there are several kinds of religion; evangelical Christianity, for instance, shows itself in a non–New Age—an apocalyptic—relation to the future. Usually, the apocalypse mind is the opposite of the New Age mind, and expresses the authoritarian sense of crisis. The approach of the year 2000 has sent the sales of apocalypse and prophecy books soaring, according to a recent newspaper article. *The Late Great Planet Earth*, a book of the 1970s with ten million copies in print, doubled its sales between July and November 1990. Sales of the Bible and books about occultist prophets, such as Nostradamus, have increased. Televangelists like Billy Graham, Pat Robertson, and Jack Van Impe have spoken of the war in the Persian Gulf as Armageddon.

People like me tend to dismiss all this as only one step away from the cult of Elvis. "To be sure," Steven Stark says in an article in *The Boston Globe*, "the religious movements that spawn these ideas are virtually invisible to East Coast intellectuals." The systematic mind gives the authoritarian short shrift. But, Stark says, it is estimated that one-third of all Americans live partly in a world of biblical prophecy. Such a number does not make them right, but it does make them important.

Those are two current responses to the approach of the year 2000, the evangelical and the post-modern. The New Age idea of history is very different from both, while reacting to the same stimuli. We must understand the New Age precisely as an alternative and voluntary response to our current situation—even though some of the other options, the less optimistic ones, will offer themselves as inevitable.

Despair, for instance, presents itself as involuntary. The Pompidou Center in Paris has an electric sign-clock, set up in 1987, which continually flashes the number of seconds left in the twentieth century. Elaine Showalter says that whatever its intention, this "Genitron" works as black humor, making everyone at best very uncomfortable, because a terminal decade always suggests a civilization's terminal moments. She looks back to the end of the last century, and quotes from Max Nordau's *Degeneration* (1892), a book of an earlier New Age, which spoke of the *Götterdämmerung* of the nineteenth century "in which all suns and all stars are gradually waning, and mankind with all its institutions and creations is perishing in the midst of a dying world."

Showalter's focus, as she moves to and fro between the last century's end and our own, is on the "sexual anarchy" that accompanies the mood of despair or crisis. That phrase, which she makes into the title of her book, is one that George Gissing used about the 1880s and 1890s. Gissing and Nordau looked at the *fin de siècle* phenomena around them without either faith or hope. It was not a New Age for them.

We have our own mood equivalent for that despair. Susan Sontag calls it "Apocalypse from Now On"; and other phrases recently devised for our sense of our age are "Endism" and "End Time." However, that mood is not singly and simply ours. We have alternatives.

My focus will be almost opposite, since it will be on *hope*, which is as natural to such periods as despair. From that same period at the end of the last century, I will examine a loosely organized movement of thought with an energetic, optimistic, "naïve" sense of reality, which was often at the time called the New Age. People found that they and/or their friends had suddenly acquired *hope*, meaning that— besides complaining about and analyzing what was wrong—they could, one at a time or in a small group, simply start living differently, and the prison walls would crumble, the cannon would melt, unjust laws would change, and so on. They did not actually stick flowers into the gun muzzles of the soldiers confronting them—that supremely evocative image awaited the coming of the 1960s—but probably they would have enthusiastically recognized that gesture as like their own.

NEW AGE REALISM

Today we probably associate "New Age" with 1960s outdoor concerts, like Woodstock and Altamont, the political activities of Abbie Hoffman and Jerry Rubin, drugs and flower children. Of really contemporary phenomena, we associate it with occultism and the scientistic optimism of the Aquarian Conspiracy, to borrow Marilyn Ferguson's phrase.

With those associations, an almost infinite perspective is already opening up before us, along with phrases that blur into "New Age" like "counterculture" and "the sixties" and "Californian." To make a single pattern out of all those—that way madness lies. I shall attempt to introduce some order into this multiplicity by first using the phrase as it was used in relation to the 1880–1910 period. So I shall describe that New Age (in the next chapter) and then the one at the end of the eighteenth century, before applying the term to the twentieth century.

This tactic involves us in some discrepancies because the term was applied rather differently in the various cases—for instance, at the end of the nineteenth century the focus was not so much on mass phenomena and media events as it was later; it was more on book-described ideas, and on individuals and small groups. However, my tactic has the advantage of bringing out, in the later period, features that we can "take seriously"—phenomena that we can meet in the spirit in which they offer themselves. Above all, the alignment of the three periods, as New Ages, is very suggestive from a historical point of view.

First of all, I must situate New Agers among other kinds of radicals. All New Ages, including the nineteenth-century one, are times of radicalism, and so in their attitude to the status quo are cynical and angry. They are motivated by passionate dissatisfaction, and aim at enormous changes. Thus they have much in common with left- and right-wing radicalism or revolutionism. ("New Age" means a period when all kinds of radicals are active, though it also means New Age radicals as distinct from other kinds—words do have that annoying way of confusing issues.) New Ages are then charged with indignation, and some of their members are ready to employ violence. Even the cause of ecology today, preeminently a New Age issue, has had its exponent of violence, in Edward Abbey. For if their solutions tend toward the gentle, the lyrical, or the sacrificial, the New Agers' problems are the same as those of violent revolutionaries.

Thus, though I have described New Age realism in terms of hope, optimism, and naïveté, of course any strong or clear mind grows by acquiring other, sometimes opposite qualities—without necessarily sacrificing its original character. New Agers do not live in a fools' paradise. I will quote a sentence from Ursula K. Le Guin, one of the New Age voices of our own time, here discussing her own early fiction, and calling its New Age character romantic: "I am still a romantic, no doubt about that, and glad of it, but the candor and simplicity of [Le Guin's early work] has gradually become something harder, stronger, and more complex." Thus one can remain naïve even while absorbing some opposite, "sophisticated" wisdom. The hopeful New Ager has more in common with the angry revolutionary than with ordinary people.

Among the dramatic political events of the nineteenth-century New Age movement we can list the attacks by terrorists or anarchists on heads of state (King Umberto of Italy and President McKinley) and heads of huge commercial corporations; the Boer War; and the 1905 Revolution in Russia. All of these were forms of violent political action. All of them failed; the revolutionaries in Russia, the anti-imperialists in South Africa, and the various terrorist groups were defeated and punished. But these events were still felt to be signs of the breakup of immense immobilities (empires) that had seemed eternal—those sharp reports that announce the melting of icebergs in the spring. The election of the Liberal Party to power in 1906, with a large majority, including a lot of members new to the House of Commons, was a promise of change within the British Empire that corresponded to Gorbachev's promise of change in Russia today.

Exactly what period in the twentieth century are we comparing to that nineteenth-century New Age? To fix the exact chronological limits of any historical period is something of a convention, a formal or aesthetic device. Moreover, New Age phenomena occur in all periods; we use the phrase only when they are unusually concentrated; and certainly what happens soon before or soon after the dates I give may be just as relevant to my argument as what happens within them. Nevertheless, it is worth trying to be clear-cut within the limits of possibility, to save us from drowning in cases, half like each other, half unlike.

Thus, looking for current equivalents for that period, 1880–1910, I shall—not being ready to engage in outright prophecy—take our present time, the most recent thirty years of our past, 1960–90. The parallelism in cases of terrorist action seems obvious: the assassination of the Kennedy brothers and Martin Luther King; and, in the world of commerce, the Baader-Meinhof assassinations in Germany. The Revolution of 1905 in Russia and the granting of parliamentary powers to the Duma have some likeness to events in Russia today. But most striking is the parallel between the Boer War and the Vietnam War. The likeness lies in both events involving a great imperial power, which prided itself on its liberalism, in a long and brutal war against a small republic far away, with whom world opinion sympathized. The parallel shows itself most importantly in the radical split caused in the home country between the patriot-imperialists (Kipling in the earlier period) and the pro-Boers or pro-Vietnamese. (Two books that summed up the indignation of the left were J. A. Hobson's *Imperialism* for the earlier New Age, and Susan Sontag's *Trip to Hanoi* for the later one.) This had a direct effect upon the world of literature and thought—after the Boer War, Kipling was an outcast from the world of letters. Indeed, the output of adventure tales (by English writers hoping for literary status) stopped as definitely after 1910 as Hollywood's production of Westerns stopped in the late 1960s.

The effect of the Boer War and of the other two kinds of events was to mobilize and radicalize liberal opinion, and to put the conservatives on the defensive, in the 1880–1910 period. This energizing of the more idealistic party helped create or sustain the mood of hope and experimentation, but also anger, however sublimated, that called it-self the New Age. The same is true of the Vietnam War.

As my examples will already have suggested, however, our 1960–90 period was not homogeneous. It contained within it a difference and a change, from that age of revolution we call the sixties to the age of conservatism in which we now live. There are New Age elements in both, but as far as political action goes, in the conservative period those remain quiescent or merely rumble. That is why the phrase has nowadays that immediate reference to "candles and crystals," and why so many turn away from it impatiently.

By the same token, the phrase could suggest—quite wrongly—that between certain dates everyone or at least most people shared ideas and activities quite unlike those shared in another decade. In fact, as I have already implied, plenty of people were doing in the 1950s just the sort of thing that was hailed as "of the sixties" a few years later. The difference between periods is largely between their contemporary myths.

For these reasons it will be profitable to compare our thirty-year period 1960–90 both with the nineteenth-century New Age and with another one that *was* an age of revolution. We shall use the end of the eighteenth century in England for that second purpose. That will compare with features of the sixties, while the nineteenth-century New Age compares better with the eighties.

HISTORICAL AND THEORETICAL CASES

I am describing the participants in New Ages, then, as people who share a sense of reality that is more open and optimistic than other people's, a feeling that the obstacles to desire are often less substantial than they look. In lightweight, light-minded people, of course, such a trait would deserve to be called mere optimism, and probably linked to those flaws of the psyche we call narcissism or hedonism.

However, two of the examples I shall refer to most often are Tolstoy and Gandhi, which should show that the naïveté I am interested in is not lightweight—or uninformed or uncritical. That *naïve* is still a meaningful word to use about them is suggested by their both saying that they had been closest to the truth, and at the height of their powers, when they were children: that education, even in the broadest sense, had obscured the truth for them. Tolstoy saw in one of his own children who died very young spiritual powers that he himself could not achieve.

These men must be said, therefore, to have aspired to naïveté, and tried later in life to retrieve their childish faith by an eager assent to the moral teachings of Christianity on the one hand, Hinduism on the other. Their vegetarianism, for example, was under one aspect simply an application of "Thou shalt not kill." Thus the New Age is—not only, but in part—a return to those childhood teachings.

Today, the most impressive poets and thinkers of the current New Age are clearly, though discreetly, preparing us to live in the aftermath of some unspeakable disaster, most likely in the form of nuclear war or accident, possibly in the form of energy failure. They direct our attention, for instance, to the economies and organizations of American Indian tribes, as our best clues to the adaptation that may be forced on us. That is not mere optimism.

Some members of the nineteenth-century New Age, also, were serious enough—one might say desperate enough—for us to see their optimism rather as a very grim kind of virtue; indeed, to think of it as like the theological virtues of Faith, Hope, and Charity. And the two of those people who remain the most interesting to us are the old Tolstoy and the young Gandhi, in both of whom a kind of innocent realism could as well evoke our sense of the despairingly heroic or tragic as our sense of the naïve.

Tolstoy declared that we have only to want no more war, and we shall have no more war. We find the same faith in Gandhi—the moment Indians really want *swaraj*, home rule, they will have it. The two men's heroic personalism, their sense that everything depends on the individual act of will, also contained a component of lightness, which facilitated that heroism: a sense that the world only exists because we wish it to—because we assent to its claims. Much of what we call, or allow to be called, the world's substance—"human nature" and "our situation" and "what history teaches"—is quite insubstantial. Reality could perfectly well be absolutely different tomorrow, and we do not need to take it seriously. As Gandhi put it, "I refuse to judge mankind on the scanty evidence of history." He was a profoundly realistic politician, as Tolstoy was a profoundly realistic moralist, but it was a paradoxical, New Age realism in both cases.

To make the idea of this New Age realism clearer, it is well to hold in mind two contrasting senses of reality. They correspond roughly to right-wing and left-wing radicalism, and so they will be useful in sorting out the three families of radicals—who sometimes belong together, but sometimes must be sharply distinguished from each other.

One of these two, and the one less like New Age naïveté, we might see embodied in nationalist leaders like Churchill, de Gaulle, or Stalin; or embodied in our confidence in such men. All three of these figures are, seen in this context, "reactionary," in the sense that they make us react against the idealistic New Age optimism that all of us have a share of, and that Tolstoy and Gandhi acted on. (In our moments of confidence in or enthusiasm for the three great national or imperial leaders, we normally do not focus consciously on their reactionariness, but it is always implicit.) In the nineteenth-century New Age, Kipling was a spokesman for this kind of reactionary radicalism.

These figures, heroes and spokesmen, are champions of the nation-state. This is an idea that—at least as a moral ideal—intellectuals are likely to dismiss too quickly. "In our own time, Gaia is goddess, and the nation is suspect," says Catherine Albanese in *Nature Religion in America*. But the nation-state is still an idea that intelligent people live and die for, and certainly has been an immensely powerful force in history. On the other hand, it stands in marked contrast with the current New Age's idea of the tribe.

These men's sense of reality—or the one we associate with them—I would describe as morally blood-stained, by the feeling that nothing can be accomplished without grief and guilt, violence and domination. It is a realism associated with royal robes, official portraits, uniforms, medals, titles, all of them stiff with guilt as well as gilt, with blood as well as glory. And insofar as they incorporate the masculine identity (which they tend to do), that in itself becomes inseparable from force, explosions, death-dealing, the nuclear winter. We expect to find this sense of reality among men of action, and women, too, when they have the same social function, whether the individuals are solitary adventurers, commanders of armies, or rulers of nations. (To evoke the contrast with New Age realism, put a photograph of Gandhi in his loincloth next to one of Churchill, his great opponent, in his bemedaled uniform.)

The second alternative realism I associate primarily with intellectuals, such as the followers of Marx, Freud, and Weber, the founders of nineteenth- and twentieth-century social science. This sense of reality is marked by its systematic character, the mutual consistency of its defined terms. Its great legendary success is the hard sciences, the triumphant achievement of Western civilization. In social life its great manifestation is the law—which as a moral ideal tends to absorb all of politics.

Taking it for granted that all three of these realisms are dissatisfied with consensus common sense, and so all employ special codes, it remains true that the systematic alternative makes the greatest effort toward translating everything into its own cognitive terms. For such people, phenomena can only be regularized and accorded reality (which is in this sense something formal and abstract), so they can only be *understood*, by being coded.

Politically, this results in a praxis that Norman Mailer calls in *The Armies of the Night* "the sound-as-brickwork-logic-of-the-next-step," and associates with Marxism. In his account of the 1967 March on the Pentagon, he said that in the 1960s a new, post-Marxist generation had arrived in America, who believed in technology but also in LSD, in witches, in tribal knowledge, in orgy, and revolution. "It had no respect whatsoever for the unassailable logic of the next step," only for the revelatory mystery of the happening. That is another way to say that that generation embodied the intellectual style of the New Age.

The systematic translation and coding of data takes an effort of reason and theory, conducted by discussion and controlled by method. This is the source of the realism of intellectuals—i.e., to name the group more concretely, people in the academic world. (Of course, it is not the mere or ordinary academic, only the ideologically energetic few, whom one would compare with the other radicals discussed here.) The most current forms of system are perhaps feminism, structuralism, and poststructuralism, though they are most prevalent outside ordinary politics. The photograph to set beside Gandhi this time would perhaps depict Freud and his psychoanalytic colleagues at one of those early conferences at which the scientific respectability of the movement was being legislated.

It may be useful to associate these three realisms with the three temperaments described before, implying by temperament an aptitude or predisposition for certain patterns of feeling as well as action. This will define the New Age mentality as a phenomenon distinct from the ideas it entertains—which are quite different at various times and in various people. It will also extend the scope of "realism" to cover more of behavior; for this is not limited to the cognitive, but covers emotional, imaginative, and indeed political activity.

For instance, the animal or human sacrifice (literal or symbolic) to be found in so many religious cults, though horrifying to the piety of the other two minds, has a ring of awful truth to men of power. It answers to that element of lawless violence (we hear it in the roar of the mob, whether in the stadium or the streets) that surrounds our rational discourse as a limiting boundary. Some modern novelists bring that violent chaos into their plots, their city backgrounds, even their own language, in narrative and analysis—see Norman Mailer's *American Dream*, Tom Wolfe's *Bonfire of the Vanities*, Martin Amis's *Money*. More traditionally, it has been a part of our image of warfare. To this experience of chaos, the stern splendor of sacrificial religion, or the execution of political assassins, can seem a counteraction, necessary to reestablish order.

It is the mild and rational piety of More and Erasmus, or the great Anglican writers of the seventeenth century, that we associate with the second temperament. Awe and splendor, power and force, thunder and lightning of all kinds—these arouse the authoritarian mind. But after the majestic strains of, say, the *Eroica* Symphony die away, the flatter voice of the systematic mind can be heard, comparing, discriminating, explaining. And the naïve mind finds its religious emblems in figures like St. Francis or Gandhi or—to take images rather than life stories—those long-haired and androgynous pop stars who sing against war or world hunger.

The word "naïve" shows its appropriateness to the New Age temperament in the latter's "childish" attachment to goodness—its stubborn insistence on the primary school or catechetical virtues. Tolstoy in his old age thought he had been taught the crucial values as a child, and then had them obscured (ridiculed and replaced) in adolescence and manhood. We are told that Queen Victoria, when told she was queen, said, "I will be good"; and that ideal remained a naïve element in Victorian consensus moralism—reflected, for instance, in the representation of sexual relations in that period's middle-brow novels. Most people today find that naïveté hard to swallow, because of specifically modernist features of our society (those depicted by Mailer, Wolfe, Amis) but also because of a traditional sense of reality that we share with, for instance, Augustan London—say, Swift and Pope. They did not believe in goodness any more than we. But Gandhi was an admirer of Queen Victoria, and he himself aspired to be good, in manhood as in childhood. He was naïve.

The ideas embodied in Tolstoy and Gandhi were very different from those embodied in Tom Paine and William Blake, not to mention contemporary New Agers like Gary Snyder. Yet all these have a right to call themselves New Age; indeed, almost any idea may be New Age if it is put forward when and where it can be applied in individual life-experiment. They all therefore have a special excitement, however they differ from each other.

There is thus an ascetic New Age, of which Gandhi and Tolstoy were great examples, contemporary with an erotic New Age, represented by Edward Carpenter in England and Otto Gross in Switzerland. There are future-oriented New Age ideas, and backward, Golden Age–oriented ideas. But the opposites often melt into each other; we shall find it just as plausible to call Otto Gross ascetic as erotic.

To take another example, the taking of hallucinogenic drugs has often been a New Age practice, but so has vegetarianism. To most people, the two practices seem very different in social character, but in New Ages they often coincide, as they did in Haight-Ashbury in the 1960s. And at the end of Gandhi's life he engaged in sexual experiments that belonged not to the ascetic but to the erotic New Age—indeed, he explained them by referring to Havelock Ellis and Bertrand Russell, sexologists of that earlier period. These practices startled all those who thought they knew Gandhi, but he had always been a life-experimenter. Such a coincidence, of Gandhi and Havelock Ellis, points us toward what I called the New Age mentality or temperament.

In any large idea or fact, such as Christianity, one will find all three of these temperaments represented. The Gospel itself, summarized in the Sermon on the Mount, speaks to the naïve mind, and is returned to in most New Ages. Theological systems and ecclesiastical policies, on the other hand, are created and administered by the systematic mind. And the warrior bishops, or Savonarolas, the literal or metaphorical crusaders, are clearly figures of authority. Of course the three temperaments blend together in actual events, as they do in individual persons, but one can understand both events and persons much better if one teases out their components.

The suggestion of the congenital, unconscious, or unalterable in the word "temperament," however, should be taken as heavily qualified. We are examining a group as much as an individual phenomenon—to some extent this temperament is a function of what people believe or intend, not something involuntary or inherited. And some individuals can change their temperaments: enthusiasts can sometimes change themselves and become what they want to be. Gandhi before 1894 was very shy and inept in matters like public speaking; Tolstoy after 1880 set himself to become meek, patient, long-suffering.

For the temperament that seems essentially proper to the New Age, I have already suggested the label "Naïve," meaning by that not any lack of knowledge or intelligence, but a generous readiness to believe in something new, and to act upon a belief. The weakness or softness that plagues that temperament as its defect is of course a lack of critical rigor, a readiness for self-deceit, or even self-indulgence.

The temperament that goes with the right-wing realism I have labeled "Authoritarian," although I don't use that word in order to condemn it. I mean that people with this temperament are especially concerned with hierarchy and power and responsibility, and with endorsing and enforcing the best forms thereof.

The other temperament I have labeled "Systematic," meaning that such people believe above all in rationally organized efforts, whether it is concepts or individuals who are being organized. They care more than the other two groups about the consistency of their thoughts and language—sometimes at a cost in substantiality—keeping the language of one field consistent with that of another, and even in hypothetical circumstances.

The mutual antagonism between these three temperaments—three realisms—takes many forms. One of the most striking is the resentment felt by the systematic mind for the naïve. Because of the circumstances of my career, I have encountered this most often in the academic dislike for Gandhi and Gandhism. (Authoritarians tend to love him, sentimentally.) This is no doubt because Gandhi—and other such figures—belong to the iconostasis of secular saints. Academia, the guardian of intellectual adulthood, regards Gandhi as grade school pabulum, to be rejected by the brighter high school student, and on no account to be allowed into college, except to be reductively analyzed. To reject him, along with many other New Age enthusiasms, is an intellectual rite of passage.

Another such example is the contempt freely expressed by men and women of letters for the Tolstoy of 1880–1910 (the New Age writer). Critics and historians whose tone about *War and Peace* and its author is reverent to the point of idolatry feel licensed to dismiss his late stories and essays as ridiculous. One example is the recent and highly praised biography by A. N. Wilson, but there are many others. Finding Tolstoy involved, in the last phase of his life, with New Age ideas, intellectuals feel no need to consider seriously what he was saying. They join their colleagues in calling feeble a mind they have previously defined as bold and powerful.

Perhaps it will also dramatize the conflict to describe the way each radical option looked at the other in the New Age of the nineteenth century. Kipling, speaking for the authoritarians, made fun of the New Agers of his time, in his story of 1913 "My Son's Wife." Frankwell Midmore is the hero of the story, which tells of this young man's recovery from the sickliness of New Age enthusiasm in London by the hearty experience of hunting and the unchanging humors of life in the country.

The unregenerate Midmore is in fact a composite portrait, representing many branches of the New Age, from the Fabians to the sexologists. He engages in Social Research, disapproves of hunting, refers to "our tomfool social system" and to marriage as a base convention. He makes love to women "whose hair smelt of cigarette smoke . . . [women of] the Immoderate Left." Amongst the women we shall discuss, Olive Schreiner is one who would probably have seemed to Kipling to fit into this category.

The story begins: "He had suffered from the disease of the century since his early youth, and before he was thirty he was heavily marked with it. He and a few friends had rearranged Heaven very comfort-ably, but the reorganization of Earth, which they called Society, was even greater fun." Midmore felt assured each day that he and his friends had "helped the World a step nearer the Truth, the Dawn, and the New Order." Kipling is of course making use of New Age rhetoric.

Such was the nineteenth-century authoritarian mind's satirical awareness of that New Age. The systematic mind's awareness we might take to be expressed by Friedrich Engels and H. M. Hyndman talking about William Morris's socialism; Engels declared Morris "un-talented" in politics, and "a victim of the anarchists," and "a settled sentimental socialist."

Or we might cite the Webbs talking about H. G. Wells: Sidney Webb commented on Wells's book *Anticipations* that Wells underval-ued the role of the professional administrator; "all experience shows that men need organizing as much as machines, or rather, much more." Beatrice Webb deplored Wells's "lack of any detailed knowl-edge of social organizations." Both disapproved his "gambling with the idea of free love." Morris and Wells were naïve by comparison with their more systematic-minded colleagues.

In a book I wrote during the 1960s (*Cities of Light and Sons of the Morning*), I also defined three temperaments. They were rather dif-ferent; partly because that book's primary focus was on writers of imaginative literature, and partly because of the focus on revolution indicated by its subtitle, "A Cultural Psychology for an Age of Rev-olution." (That was a sixties book.) An age of revolution is an ex-treme case of a New Age when the pressure to take everything to the point of immediate action makes a difference to ideas. Nevertheless, what I call the authoritarian temperament here is roughly the same as what I call the Faustian temperament there; and what I call the systematic here I there call the Calvinist.

I used those terms to stress the idea of a psychic bargain, or an exchange of one set of possibilities of personal development for another—the famous one traditionally being Faust's bargain with the Devil, selling his soul for forbidden powers. (I contrasted "Calvinist" and a third term, "Erasmian," partly because Calvin, Erasmus, and Faust have a certain epochal and imaginative congruence.) To use another metaphor, such a bargain or contract is an investment-transfer of one's psychic resources, capital, and work force from one enterprise to another. This is important not so much because either capital or work force is limited in quantity, but because the act of transference arouses and energizes the whole psyche. The mind has its self-consciousness, and is profoundly responsive to its own actions. The larger the action, the larger the responsive effect. This is not limited to the conscious mind, and some of those transferences are very large in their compass, and have the character of being for life. These are temperamental contracts.

Most people make many contracts, some of which compromise the effects of others, in order to take care of all their needs to some degree. But though to make just one contract is to risk large failures, it is also to acquire large energies, because of the mind's power of self-excitation. This is what Nietzsche meant when he said that a man of just one virtue is stronger than a man of many.

Such a man will be a radical, in one or other of the three ways described, and we will find all three kinds of radical conflicting with the status quo, and with each other, in most Ages of Revolution.

CONCLUSION

We find all three temperaments side by side in Tolstoy's great historical novel, *War and Peace,* and to locate them there has the advantage of leading our minds back to the radical difference between this younger Tolstoy, the novelist, and the later spokesman for the New Age. In his novel, he is espousing the authoritarian, the national-military option, and he makes as good a case for that as can be made. Moreover, he does so in conscious opposition to the systematic option; and he makes an exception in favor of the naïve that became significant later in his life.

Tolstoy's novel was written at a time when the Russian intelligentsia contained many highly systematic and combative thinkers, and *War and Peace* was greeted by them with a good deal of contemptuous anger. The novel's characters had no ideas, they said; its mood was merely nostalgic; the message was irrelevant to the problems of Russia in the 1860s. Dmitri Pisarev, the radical critic, said all it did was show how Russian aristocrats managed to live without knowledge, without ideas, without energy, and without work.

Simply by choosing to write about a patriotic war, a time when Russia was fighting for her life against the French invasion, Tolstoy was making a move against the intelligentsia, since the emotions associated with such national memories are necessarily authoritarian. (The three men I chose to associate this realism with—Churchill, de Gaulle, Stalin—were heroes of patriotic war.) Tolstoy describes a military parade at which, as Czar Alexander I approached each regiment, "Every man felt self-forgetfulness, a proud consciousness of might, and passionate devotion." Nikolai Rostov, one of the novel's central characters, seeing Alexander's handsome and happy face, "experienced a feeling of tenderness and ecstasy such as he had never before known. Every trait and every movement of the Czar's seemed to him enchanting."

Of course, as the title implies, there is another interest in the novel, the life of peace, the life of love and marriage, which is complementary to (and temporarily supportive of) the life of war. Natasha Rostova is a more important character than her brother Nikolai. The story shows how the values of marriage meet those of dandyism and conquer them, and then they merge with the values of war and establish a hegemony over *them*.

Both these interests (equally conservative in political tendency) are saved from a merely political label for the sympathetic reader by their being rooted in the "unconscious" life; and indeed this ideology of life values is often invoked by others who see reality in the first way I described. (Take the political novels of D. H. Lawrence as an example.) From the point of view of the systematic mind, this is of course mystification. To the naïve mind, it is the cult of power.

The most important representative of systematic thinking in the novel is Mikhail Speransky, the Czar's adviser, whom contemporary readers were able to associate with the sixties intellectual Chernyshevsky. Tolstoy identifies Speransky above all by means of "the whiteness of his plump hands and face . . . and his awkward, ungainly movements." Those hands tell us that their owner has no contact with the sun and the wind and the soil, they do not make things, shape things, cultivate things, they only manipulate symbols. Paradoxically, Speransky is linked—as a character type—to Napoleon. The latter has the same hands. But he might more naturally be associated with the Czar, except that Tolstoy wants to save the phenomena of patriotic war from any association with militarism and imperialism. The Czar, and General Kutuzov, are presented as morally innocent, because in some sense unconscious, agents of Russia's destiny.

Speransky produced a Civil Code in 1812, based on Napoleon's, which was part of his blueprint for the reconstruction of Russian society. Napoleon is the novel's villain, in life-values terms, because he is an entirely "produced" personality, entirely conscious of his own effects, all intention, calculation, rhetoric, theater, and theory. We hear him telling himself, "I shall speak to them as I always do: clearly, impressively, and magnanimously." He has no hidden sources, no unknown self, no fertile darkness or hinterland. This wrongness in him coincides with his role as national enemy (the French being less natural than the Russians) and with his role as representative of revolution. For Tolstoy this concept referred not just to the French event of the 1790s but to the potential Russian revolution of the 1860s, which also seemed to Tolstoy rhetorical, ideological, theoretical, and theatrical.

The third option, the New Age temperament, is represented in the novel first by the self-renewing naïveté of the central figure, Pierre Bezukhov, the autobiographical hero, who is unlike his friend, Prince André, because never long committed to any course of action. But neither is he, on the other hand, scornful of action; he is instead always on the point of self-commitment. He is all becoming. And secondly we see naïveté in the peasant Platon Karataev, met only briefly by Pierre as a prisoner after battle, but exerting an oracular effect upon both Pierre and Tolstoy. Karataev "had no attachments, friendships, or love, as Pierre understood them, but loved and lived affectionately with everything life brought him in contact with." His talk was all folk sayings, barely conscious, unintentional, transparent, innocent of ego. He and Pierre are, in somewhat different ways, innocents, one demonstrating naïveté in psychological terms, the other in social terms.

What these two personalities mean in the terms of the novel's national-military politics is—a priori—impossible to say; i.e., they mean nothing in such terms, and thus the effect of admiring them is to justify political inertia, or conservatism. What happened to Tolstoy in his later life is that he decided to "say," indeed to live by, what these figures would mean if taken seriously. Whereupon he discovered that their (Christian) naïveté was just as hostile to the authoritarian kind of realism as to the systematic. That is, to spell out these characters' meanings is to discover one New Age ideology.

Prophetic Voices: 1880–1910

> The first duty of the British workers is to refrain from enter-
> ing the Army or Navy, these being the tools whereby their
> land-owning class defend their own possessions at home and
> seize on the land of others abroad. . . . Britain has just
> passed through the throes of changing Governments. She has
> rejected, even with obloquy, some of the men who were her
> demi-gods only two or three years ago. . . . Have the party
> politics of a democracy any more real principle behind them
> than has the irresponsible will of a despot?
>
> Isabella Fyvie Mayo,
> applying Tolstoy's teaching to England, in 1910

The nineteenth-century New Age movement was a worldwide phenomenon, at least wherever Western culture was established. I shall
limit my concerns to its manifestations in England and the Empire,
but with one exception: the colony of radical New Agers in the Swiss
lake village of Ascona. This had important connections with the English equivalent, principally via the Simple Life and Nature Cure
enthusiasms, but it belonged primarily to Central and Eastern Europe. However, it deserves to be described here because it was a
concentrated epitome of all that was elsewhere feebler and more
scattered.

ASCONA

In the year 1900 a group of seven young people, from several different
European countries, met in Munich and decided to turn their backs
on the city civilization about them. Some of them had attended the
centennial celebrations in Paris, but had felt disgusted rather than
enthralled by the triumphs of progress exhibited. They walked into
and across Switzerland, looking for a place to settle, and found the

lake village of Ascona, in the Italian-culture canton of Ticino. Its beautiful landscape and underdeveloped economy had already attracted some anarchists and theosophists. The best off of the seven (a Belgian called Henri Oedenkoven) bought land on a hill called Monescia, and there set up a Nature Cure sanatorium called Monte Verita.

Even before they bought land, they talked with Albert Skarvan, a Tolstoy enthusiast, who seems to have broadened their ideas and given them a more political cast. Skarvan had been a doctor in the Austro-Hungarian army, until his Tolstoyan pacifist convictions had caused him to be stripped of both his commission and his license.

Tolstoy was therefore one of the masters and teachers of the Ascona New Agers. Two others—very unlike Tolstoy—were Wagner and Nietzsche. The latter was the great philosophic rebel against conformism and the status quo. Wagner they sang and read aloud, and his 1880 essay, "Religion and Art," had almost scriptural authority for them. Wagner there called for a league of noble spirits to lead the rest of Europe out of its enthrallment to materialism and to help regenerate the race. That revolt against contemporary materialism was what linked the three prophets in the Asconans' eyes. Like the Asconans, Wagner had become a practicing vegetarian—in Wagner's case after reading an essay on the subject by Tolstoy—and his hero Tannhäuser wore sandals, as they did. (Sandals were symbolic footwear.)

The seven soon disagreed over ideological issues like the owning of property and the charging of fees by the sanatorium. Only two of them, Henri Oedenkoven and Ida Hofmann, continued with the project of the sanatorium, but nearly all the others settled in Ascona, setting up their shelters (of a primitive and temporary nature) on the same hill or nearby.

The most extreme in his life-style was "Gusto" Graeser. Born in 1879, in an eastern province of the Austro-Hungarian Empire, Graeser was baptized Arthur Gustav, but renamed himself to express his joy in life, his gusto. He also told people that Graeser was the plural of *Gras*, grass, and offered a blade as a visiting card. He lived some of the time in a cave, and at other times wandered, doing without money and employment. When a common-law wife attached herself (and her five children) to him, they and their children (there came to be eight altogether) lived in a caravan. He made himself an embodiment of health, as Walt Whitman and Edward Carpenter had. One of his early friends, who wrote articles about him, was Johannes Schlaf, a translator of Whitman. Another friend was Hermann Hesse, who was strongly drawn to vagabondage, and much influenced by Graeser's example.

He wrote poems, which he gave away, or offered for whatever price the purchaser thought fair. In one, he says that he too had once smoked, worn gloves to stroll in, and strangled himself with a silk tie, but never again:

> I knotted me into the father-noose—and even bragged about it
> Hung myself by the silken tie—by manhood's executioner.

Now he wore a tunic and sandals, and offered the spectacle of himself as an antidote to a poison that many people felt to be in the air—the poison of civilization and culture.

In Kronstadt, his hometown, Graeser refused to do his year of military service, in 1901, and was sent to jail. Returning to Ascona, he was offered a piece of land by the villagers of Losone, but would not accept it as his property. His early "home" was formed by two slabs of rock, with a few boards on the ground to lie on, and a trough into which he threw fruit stones, later to be scattered wherever he thought trees were needed.

He was deeply influenced by the *Way of Life* of Lao-tzu, and translated it into German. One of the Chinese poet's most important concepts is *wu wei*, quietism or deliberate inactivity, the voiding of the self so that Tao, the Way, may take control of all one's being and doing. Lao-tzu, important to Tolstoy also, acquired authority in the New Age generally, as he has again in our own day.

Graeser was one of the stylemakers of the vagabond life. He is credited with inventing both the headband and the version of the poncho that wanderers then wore. He cut out his own tunic and made his rope sandals, which usually laced up the calf. His hair was untrimmed and he had a noble beard.

He also applied his aesthetic to the rubbish-dump aspect of his life—his use of pickups and throwaways. Adolf Grohman, in 1902 or 1903, described Graeser's cave home, the *Felsenheim*, which was an hour's walk northwest of Ascona, as picturesquely adorned with "bits and pieces." (And at the end of Graeser's life, in the 1950s, the Munich garret he died in made use of twigs to hang things on, and hollow logs to stuff things into, and conveniently shaped stones and bones and rinds.) The landscape around, Grohman tells us, was full of caves and waterfalls, goats and hollow chestnut trees. At this time, Graeser was looking for a *Felsenweib*—a cavewoman for his cave home. Elizabeth Doerr and her five children answered his call.

He was a handsome man, with abundant hair, a noble posture, regular features. There are pictures of him walking down a Munich street, the cynosure of all eyes, seeming to tower over others, physically and morally. Besides accosting people and presenting himself in this way, Gusto gave "lectures," formal and informal, on his life-style and his development, his *Werdegang*. He talked about health and healing, and in effect announced himself as the way, the truth, and the life. He attacked Christianity and its dynamic of guilt, in the name of Germanism and its dynamic of joy.

He did not publish his poems, in any ordinary sense, but he worked seriously at them. From his Tao translation, we can take part of the first poem.

> Do you hear me?
> Give over the drudging and clawing, just
>   let yourself rest—
> Let yourself fall in good faith with the faithful
>   Whole, like the dew
> That falls to the ground.
> Outside us beats the all-holy pulse.
> Flow-fall with the TAO into life! . . .
> Don't name and take, from yourself and me,
>   what It saves and brings
> By way of gifts.
> Unnamable is the unending One and
>   namable only
> The passing part—

NATURE CURE

Ida Hofmann, another of the original seven, and one of the directors of the sanatorium, wrote a pamphlet in 1905 called *"Vegetarismus!*

Vegetabilismus!" The second word meant eating vegetables instead of meat; the first meant also nature cure, the rejection of vaccination, the wearing of clothes that needed no starching or ironing, and the sharing of housework among men as well as women. Thus vegetarianism reached out toward feminism and dress and medical reform.

Besides the diet and the fresh air and sunbaths, Monte Verita offered medical treatment, though of a kind very unlike the surgeries and hospitals of the day. Mud poultices were applied to burns, cuts, inflammations, and high blood pressure. Patients sunbathed in the nude, slept out of doors, sat in cold baths, dieted, fasted. The cure was a system of ascetic exercises, a denial to the body of the harmful luxuries of modern food and comfort, with the aim of self-strengthening. The ethic-aesthetic was a hard, clean strenuousness, a scouring out of the alimentary system, a stripping off of subcutaneous fat, a bare vigorous intercourse with wind and water, hill and stars. Above all, it meant sun worship. Hofmann and Oedenkoven had first met at an Austrian sanatorium run by Arnold Rikli, known as the sun doctor, the *Sonnendoktor*.

This nature cure was a widespread movement in Germany. The first nature-cure doctor to practice outside the villages was Louis Kuhne, born in 1853, whose *New Science of Healing* eventually appeared in twenty-four languages. He saw the nineteenth century as the century of nervousness, especially of "progressive paralysis of the insane"—a city disease that does not occur among poor people and peasants. In South Africa, Gandhi and his friends took Kuhne baths.

Adolf Just, born in 1859, brought out his *Back to Nature!*—also very widely read—in 1896. He said everyone should be his own doctor, and should make use of the four great therapeutic means that nature supplies—mud, diet, light and air baths, and the cold rub-down. His subtitle runs, in translation, *The True Natural Method of Healing and Living and the True Salvation of the Soul—Paradise Regained*. (This doctor, too, was well known to Simple Lifers in England, and to Gandhi and his friends in South Africa, who faithfully imitated his recipes and diets and therapies.)

Sebastian Kneipp (1821–1897) was a Roman Catholic priest who developed a water cure. He was the teacher of Elizabeth Doerr, Graeser's common-law wife, and a prominent figure in Ascona.

Kneipp, having suffered with his lungs, and finding no relief with regular doctors, worked out a system of rubs, showers, and douches with salts to dissolve in the water. In 1889 he founded his first *Badeanstalt,* which had a great success.

Such are some of the figures who stood behind the medical work of Monte Verita, and behind the Simple Life and Nature Cure taught by Carpenter in England, Gandhi in South Africa, and the Tolstoyans everywhere.

Ascona and Nonviolence

Ascona was also a center of anarchist and antiwar activities. Gusto Graeser refused military service both before and during the Great War. Indeed, he lectured against the war, and for that reason was arrested in Stuttgart in 1915, condemned in Budapest, and confined in Kronstadt. The commanding general there gave him an ultimatum: put on a uniform (he was still wearing his tunic) or be shot in the morning. He chose the latter, with his wife's approval. But in fact the military authorities then put him into a mental home for six months, and finally released him.

There were others like him among the New Agers. Ascona was a station on an underground railway for young men evading military duty in Germany. They could cross into Switzerland by boat, and then from Ascona could get into Italy.

Graeser carried the gospel of nonviolence into postwar politics, too, in 1918. When a revolutionary government was set up in Munich at the end of the war, it included some New Agers: some, like Erich Muehsam, had been living in Ascona; others were the friends of Asconans, as Gustav Landauer was a friend of Muehsam. But there were also men of violence there, adventurers and Communists of another kind. Hearing this, Graeser felt the call to go down from the mountains into the city, to preach nonviolence. He called on Hermann Hesse to accompany him, but the latter was too prudent, and Graeser had to go alone. His speech—delivered on April Fool's Day, 1919, with the title "The Communism of the Heart"—was mocked and ignored. (Being politically insignificant, he escaped with his life, as Landauer did not.) The episode, and its moral implication, left a deep scar on Hesse's sense of himself, which can be traced in his literary work.

Eroticism

Ascona was one of the great centers of erotic and gender liberation in the New Age, and the doctrine as it reached, for instance, England, bore the Ascona imprint. The most striking case of that is no doubt D. H. Lawrence, whose wife had been an Asconan (of the spirit), but there are several other cases, like H. G. Wells.

That doctrine can be read in the form of two or three legends. One appeared in various works of fiction in this period. We can take Gerhart Hauptmann's once famous novel *Der Ketzer von Soana* (*The Heretic of Soana*) as our example. This tells the story of a young Catholic priest in a Swiss mountain parish very like Ascona, who leaves Christ for Eros. He encounters and succumbs to paganism in the form of a beautiful girl who has been brought up outside the Christian religion and civilization, and so is innocent in her sexuality. When we first see the ex-priest, he works outdoors all day as a goatherd, wearing a goatskin instead of a soutane, and is as proudly beautiful as a Donatello statue.

This novel had great and international success. By 1925 it had sold 140,000 copies, and was translated into every literary language. It formed part of the literary propaganda for eroticism. At the end, the narrator, to whom the priest tells his story, sees for the first time the woman who had such an effect. He is going down the mountain as she is coming up, and he feels weak and small before her. "There was no protection, no armor against the demands of that neck, those shoulders, and that breast, blessed and stirred by the breath of life. She climbed up and out of the depths of the world, past the wondering scribe [the narrator]—and she climbs and climbs into eternity as the one into whose merciless hands heaven and earth have been delivered."

That image—the incarnation of triumphant erotic values in a figure, male or female, emerging from nature toward a story's central figure—is to be found in Joyce (the wading girl in *Portrait of the Artist as a Young Man*); and in Lawrence (peasant or gypsy men in stories like "Sun" and "The Virgin and the Gypsy"). In an earlier version, Hauptmann's novel was entitled *Die Syrische Gottin* (*The Syrian Goddess*), one of the titles of Magna Mater, the Great Goddess. In *Women in Love*, Lawrence spoke of Syria Dea.

In 1905 H. G. Wells published *A Modern Utopia*, a semifictional account of modern social ideas, which is set in Ticino and includes a description of the beliefs and life-styles of the *Naturmenschen* of Ascona. Five years later, in his autobiographical novel, *The New Machiavelli*, he described a walking tour like the one he himself had taken, in which his hero, like Hauptmann's, receives a revelation of female beauty and strength from the peasant women harvesting in the valleys (their "deep breasts and rounded limbs" inflame his imagination), and has his first erotic experience in a Ticino hotel. In fact, the name "Locarno," the town next to Ascona, recurs throughout the novel as a code word for eroticism.

The second legend important to Asconans was more mythical. It was about the Primal Crime, humanity's Original Sin, which had been committed by Man—that is, by the patriarchal Father/Husband/ Master who dominated imperial Germany. This story comes to us in fragments: one of them was invented by Otto Gross toward the end of his life. He had a vision of a turning point in world history when a horde of ambitious half-apes burst out of a clump of bushes and flung themselves on the naked and unsuspecting women who had, till then, in matriarchal innocence, directed human life. They enslaved these women, making them wives, and with that event our miserable history began.

Gross depicted these men in cartoon terms, as war-mad bureaucrats, administrators, academics, who wore professorial beards and official decorations on their breasts. That is, he saw them as being like his own father, Hanns Gross, who had been a professor of criminology, and who had volunteered to fight in 1914, although in his sixties. At the beginning of our history, men like Hanns Gross hung up, in the women's innocent temples of sensual love, their weapons of war and their tablets of the law.

Another fragment or version of this story was the dance drama conceived by Rudolf Laban and Hans Brandenburg, and worked out by Laban's women dancers in Ascona in 1914. In this the men's symbolic crime was sexual; a father—danced in a gigantic and terrifying bearded-idol mask—destroys his wife and then invades and ruins the erotic lives of his son and daughter. At the funeral of their mother, his wife, he fixes his desire upon his daughter.

Such a version of Original Sin is Asconan and not Freudian, because it accuses Man. The Oedipus complex here is not a matter of infantile feeling but of historical fact; it is acted out, not in the child's mind, but in the adult's behavior. And such facts were part of Ascona's history, in for instance the Gross scandal. In 1913 (the year Laban brought his dancers to Ascona) Otto Gross was arrested on his father's deposition that he was a dangerous psychopath. At the age of thirty-six he was declared incompetent to manage his affairs and incarcerated in an asylum. Hanns Gross was declared his legal guardian. Moreover, Hanns petitioned to have Otto's son handed over to *him*, to have the boy removed from his mother's care in Ascona, because she—following Otto's teaching as she did—was not a fit mother.

The English poet Harold Monro, during his time in Ascona (just before 1913), began an epic poem called "Jehovah," which he worked on for the next fourteen years, and which seems to have had a similar message, judging by the surviving fragments. He presented his Jehovah as "an ignorant and boorish ogre," the god of aggressive nationalism, like the Father in the dance; and some lines suggest the Otto Gross story:

> Devourer of your first-born, unbeloved . . .
> You will not claim to be father of Jesus? . . .
> War lords are your archangels, O Jehovah

The poem showed how Jewish monotheism historically replaced the animistic worship of rocks and plants and water. (Laban's autobiography ascribes a great importance to rocks, sands, and crystals in his early experience.) Monro quoted Shelley, saying that the overthrow of the idea of God would bring about the supreme good of earth.

When we put these three legends together, we have an idea, a program—an impeachment of Man and his God, an enthronement of Magna Mater—that was dear to all Asconans. The conflict between Hanns and Otto Gross was, as we have seen, an anecdotal equivalent of this idea.

HANNS AND OTTO GROSS

Hanns Gross may be said to represent both the authoritarian and the systematic temperaments I have described. His is not a generally famous name now, but he was an important man in his day, and his son Otto was a key figure in the nineteenth-century New Age in Central Europe; the son's convictions began in his rebellion against his father.

Hanns (1847–1915) introduced criminology, as a modern social science, into the Austro-Hungarian Empire. He traveled all over the province of Styria, enforcing justice by the most modern methods—investigating crimes as well as sitting in judgment—and his work was systematic: he was scandalized by the haphazard enforcement of the law in country districts. Austria was still debating the desirability of entering the iron cage of modernization and centralization, and in that debate Hanns Gross spoke for everything modern.

He wrote up his cases and described the scientific methods by which he tracked down criminals in his *Handbook for Examining Magistrates* of 1893. Footprints, fingerprints, bloodstains all turned into clues in his hands. (We, coming after, find it hard to imagine such things being anything but clues, but this is one of the classic cases of encroaching positivism.) He dealt in facts, and therefore put little credence in eyewitness reports. People were less reliable than facts, and typically he held menstruating women to be especially unreliable witnesses. He was also especially suspicious of gypsies, who were for him prototypes of the untrustworthy. His son made himself into a sort of gypsy, in revenge. Gross's *Handbook* has had many editions, has been used by Third World countries in setting up their own police forces, and is referred to today in Simenon's police procedural mystery novels, among others.

So far we have described him as a man of system; but he should also be seen as a man of authority, intuitively enforcing the interests of his class and country, like a *War and Peace* Kutuzov. In personality, Hanns Gross was an all-German father figure—what German New Agers called *ein Baertige*, a Beard. He was a big man, with a dominating personality as well as physique, who relegated to his wife and son a very subordinate role in the family. Athletic, with a bull neck, he was a semi-soldier all his life. His scientific work was done with soldierly precision and punctuality, and his institute was put at the service of his fatherland's defense, against internal and external enemies. As a boy, he was active in escapades and ingenious in mechanical devices—a young Tom Sawyer. He grew up to love the army (his father had been a professional soldier) and he died at sixty-eight of a lung inflammation contracted as a wartime volunteer in the army. His admirers described him after his death by saying that the three roots of his personality were the military, the judicial, and the scientific.

His son Otto's personality was an opposite type—rooted in art, love, and introspection. Otto declared that he had no sense of community, no sense of duty or patriotism. He rebelled against both authoritarian reaction and scientific systematization. He was in every way opposite to his father. As part of his lifelong rebellion, in 1905 he made his way to Ascona, where people like himself were gathering, to start a new way of living. His case represents the strengths and weaknesses of the New Age idea with great intensity.

By means of both personal, therapeutic encounter and the preaching of his ideas, Otto Gross liberated many individuals from emotional and ideological imprisonment. Some of the force of his personality, however, was rooted in a destructiveness that he aimed primarily against himself, and he ended as a virtual suicide. Indeed, he spread destruction around him (encouraging recklessness in his disciples, and supplying some of them with the means of suicide) and was a sinister figure as well as a martyr and hero of the New Age. He was in effect suppressed, and his memory erased, by the authorities invoked by his father, but also by the psychoanalytic movement as organized by Freud. (Freud saved him from Hanns Gross, Otto said, but then replaced Hanns as the father against whom he must rebel.) But Gross's memory, carried mostly underground in the minds and work of those who knew him, especially artists, has been part of the heritage of the twentieth century.

Otto Gross died in 1920, and in the same year Hofmann and Oedenkoven sold Monte Verita. Ascona's heyday was over. But many life experimenters continued to live there, and it was no accident that the famous series of Eranos Conferences were held in the years that followed. Many famous names were associated with these discussions of religious and occult ideas and icons, but the dominant presence was C. G. Jung. He had of course known Gross and many other Asconans, and his ideas—in transformed shape—incorporated much of their thinking. This will be important in considering later New Ages. Ascona was forgotten, but via Jung some part of its heritage reached as far as California in the 1960s. (Indeed, the California communes founded at the beginning of this century had much in common with Ascona.)

THE ENGLISH MOVEMENT

In England at the end of the nineteenth century, the closest equivalent to Ascona was probably Whiteway, a Tolstoyan colony near Stroud, in the Cotswold hills. It was a smaller-scale phenomenon in every sense, but was set up for much the same reasons, and had many of the same features. We will notice recurrent themes of eroticism, antimilitarism, imprisonment, nature cure, and others.

Whiteway was an agricultural colony, founded by a group of radicals coming from the London suburb of Croydon. John C. Kenworthy, a disciple of Tolstoy, was pastor of the Croydon Brotherhood Church and editor of the Brotherhood Publishing Company. The church, founded in 1894, ran a store, a laundry, and a dressmaking establishment before it set up its agricultural colony. "Brotherhood" stood for "Brotherhood of Man"; such churches were sometimes called Labor Churches.

The colonists made their big decision in 1898, just two years before the Asconans. Three of them officially bought the land, but they then burned the title deeds, so there should be no owning or owners. The twelve of them—some of whom were Quakers—lived communally but also spontaneously. They shared even their clothes, and took no vows, made no promises or pledges even to each other. During their very first winter their money ran out, and they lived on potatoes and parsnips.

Though many left, many more came, with various intentions and from various countries. Let us take as an example Francis Sedlak, the neo-Hegelian philosopher. He was born into a farming family in Moravia in 1873. A rebellious boy, he contradicted his teacher's pious doctrines about kings and priests, and denied his father's authority over him—and so while away at school got sent from home twopence to buy some rope to hang himself.

He was an intellectual from the start, attempting while young to devise a system of ideographic writing. He did not want to work on the family farm, and ran away from home to join the French Foreign

Legion. After a short time he deserted, was imprisoned, and returned home in time to be conscripted into the Austrian army.

He soon came to have conscientious objections to obeying officers' orders, refused to be a soldier, and was imprisoned. He studied the anarchist doctrine of Max Stirner with enthusiasm, and—as soon as he was free from the army—set out for England where he had heard of an anarchist colony in Newcastle, headed by an Austrian anarchist. By the time he got there, the colony had been turned into a private enterprise, in which he took work; but he soon set off for Russia, as a fireman in a steamship.

He had not at this point read Tolstoy, though he had heard of him; indeed, the Austrian military authorities assumed Tolstoy's pamphlets were the source of Sedlak's recalcitrance. But in St. Petersburg (in 1899) he bethought himself that the great man was not far away and set off to visit him. (He assumed that Yasnaya Polyana was an anarchist colony.)

He kept a diary as he tramped and begged his way there. "Well, I am about to see the most famous and original thinker of the dying century." Arriving at dawn, he had breakfast with Tolstoy, and told him his life story. The old man (having no money of his own) borrowed three rubles from the cook to send Sedlak back as far as Tula, asked him to write up his army experiences to help the antiwar cause, and told him about the English colonies set up by Tolstoyans at Purleigh and Whiteway.

When Sedlak arrived at Purleigh (founded by Aylmer Maude), he discovered that it had reverted to private property; but at Whiteway he finally found a welcome, and in fact stayed there till he died in 1935, living in a free union with Nellie Shaw, one of the original founders. He began as a Tolstoyan, but then was attracted to Theosophy, practiced yoga, and wrote *Counterblast to Tolstoy*. Then he turned to Hegel, whose ideas absorbed him for the rest of his life. He published a book on the Hegelian philosophy, which was reviewed in sympathetic journals like *The Theosophist* and *The New Age*.

Like Graeser, Sedlak was a figure of splendid manliness and perfect health—such are the terms in which the colonists described him. (It is notable that these living icons were most often male.) He went barefoot, dressed in white cotton pants and shirt, and wore his hair long. He was often photographed by strangers and compared with paintings of Christ's apostles; the same thing happened to Graeser and other German wanderers. And Sedlak, too, was a vegetarian and practiced Nature Cure.

There are then manifold likenesses between Whiteway and Ascona. It is no exaggeration to say that they were both manifestations of the same idea. But in England the general situation as regards both sexual and orthodox politics was less patriarchal, and the New Age movement as a whole was less extremist in its resistance. As a result it was, in the short run, more widespread and more influential.

The New Age was the title of an important radical journal, one of the few to review Sedlak's book on Hegel. Under the editing of A. R. Orage, *The New Age* was often described as the leading left-wing weekly, and left-wing culturally as much as politically. More generally the phrase was used, together with its alternate, the New Life, as the label most frequently attached to that powerful though diffuse movement of ideas, that idealistic faith generally thought to have been broken by the outbreak of war in 1914. There was also a New Order publishing house and journal, which published Sedlak, a *New Era* magazine, and other such variants on the idea New.

Finally, there was a Fellowship of the New Life, the stimulus for which came from an itinerant Scottish teacher, Thomas Davidson. The meetings he convened in his rooms in Chelsea between 1881 and 1883 are said to be the *fons et origo* of ethical socialism in England. (Ethical socialism was the New Age alternative to scientific or Marxist socialism, and the Fabian Society in fact began as a branch of the Fellowship.) Havelock Ellis the sexologist and Hubert Bland the socialist are two members whose names have not entirely faded from the record.

The movement was international, and its two greatest members, even for the English, at least by now, are a Russian born in 1828, Leo Tolstoy, and a Hindu born in 1869, Mohandas Gandhi. Quite apart from their foreignness, however, seen from the perspective of the English movement then, Tolstoy was too old, and Gandhi too young, to count among its most typical representatives; Tolstoy was a precursor of, Gandhi a successor to, that New Age. But they are the ones we look back to now.

This is partly because, as well as their incarnation of specifically

New Age qualities, they had other extraordinary gifts and achievements. Tolstoy was one of the greatest imaginative writers of the nineteenth century, Gandhi was one of the greatest political leaders of national independence. Thus they give the New Age the endorsement of great achievers—of various kinds of greatness, as common sense and the establishment have understood that term.

It is worth noting that they came to know each other in the medium of that English environment. Tolstoy was a member of the New Age movement as well as a leader. In a list of the magazines he read, drawn up on March 15, 1890, he put down a Swedenborgian journal called *New Christianity*, the American *The World's Advance Thought*, the *Religio-Philosophical Journal*, the Orientalist *Open Court*, the Theosophical *Lucifer*, *Theosophical Siftings*, and the Brotherhood Church's *Dawn Sower*. That is a very representative list of New Age publications. Another such list can be found under "Recommended Reading" in Gandhi's *Indian Opinion*.

Gandhi first heard Tolstoy's name in the vegetarian circles he moved in during his years in London, 1888–91; and first read him (*The Kingdom of God Is Within You*) in South Africa in 1894; wrote to him (in English) in 1908, when Tolstoy was eighty; exchanged letters and documents with him in 1909 and 1910; and founded Tolstoy Farm in South Africa in 1910, the year the old man died. They read each other's writings in English, sent each other books and pamphlets printed in England, and wrote letters to each other in English, and—sometimes literally—via London. How else could a Russian and a Hindu of different generations, different social classes, different religions and languages, never in the same city or country at the same time, come together? It can sometimes seem the greatest achievement of that New Age that it put these two minds in touch with each other.

WRITTEN INVITATIONS

The movement's beginning can fairly, if symbolically, be attached to the year 1880. We have already come across Wagner's pamphlet of that year, and in another pamphlet of 1880, "Spirit of Revolt," the Russian geographer/ecologist and anarchist Peter Kropotkin declared, "There are periods of human society when revolution becomes an imperative necessity, when it proclaims itself as inevitable. . . . The need for a new life becomes apparent." Kropotkin—exiled from Russia for his politics—lived in England and visited Ascona. He was one of the prophets of this period and voices of this temperament. His politics, as opposed to Marx's, and his science, as opposed to Darwin's, were both New Age.

So loosely self-defined a movement naturally included a variety of people and ideas, some of whom belong rather with the authoritarian or systematic kinds of radical, if one is trying to distinguish those two *from* the New Age type. But all three can be, and often were, lumped in together, to contrast the radical with conservative or liberal options. For instance, the Fabian Society and the (Marxist) Social Democratic Federation both were (being radical) and were not (being systematic) parts of the New Age in England.

That movement was often imagined in terms of literal movement, of people leaving their homes, which is of course a traditional gesture of or metaphor for conversion—being called to come out. Thus accounts of Ascona, given us by Hermann Hesse, Mary Wigman, and Emil Szittya, often begin with the sight of bare-legged, long-haired hikers passing through a village, on their way to the center of the New Life, attracting the attention of the settled people, and being followed. Such people went from one such center to another; for instance, to Whiteway, and to Yasnaya Polyana. Dr. Skarvan visited the latter and also the Brotherhood Church in Croydon. Gandhi visited Whiteway. Tolstoy died coming out—running away from home.

But let us begin with written invitations to the New Life, by Tolstoy and by Edward Carpenter, from which we can pass to the people who responded to those invitations, and their equivalents today. The tendencies of the two men's ideas were diametrically opposite, from most points of view. Tolstoy's was an ascetic New Age, Carpenter's one of erotic liberation. But both were part of the same movement, and acknowledged each other as such; both were generally recognized as prophets of the New Age; above all, however different their ideas, they shared the same mentality.

Both the erotic and the ascetic New Ager sought to harken to and obey their inmost voice—something remote from worldly common sense, and requiring no other sanction. The difference was that the ascetic enthusiast located that inmost voice in the soul, as traditionally defined; the erotic enthusiast located it in the body. (Of course, the former paid great attention to the body—witness Gandhi's constant preoccupation with diet and health; and the latter was concerned with the body-soul—see erotic novels like D. H. Lawrence's *The Rainbow*. But the difference is so fundamental that it deserves to be fixed in terms as contrastive as possible.)

From this contrast flowed all the differences between Tolstoy's teaching and Carpenter's. But we should not forget that likeness, which they themselves saw quite clearly. Both engaged in radical critiques of scientific medicine and other systems of modern life and thought. More generally, both demanded that their readers resist all systematic thinking and listen to the inmost voice.

TOLSTOY

An important document of the movement at its most serious was Tolstoy's *The Kingdom of God Is Within You*, written in 1893, of which the subtitle was "Christianity Not as a Mystical Teaching But as a New Concept of Life"—the last phrase making Christianity itself a New Age phenomenon. This was obviously not in any exclusive sense an English book, but it was first published not in Russia, where it had been banned while still in manuscript, but in England at the "Free Age Press." Tolstoy's principal disciple, Vladimir Chertkov, was living in England (he too was an exile from Russia) and publishing the books that Tolstoy could not bring out in his homeland. Indeed, the Tolstoyans in several countries constituted one radical section of the international reading public.

The person we call "the late Tolstoy" was in fact born in 1880 and died in 1910—his life span was the period of the New Age. In 1881 the famous writer of *War and Peace* and *Anna Karenina* moved his large family from the country to Moscow, so that his children could have the advantages and pleasures of city life. But he himself had to meet the harsh and strenuous moral challenges of living in a large industrialized city, with a mixed population that included the very oppressed and the very powerful. This was also the time of the assassination of the Czar, Alexander II, by idealistic young radicals and the execution of his assassins. The effect of these events was to upset for good the delicate balance of interests, policies, and values (domestic, artistic, worldly) by which Tolstoy had hitherto lived. For the next thirty years, he tried to discover both the theory and the practice of a different—and radically religious—attitude to life. *The Kingdom of God Is Within You* was an important step forward in that progress.

Historically, the newness referred to in the subtitle means the way early Christianity differed from the Roman imperial culture in the midst of which it developed; but ultimately it points to the incompatibility between Christian concepts and the Russian Empire of the nineteenth century (and modern Western civilization in general). It denounces that civilization, and prophesies its doom on the authority of true Christianity.

In the 1890s, the modern world system seemed to many people to be trembling, in London as in Moscow, and a new idea to be burgeoning, which might in fact be that old idea of "true Christianity." Aylmer Maude, representing the British New Age, named the period 1897–1907 as the Tolstoy period of history, when it seemed as if Tolstoy groups and colonies were springing up everywhere. A somewhat extended summary of the book will help us to understand what happened.

Tolstoy began by referring to the seventeenth-century Quakers as his spiritual ancestors, and then to some of the nineteenth-century American abolitionists, quoting from William Lloyd Garrison's "Declaration of Sentiments" of 1838. (The former could be called an example of seventeenth-century New Agism.) He described the Quakers' repudiation of patriotism, politics, and the courts, and contrasted with them the radicals of violence he called the jacobins or terrorists: "The spirit of jacobinism is the spirit of retaliation, violence, and murder." Then he expounded the lost truths taught by the fifteenth-century Bohemian Chalicky in his *Drawnet of Faith*.

The latter denounced the adoption and adaptation of Christianity for state purposes by the Roman Emperor Constantine, using the metaphor of fishing in his denunciation. He said that the larger fish, like emperors, tore their way out of Christ's drawnet, and through the holes they made lesser folks followed. Tolstoy agreed, saying that the ruling class everywhere and at all times is hostile to Christianity, and tends to suppress it, even in the books they write. That is why these truths have been lost so many times.

Social obligation has always worked to the advantage of society's ruling class, he said, and nowadays that class is morally retarded, compared with those they rule. For 1,800 years there has been a development of moral sensitivity, but also a development of material power, with opposite moral tendencies. The contradiction is concealed by social hypnosis, which modern methods of communication extend into private life. And the great example of such hypnosis is in the preparation of whole peoples for war. (He cites the effect of military parades—so dear to Russian czars—and the selling of toy soldiers for middle-class children to play with.) All the Western nations, he says, are stockpiling weapons and spreading war propaganda. The German kaiser, "this miserable sick man who has lost his mind from the exercise of power," is the *enfant terrible* of European politics who reveals the mania that others discreetly conceal.

And yet men today pride themselves on "that high degree of culture on which European civilization now stands, with its Krupp guns, smokeless powder, the colonization of Africa, the government [subjection] of Ireland, parliament, journalism, strikes, and the Eiffel Tower." Tolstoy contests the American Colonel Ingersoll, who said that Christ's teaching is no good today, since it does not harmonize with our industrial age. Tolstoy reverses the proposition: since Christianity is the abiding measure of our lives, it is industrial civilization we should get rid of, together with its attendants, science, art, and theology. Unbelievers are deceived by science, as believers are deceived by the churches.

Tolstoy's view of religion was essentially progressive and idealist. The scholarly study of religion (in the 1890s) explained it as a symbolic representation of the forces of nature, which persists in our minds, a survival from the past. But in fact, Tolstoy said, religion refers to the future, and represents the path that humanity must in the future travel.

We are now, according to him, in the third phase of religion's development, the universal (the first was personal or animal, and the second was social or pagan). The process of its realization will go on to an infinity, to an absolute, morally as well as metaphysically speaking. Consequently, to understand religion as something historically conditioned, and so to lower its demands on our conduct, to make religion practical, is to destroy it.

It is now time for society as a whole to change its life because material conditions now make that possible, and because the contradiction between Christian ideals and social facts, above all those of war, is now so great. There is a contrast between our consciousness and our life, and the latter needs to catch up. But this does not mean that people of culture should be our leaders. "The indefiniteness, if not the insincerity, of the relation of the cultured men of our times to this phenomenon [war and conscription] is striking."

Tolstoy's enthusiasm for definiteness and clarity is reflected in his own style and structure, which tend toward the effect of a geometrical theorem. "We must take the Sermon on the Mount to be as much a law as the theorem of Pythagoras." This comes as a surprise and shock to any devoted reader of Tolstoy's novels, whose art it is to represent so much of life in suggestive (i.e., indefinite) relatedness. But this kind of simplification is one of the New Age characteristics—a simple literary style and a simple set of concepts.

A man need only make the new life concept his own, Tolstoy said, for all his chains to fall off. But this means that he must not let the state make moral decisions for him. Indeed, a man must never take an oath of obedience to an army or to the state, however Socialist the latter may be, because he belongs to God. A Christian need not, must not, pass judgment on a government, but he must for himself refuse to support it. "Christianity in its true meaning destroys the state." That is why Christ was crucified.

We hesitate to believe this, Tolstoy says, because we feel that if we lost the protection and order the state gives, we would lose everything else in culture. But that is mere superstition; the state's claim to be guardian of the good is not to be credited; in fact, we know that the individuals who are set in power by the state become evil. We know that thanks to Christ's "lucid and exact" definitions of evil.

Such is the message of this book of 1893, read by Gandhi in South Africa, and felt by him as a calling to a life of social action. It was, in the words of the official Soviet edition, the culmination of all Tolstoy's publicist work of the 1880s. It was praised by Lenin as posing concrete questions of democracy and socialism, and expressing a sincere protest against class domination, although it pointed in a direction very different from that which Lenin followed.

To represent Tolstoy's discipleship in England we can take Isabella Fyvie Mayo (1843–1914). She was a novelist and writer on women's issues, already past her youth when the New Age began, and in most ways a very limited thinker in a very Victorian manner, but under Tolstoy's inspiration she entered the New Age. She was invited by Vladimir Chertkov, Tolstoy's close friend who lived in England, to collaborate in the translation of Tolstoy's work.

Chertkov first settled in a farm near Croydon, because of Kenworthy's Brotherhood Church there, but then moved to the Mill House, Purleigh, toward the end of 1897, where he set up his own colony. In 1900 he bought a house in Eastbourne, where he established the Free Age Press, which put into print four million pages of Tolstoy between 1900 and 1903. Chertkov made himself the official center for the translation and publication of Tolstoy outside Russia, and he chose his collaborators in the cause very carefully. (Albert Skarvan, adviser to the colonists of Monte Verita, translated the novel *Resurrection.*)

Mayo helped Chertkov with the translation of some of Tolstoy's late pamphlets for the Free Age Press, and wrote some quite fiery "Notes" to accompany some of them. (A quotation from one of them forms the epigraph to this chapter.) Her comment on his "The Crisis in Russia" begins, "It is often said that in order to understand Tolstoy one should take into consideration the peculiar conditions of Russian life. It would perhaps be more correct to say that this is just the way to misunderstand Tolstoy. Tolstoy examines and solves the problems of life from the standpoint of Reason and Christianity . . . a moral universal ideal."

In her autobiography, *Recollections of Fifty Years,* she describes her progress from pious Anglican beginnings in London to Tolstoyan convictions in Scotland. She had always supported Christian and feminist causes: in 1877 she attended the meeting to found the Working Ladies Guild, and she listened to the sermons of the great Nonconformist preachers, like Charles Spurgeon and Thomas Guthrie. But by 1910 she was deeply into the Tolstoyan New Age. Thus she implies that she or her friends are vegetarians by remarking that in the recent past vegetarianism had seemed a dangerous eccentricity, and she now prefers the Brotherhood labor churches (such as Kenworthy's) to any regular church. "Since I have lived in Scotland [after 1877—the birth of the New Age] I have not come into any close relation with churches or church work." Her advice to young people is the Tolstoyan and Gandhian "keep a diary and draw up scrupulous accounts." She has just, as she finishes the book, received a message from Tolstoy: "We can imagine nothing better than life, if only in it we fulfill what God desires of us." Nineteen-ten was the year in which Tolstoy was to die; this last message can remind us of the New Age exaltation that accompanied the asceticism.

ICONS AND IDEAS

Books and arguments always incorporate only part of the life of the mind, and this is especially true of movements like New Ages, which distrust the formalities of intellect and aspire to spiritual values. Besides summarizing Tolstoy's book, therefore, we should remind ourselves of the person who wrote it, as he was seen by its readers.

One of the icons of the nineteenth century's New Age was Repin's painting of Tolstoy at the plough, wearing his peasant's blouse, a figure of age and labor, severe and worn. There were innumerable reproductions of this (for magic lantern and stereoscope and so on, as well as simple prints) and many photographs of him in the same costume. Several bitter quarrels in the Tolstoy family were touched off by the questions of by whom his picture should be taken, wearing what, with whom, against what setting, and so on. Pictures like Repin's were a statement that Tolstoy did not belong to his wife and children, or to the class and age he was born into, but to the peasants and the New Age.

His family used to call those who came to Yasnaya Polyana to meet the New Age Tolstoy "the dark people"—to distinguish them from *their* visitors. In fact, a good deal of Tolstoy's thinking did derive from those visitors. His vegetarianism, for instance, was taught him by a Swedish wanderer who called himself Wilhelm Frei. Syutaev, a muzhik from Tver, taught Tolstoy the evil of upper-class philanthropy; and Bondarev taught him the need for everyone to perform bread labor (the daily physical work needed to produce the food one consumed). The last two men were both Bible searchers and sectarians (roughly speaking, the Russian equivalent of nonconformists or dissenters), but they can stand for many more peasants and pilgrims, often orthodox in their Christianity, with whom Tolstoy held long conversations, out of which evolved his writings and his life after 1880.

Another source was the revolutionary movement, which entered Tolstoy's home in the form of the children's tutors. Most importantly, V. I. Alexeiev came to be mathematics tutor in 1877, and had a strong influence on both the eldest child, Sergei, and Tolstoy himself. Alexeiev was then twenty-nine years old, and one of the eight children of a marriage between a peasant woman and a landowner from Pskov. While at the University of St. Petersburg, he had read John Stuart Mill and George Henry Lewes, and became a "Narodnik" (a populist radical).

He had made political propaganda among the workers and joined a famous revolutionary group headed by Nikolai Chaikovski. He then fell under the influence of a man called A. K. Malikov, who preached a mystical-social religion of God-manhood—of God realizing himself in man. Malikov's group founded a commune in Kansas, where Alexeiev and his brother went to live and which lasted from 1875 to 1877. By the time he returned to Russia, moreover, the Alexeiev who went to the Tolstoys' was husband to Malikov's wife and father to his children.

He lived in the village of Yasnaya Polyana, refusing a room in the manor house, because he refused to be served by the white-gloved servants. Sergei Tolstoy, who is our main informant about Alexeiev, calls him the first Tolstoyan, but one might call Leo Tolstoy the first Alexeievan. Tall, thin, beardless, narrow-shouldered, neither strong nor passionate, Alexeiev was an opposite to the temperament Tolstoy had always aspired to—as officer, as lover, as artist. He was what Britishers like D. H. Lawrence and George Orwell, in their anti-Christian outbursts, called "a creeping Jesus." But Tolstoy now apprenticed himself to Alexeiev, in ideas and temperament. Alexeiev took down from Tolstoy's lips the nonecclesiastical version of Jesus' gospel they worked out together and helped him compose his 1881 letter to Czar Alexander III, begging him not to punish the assassins of the previous Czar.

Sonia Tolstoy burst in upon them when they were so engaged and made a terrible scene (about the danger in which they were putting the family), which ended with Alexeiev being exiled to the Tolstoys' estate in Samara. A little later, after some disagreement, Tolstoy wrote him, "We have the air of having forgotten that we love each other. As far as I am concerned, that it is not true. I don't want to forget that I owe you much of the calmness and clarity in my present conception of the world. You are the first educated man I met professing not only in words but in your heart the religion which has become pure light to me. That is why you will always be dear to me."

Via Alexeiev, Tolstoy also met three of the "hundred and ninety-three" radicals, a famous group arrested in 1866, including Malikov, and Bibikov, who acted as bailiff on the Samara estate. Thus the revolutionaries as well as the peasants and the vagabonds like Frei contributed to the New Age ideology as Tolstoy worked it out and spread it through the world. All this is to be seen in those iconic pictures of Tolstoy at the plough that New Agers nailed up on their walls, gave each other as remembrances, stowed away in their packs as they migrated from province to province or from continent to continent.

In the case of Gandhi, the skinny figure in shawl and dhoti with toothless mouth and spinning wheel was familiar from cartoons as much as from photographs. He is alluded to as a joke in 1930s movies and comic songs (for instance, Gracie Fields's). But he too was an icon, and his image was treasured in thousands of homes as something holy, though in it the comic aspects blended together more obviously with the serious. We shall find the picturesque and comic aspects of later New Age leaders important, also.

CARPENTER

Another side of the New Age, almost opposite to Tolstoy's in its recoil from asceticism and evangelical religion, is represented by Edward Carpenter, who wrote in his autobiography that we should learn to understand Christianity as a version of a universal solar religion, and that "the world is coming round again to a concrete appreciation of the value and beauty of actual life, and to a neo-Pagan point of view." Carpenter's work includes such titles as *Love's Coming of Age* and *The Art of Creation*. The latter, of 1904, begins, "We seem to be arriving at a time when, with the circling of our knowledge of the globe, a great synthesis of all human thought on the ancient and ever-engrossing problem of Creation is quite naturally and inevitably taking shape. The world-old wisdom of the Upanishads, with their profound and impregnable doctrine of the Universal Self, the teachings of Buddha or of Lao-tzu, the poetic insight of Plato, the inspired sayings of Jesus and Paul, the speculations of Plotinus, or of the Gnostics, etc., . . . all this, combining with . . . modern physical and biological Science, and Psychology, are preparing a great birth, as it were." This sort of expansive speculation was New Age thinking, as much as Tolstoy's asceticism.

No single text by Carpenter was as important as Tolstoy's *The Kingdom of God Is Within You*, but I can mention a few and dwell briefly on one that is very representative. This last is *Civilization: Its Cause and Cure*, of 1888. Together with Tolstoy's, this was the most important of all books in forming Gandhi's philosophy. It is primarily an attack on modern medicine and health care. Health is wholeness and a positive presence, says Carpenter, and yet we treat it as the mere absence of disease. Medical science makes a fetish of disease, and dances around it.

"The words health, whole, and holy, are of the same stock," he says. (Wendell Berry and Gary Snyder are still telling us the same thing today.) Carpenter quoted Captain Cook on the healthiness of Tahitians, and declared that Africans are the children of nature. The "wild" races—the ancient Greeks, the American Indians, the Africans—are at one with nature in their keenness of sense, and much more. (Gandhi advances many of these ideas.) We should eat fruit and nuts, and avoid even those vegetables which have to be uprooted, like cabbages. In *Towards Democracy*, Carpenter wrote an extremely long poem in Whitman-like blank verse, and presented himself, as Whitman had done, as a figure of perfect health.

Carpenter was sixteen years younger than Tolstoy. Clever, handsome, mild-tempered, he was a favorite of fortune in his early years. He graduated from Cambridge in 1864 and was ordained and made a fellow of his college in 1869. In 1870 he became curate in a Cambridge church where the incumbent was F. D. Maurice, a leading Victorian intellectual.

But Carpenter had always been under the influence of poets like Shelley, Wordsworth, and Whitman, as much as that of theologians—he was oriented toward beauty as much as faith—and after a visit to Italy in 1873, he fell in love with Greek sculpture. Moreover, this development was entwined with his discovery of his own homosexuality. In 1874 he left the church and began a new career as a university extension lecturer. He bought a country cottage in York-shire (near where Ruskin's followers were creating a commune) in 1883, and lived with a working-class family there. He became largely vegetarian and a teetotaler, and lived a great deal in the open air. He grew fruit and vegetables, and took them some miles to sell them in a market. He liked the working people of Sheffield, whom he saw as "natural"—rough but shrewd and good-natured. He preferred them to the guardians of official culture.

Like Tolstoy, Carpenter began his New Age career in the spring of 1881, the beginning of the New Age period. It was then that he found his poetic voice and his philosophic message, in the long poem *Towards Democracy*. He explained later that he had been liberated by the sudden discovery of a new region of his Self, which existed equally in others and which became the subject of his poetry. He knocked together a sort of sentinel box in his garden, in which he wrote—the free open air being as necessary as the free-verse form to his inspiration. He became the guru of the Simple Life.

Today a powerful movement in ecology and protection of the environment is heir to the nineteenth century's pioneers. Everyone thinks of Thoreau, of course, but Edward Carpenter, till recently a forgotten figure, is again being referred to. For instance, Marilyn Ferguson, in her widely read *The Aquarian Conspiracy*, refers to Carpenter nine times, as well as to other figures of the English New Age, like D. H. Lawrence and John Middleton Murry.

In *Love's Coming of Age*, written in 1896, Carpenter had an essay, "Man the Ungrown," in which he criticized the orthodox masculine persona, and saw it as then coming under attack from Woman on the one side, and from Workmen on the other. Of course the hint of sexual as well as gender heresy, developed further in Carpenter's essay on "The Intermediate Sex," and his general propaganda for sexual liberation, was not part of what was congenial to Gandhi or Tolstoy in his work.

Civilization: Its Cause and Cure, on the other hand, *was*. This book had a profound effect on both of them, and it touched on much more of "civilization" than just the nature cure subject discussed before. In it the whole modern structure of material and mental life is as radically condemned as it was in *The Kingdom of God Is Within You*.

Carpenter's rhetoric was much more pagan than Tolstoy's. "On the high tops once more gathering he [Man] will celebrate with naked dances the glory of the human form and the great procession of the stars." (This was quoted by Stanton Coit, the Ethical Culture leader, in his lecture *Is Civilization a Disease?* We see how different branches of the New Age reflected each other.) This is the kind of rhetoric we associate also with Hermann Hesse, and the erotic writers of Ascona.

We don't know whether Carpenter ever stayed in Ascona, but in 1910 and 1911 he was in Florence and held long conversations with Harold Monro, who owned a house in Ascona and moved to and fro between there and Florence. Monro was later the proprietor of the Poetry Bookshop in London and sponsor of contemporary poetry in England. He had just left his wife, and was acknowledging his identity as a homosexual. Thus Carpenter's influence on Monro was like his influence on E. M. Forster; he encouraged both men's erotic liberation. Whether or not Carpenter spent any time in the Swiss lake village, he clearly knew about it, as a center of both erotic liberation and diet-and-nature cure. His attack on "civilization" was an eloquent statement of the values by which the Asconans lived.

This book was actually published in the year of Gandhi's arrival in England, but whether or not he read it then, the latter must surely at that point not have been ready for its sweeping condemnation of Western civilization and its call to simplify social as well as individual life-styles. However, it was reviewed by Henry Salt in *The Vegetarian* in September 1888, so it is quite likely that Gandhi knew about Carpenter's ideas, in abbreviated form, long before 1909. For over the twenty years to come (before Gandhi wrote his own book), Carpenter's teaching persisted and indeed spread.

In his autobiographical *My Days and Dreams*, Carpenter says that even Sidney Webb and G. B. Shaw, the Fabians who had at first most attacked his ideas, had since then themselves ceased to use the word civilization as a self-confident and self-evident value—in its "old optimistic and mid-Victorian sense." In the 1880s and 1890s Carpenter was the greatest teacher of "simplification" in England, as Gandhi was to be elsewhere later.

To complete the symmetry in the treatment of Carpenter and Tolstoy, we should glance at disciples of the former who stood in something of the same relation to him as Isabella Fyvie Mayo did to Tolstoy. Olive Schreiner and Kate Joynes Salt were two women of intellect who were frequent visitors to Millthorpe and members of Carpenter's circle there. They received many of his ideas, and were personally devoted to him. His "ideas" meant most importantly the Simple Life, so the fact that Schreiner did her own housework had an ideological bearing that Gandhi recognized and valued in her later. Schreiner was of course a famous author and thinker in her own right; Kate Salt was for a time secretary to George Bernard Shaw, and was said to be the woman from whom he drew the character Candida in his play of that name. She was of that third sex that Carpenter called Urnings.

Schreiner had intense platonic love affairs with both Carpenter and Havelock Ellis, the sexologist, and those affairs and the other woman's can represent to us the New Age's patterns of sexual experiment. When in 1885 Kate Salt and her husband, Henry Salt, left Eton College, where he had been a master, they put on their sandals and made for the simple life, as Michael Holroyd puts it, "the lemonade and potato digging of Edward Carpenter's world." Like Schreiner, Kate Salt had a platonic affair with Carpenter, and also one with Shaw. Shaw was her Sunday husband, but her heart was given to Carpenter, as Shaw acknowledged.

Of these relationships, we know most about Schreiner's with Ellis. They got to know each other in 1884, and gave each other both a strong affection and physical intimacy (Schreiner would stroll downstairs in the nude to talk with Ellis), without apparently feeling the desire for each other in which an ordinary sexual relationship is rooted. She apparently wanted physical nearness without excitement; and he, she decided, was a true decadent, interested only in the abnormal. But at the same time they discussed sexuality, marriage, prostitution, and deviancy more than any other topics. They gave each other detailed sexual autobiographies. Ellis's wife, Edith Lees, was a feminist devoted to Schreiner and herself more interested in women than men. This pattern of people and their relations can be called paradigmatic for New Age eroticism.

Carpenter and Tolstoy profoundly admired each other's work and acknowledged each other as coworkers in the New Age, although the former's aestheticism, putting all life under the aegis of Art and Creation, expresses a moral philosophy quite unlike Tolstoy's asceticism. As vegetarians, Carpenter and Tolstoy were both heroes and comrades to the Asconans. In 1910, when Tolstoy died, the people of Monte Verita wrote in the local newspaper, the *Locarno-Ascona Boten*, "We as vegetarians have lost our greatest comrade of all ages, literature has lost one of its giants, and humanity a master and teacher, a patriarch and a prophet." Erich Muehsam, one of the young enthusiasts there, wrote a poem celebrating Tolstoy's flight from domesticity and respectability.

> He went to die, as never a man yet went,
> Not weary-cursing, not in fear of death,
> He burst the ring of gold that held his fate . . .
> An old man left his wife, his goods, his house.

Thus even in his death Tolstoy was an inspiration to these New Agers, many of whom disagreed with most of his beliefs about how to live well but who agreed with his rebellion against the status quo.

NEW AGE JOURNALISM

These prophetic voices are the part of the New Age most impressive to us now. But they reached the general public indirectly as well as directly, as parts of a general discourse. If we had asked about the New Age during this period, we might have found most book readers identifying the idea primarily with some very popular journalists. (I am using that category to include writers of plays and novels, as will be seen; they were tagged as journalists at the end of the New Age, as a way to discredit both them and it, but I shall use the word in an honorific sense when it does validly characterize New Ages.) We have already mentioned A. R. Orage, whose journal, *The New Age*, promoted so many of our themes; but his fame was comparatively narrow, being limited to a highbrow audience. Much more widely known were Robert Blatchford, H. G. Wells, George Bernard Shaw, G. K. Chesterton, and Hilaire Belloc.

Wells, who was born in 1866, began publishing science fiction in the middle of the 1890s: *The Time Machine* in 1895, *The Invisible Man* in 1897, *The War of the Worlds* in 1898. In their way, even these stories were New Age; they increased the range of imaginative possibility and suggested ways out from contemporary "reality," which is the reason New Agers have usually liked fantasy and futurism. Wells then turned to nonfiction works like *Mankind in the Making* in 1903 and *A Modern Utopia* in 1905, books that invited readers to speculate about the possible and the future. He was especially concerned with gender and sexual changes.

Thus *A Modern Utopia*, with its Ticino setting, discussed a hypothetical social order of modern Samurai, based on the Samurai of Japan. This inspired Harold Monro and a friend to found an order of Voluntary Nobility and a press to print books devoted to that idea. This was an ascetic New Age idea. The Samurai were to practice chastity, vegetarianism, and early rising, to renounce drink and smoking, and to spend some days each year in fasting and meditation. Wells came to some of their meetings.

Even Wells's social comedies, which began with *Kipps* in 1905, gave his heroes and himself a cheerful, impudent, Cockney style that was the very opposite of official England, and seemed to stand for a radically new society.

In his attitude to socialism, Wells was strikingly like Robert Blatchford, a popular radical journalist who set up his own paper, *The Clarion*, in 1891, whose circulation went as high as sixty thousand. His book about socialism, *Merrie England*, of 1893, sold two million copies, two hundred thousand being ordered before publication, and is said to have converted far more Englishmen to the cause than Marx's *Capital* ever did. He was one of the small group who founded the Independent Labor Party in 1894. His immense success was a sign of the power of journalism in those years, and a sign of a hopeful mood.

His *Britain and the British* began, "The purpose of this book is to convert the reader to Socialism," but in fact it is Emerson who is cited rather than Marx. He wrote for those he called "unattached Socialists." Chapter 2 of *Merrie England* ends by citing Ruskin, Carpenter, and Morris as recommended reading. Blatchford called himself a Tory Democrat and an Anarcho-Communist, in other words, an antisystematizer. Though he used Fabian pamphlets as sources, he called the Fabians themselves Gradgrinds in Socialist clothing. (Thomas Gradgrind is the character in Dickens's *Hard Times* who justifies the industrial system in all its harshness.) Later in life he became more conservative, but in his radical days he was a classic New Ager.

Wells and Blatchford were great simplifiers and popularizers, both in the literal sense of reducing to common sense complex ideas like socialism and in the metaphorical sense of promising that the powers and mysteries of authority would dissolve at the touch of common-sense criticism.

Shaw was more of an intellectual virtuoso, a paradoxist and self-displayer, whose sincerity in professing socialism Blatchford distrusted; but Shaw was also a true New Ager in his own way. He was, for instance, much more ardent in understanding and appreciating the late Tolstoy and the early Gandhi than any other man of letters. He corresponded with Tolstoy and was eager to meet Gandhi when the latter came to England in 1930–31. Shaw told reporters that he and Gandhi were two of a very rare kind, and that theirs was a meeting of Mahatma major and Mahatma minor.

After a rather miserable youth, Shaw "found himself" in the 1880s, in the New Age and *as* a New Ager, in many matters of faith and opinion. Both Shaw and Wells were also New Agers by virtue of their costumes, their self-stylization: Shaw was depicted in a thousand cartoons with his ginger beard, his Jaeger suits, his sandals, his bicycle; Wells, too, and Gandhi on occasion, were to be seen cycling. (The bicycle, mildly comical appropriate technology, was *the* New Age transport form.) Wells depicted his autobiographical heroes again and again as short, fat, bouncy, untidy, exclamatory men. The same stress on comic self-styling was to be seen in G. K. Chesterton, with his cloak, long hair, and big belly, and Hilaire Belloc, dressed—so Blatchford said—like a Catholic priest. All these journalists were public entertainers. New Agers used costume as an answer to both the authoritarians' uniforms and the systematizers' three-piece suits.

The journalists gave their loyalty, however, to systematic ideas (that being the mode of *seriousness* they endorsed) and so were to some degree disloyal to the New Age movement. Shaw allied himself to Sidney and Beatrice Webb in the Fabian Society and helped to keep it devoted to statistical analysis and the "permeation" of existing institutions as the most practical of socialist options. Wells would have made the society more experimental, more New Age. But his own energies were invested in encyclopedist projects, combining all sorts of knowledge systematically. The same is true of Chesterton and Belloc's Catholicism: their personas were New Age, but their serious recommendations were quite different.

Nevertheless, on his visit to England in 1909 Gandhi took some of the ideas that most struck him from Chesterton. In an article in the *Illustrated London News* on September 18, Chesterton exhorted Indian nationalists to remain true to their own culture, and to turn away from the ideas they were absorbing from the West. It was particularly the systematizing influence of Herbert Spencer he deplored. "One of their papers is called the *Indian Sociologist.* Do the Indian youths want to pollute their ancient villages and poison their kindly homes by introducing Spencer's philosophy into them?" Spencer's sociology was at that time taken to be an extreme example of systematic thinking.

The *Indian Sociologist* was the organ of the London Indian terrorists, including Savarkar and Krishnavarma, who were Gandhi's main enemies. Gandhi's friends in South Africa, like Joseph Doke, thought Chesterton must be joking, but Gandhi wanted to have Chesterton's article translated for his journal, *Indian Opinion.* As the Gandhi scholar Geoffrey Ashe says, Gandhi found his "true India," as Chesterton found his "true England," in the legendary epoch of heroes and sages.

Chesterton wrote a book on Blake, admired Shelley, and was deeply influenced by Whitman—principally as the voice of a buoyant and direct vision of reality. These were all leading New Age lights. And even after his conversion to Catholicism, in 1922, he never entirely turned away from the milieu of Carpenter, Annie Besant, and Edwin Arnold, as Ashe says. Like Blake, he hated generalizations, and set great store by "minute particulars," and his book on Christ has the Blakean title *The Everlasting Man.* He was therefore as hostile to the Fabians as to Spencer. He held that "free thought," agnostic and atheist, was a prison cell of determinism. Like Blake, he wanted to startle his reader into seeing freshly, without the myopia of the conditioned response; his paradoxes were intended to have that effect.

In their negative thinking, of course, Chesterton and his friends took much the same line as Gandhi in criticizing modern society, and at the same moments. Hilaire Belloc entered Parliament in 1906 as a Liberal, but withdrew, embittered by the Parliamentary process, in 1910. He and Chesterton's brother, Cecil, wrote an attack on Parliament called *The Party System.* (Gandhi is unusually harsh in his remarks on Parliament in *Hind Swaraj*, published the same year.) Belloc saw Fabian ideas as leading to bureaucracy, and called another of his books *The Servile State.*

Thus we see, in the two "conservatives" of the famous quartet, as in the two "liberals," a blending of New Age ideas with the systematic thinking of the time. Gandhi was able to draw on them, as well as on those more profoundly similar, like Tolstoy and Carpenter.

CHAPTER THREE

Gandhi's London

> On the boat I had worn a black suit, the white flannel one
> which my friends had got for me having been kept especially
> for wearing when I landed. I had thought that white clothes
> would suit me better when I stepped ashore, and therefore I
> did so in white flannel. Those were the last days of Septem-
> ber. . . . The shame of being the only person in white
> clothes was already too much for me.
>
> M. K. Gandhi, *An Autobiography*

This English New Age was the community of which Mohandas K.
Gandhi became a citizen at the age of nineteen in 1888. We can
follow him—a quiet, timid, impressionable youth, new to everything
in England—as our guide through his parts of the New Age carnival
during the three years he stayed there, and beyond.

When he landed in London, Gandhi had known only life in a small
town in a small state on the Arabian Sea coast of India, and he was
deeply impressed by what he knew of official authoritarian England.
He had very little sense of India as a civilization, much less as a
political entity, that could rival the West. Morally, as became obvious
later, he was stern, and would say no forever to what offended him,
but imaginatively he was labile, ready to believe and believe in all of
official England's tales of material and moral power.

LONDON 1888–91

It is, however, worth taking note of a single London event a few
months before Gandhi arrived: "Bloody Sunday," a defiance of that
official England, which brought together a number of the people to

whom he would be finally closer in sympathy. "Bloody Sunday" took place on November 13, 1887, and was a clash between protesters and the authorities of a kind we are familiar with in our own times. The former wanted to hold a rally in Trafalgar Square, but the latter had forbidden it, and fifteen hundred police and two hundred mounted Life Guards were called out to prevent it.

The protesters assembled at various points around the city. William Morris, George Bernard Shaw, and Annie Besant made speeches at Clerkenwell Green, before their section began its march. Shaw and Besant marched together. Edward Carpenter and Henry Salt were among the protesters. Heroes of the day were the labor leader John Burns and the author Cunninghame-Graham, who chained themselves to the railings outside a hotel. They and the Marxist Maurice Hyndman were sent to jail for their actions.

The impact was considerable. Besant, who tried to organize a line of carts and wagons to check the police charges on the day, founded the Socialist Defence Association after it. William Morris thought this might be the beginning of revolution, and withdrew from overt militancy. And in the immediate future came the Match Girls' Strike of 1888, led by Besant, and the Dock Strike of 1889, led by Burns. These were the English people and ideas that finally meant most to Gandhi, but his discovery of them—and himself—was gradual.

Slender, broad-cheeked, glowing-eyed, Gandhi was full of maladroit enthusiasm and naïve curiosity. He arrived in London dressed in white flannels, in late September, having been misdirected as to English dress codes, and then was mortified to be unable to change to something less conspicuous because his luggage was delayed. When an Indian acquaintance came to his hotel to greet him, Gandhi played with his friend's headgear, the symbolic top hat. "I casually picked up his top-hat, and trying to see how smooth it was, passed my hand over it the wrong way and disturbed the fur." Dr. Mehta looked angrily at what he was doing and stopped him. "But the damage was done." He was lectured on being overfamiliar.

A recent book about Gandhi remarks on his tactile sensibility, even at the end of his life, when his habit of touching women gave rise to sexual scandal. "Like most Indians he was a highly tactile person and found physical touch irresistible. It is hard to find an informal photograph of him in which his hand does not rest on someone's shoulder or he is not patting someone on the back." Gandhi was, I think we can guess, absorbing through his fingertips the magic of Victorian London from that strange black cylinder, but he obediently put the hat down and absorbed his friend's advice instead.

This confiding naïveté, both toward his friend and toward England, was situational, in part—most young Indian students arriving in London must have displayed something like it. But in part it was Gandhi's special way of believing in himself (and so in other people) and this was to remain a valuable gift of his to the end. He believed all they said, and expected to see their promises fulfilled. Other students in much the same position, like his rival-to-be, Mohammed Ali Jinnah, mastered the forms of English life—and were mastered by them—much more brilliantly.

Gandhi, however, at first took lessons in Western dancing and violin playing and elocution. He learned to comb his hair, shine his shoes, and read the daily paper. He was ready, out of a kind of love, to make himself into an Englishman of the official kind. His enormous change of attitude—to quite an opposite readiness—was very gradual. He first saw London as a city grouped around Buckingham Palace, the Tower of London, and the Houses of Parliament.

He attended church services, though mostly in nonconformist chapels: one of the famous preachers of the day he heard was Dr. Spurgeon, in the Tabernacle; another was Joseph Parker, at the City Temple Congregationalist Church, on Holborn Viaduct. Parker was famous for his "appeal to the thoughts of young men," especially men of business. (It was still possible then to link Protestant piety and business efficiency, in the way that Defoe linked them, as twin tendencies). Parker's Thursday noon services brought merchant and clerk alike trooping in, we are told—clerks drew lots to see who should be given the time off to attend.

It is pleasant to think that Gandhi might have brushed shoulders with the future prime minister David Lloyd George (who also attended) at one of these occasions. Such commerce-minded evangelism was not in general to be counted as New Age enthusiasm, but this was a time of group self-assertion for the dissenting sects, and a little later, as we shall see, they were to stimulate Gandhi to social and political action of their own kind.

But his attention and allegiance were most significantly engaged by the quite different institutions of the New Age. Bewildered at first by so many challenges and solicitations, he began to orient himself and find his feet when he discovered a vegetarian restaurant in London. As he opened that door, he entered the New Age. There were about ten such restaurants in London then; the Central, in Farrington Street, was next door to the Vegetarian Society, which had launched *The Vegetarian* magazine in January 1888. Besides literal food, these offered Gandhi reading material, and discussion groups and social life. Above all, by refusing to eat the roast beef of old England, they refused to join in the hearty rituals of English power. Beyond the vegetarians themselves, moreover, stretched perspectives of other groups with comparable interests, and other people ready to welcome a young Hindu.

As we already know, vegetarianism was then not just a diet option; it was at the center of a web of idealistic thinking and action. A. F. Hills, the chairman of the Thames Iron Works, was president of the Vegetarian Federal Union, formed in 1889. He described its aim as "to formulate the essential conditions necessary for the attainment of the Ideal, first in the physical, and then in the mental, moral, and spiritual life . . . man made one with God by obedience to His will."

Mr. Hills financed *The Vegetarian* almost single-handedly and was an enthusiastic and puritan idealist. His company built ironclad battleships, and he is said to be the man from whom Shaw drew the armaments manufacturer in *Major Barbara*. He spoke quite a Shelleyan rhetoric about the great battle between Good and Evil in the world. Josiah Oldfield, editor of *The Vegetarian* and a man with whom Gandhi shared rooms for a time, also employed a Shelleyan or Blakean rhetoric. "When the inspiration of a diviner love has burned in the national life—when once the laws of men are made harmonious with the laws of God, then the new Jerusalem, perfect in its political purity, lovely in its moral strength, will descend as a bride adorned for her husband." This is something Oldfield wrote for *The Vegetarian* in November 1889, during Gandhi's time in London. Both he and Gandhi himself declared that Gandhi got his first lessons in political organizing during the months he was on the Executive Committee of the Vegetarian Society, staring in September 1890.

THEOSOPHY AND ETHICAL CULTURE

Toward the end of Gandhi's stay in London he joined, or was a candidate to join, the Theosophical Society. There was a considerable crossover in membership and ideas between this and the Vegetarian Society. But Gandhi was wary of its occultism (for instance, the attempt at thought transference). He stayed interested in the society for many years, however, and seems to have been attracted by its brilliant women leaders, Helena Petrovna Blavatsky and Annie Besant, and its revival of Hindu religion.

Theosophy was perhaps the major example of the Orientalizing mood that Gandhi met in London (and later in South Africa). It was a new religion, officially founded in New York in 1875 by Blavatsky and Colonel Olcott. It derived from combining all the old religions and extracting the essence of each, but also from appealing to certain ancient, esoteric doctrines and powers handed down secretly through the ages from master to disciple and particularly associated with India and Tibet. Thus, if its one face was close to Unitarianism and Transcendentalism, the other was close to magic, alchemy, and witchcraft. (Only the first face was attractive to Gandhi.) This was a central New Age phenomenon: Blavatsky and Olcott set off for India in 1879—at the beginning of that New Age.

Gandhi's career ran parallel to Annie Besant's in several ways, and in more than one time and place, for she was established as a nationalist leader in India before Gandhi himself arrived there in 1914. The main interest of that parallelism for us is the fascination that India held for both. Each had many interests and many opportunities, in religion and politics and other things; but in a way that is typical for other New Ages besides their own, Asia in general, and India in particular, drew them irresistibly. India was, perhaps is, *the* New Age country, for Westerners.

There were Theosophists at Ascona even before the enthusiasts of Monte Verita arrived there. In 1889, Alfred Pioda, a liberal local politician with New Age ideas, proposed to found a colony of Theosophists there. He formed a joint stock company for the purpose, and one of his allies in the scheme was Countess Wachtmeister, a close friend of Madame Blavatsky. Another ally was Franz Hartmann, also a friend of Blavatsky, who translated, among other things, the

Bhagavad Gita in 1898. Hermann Hesse, who was reading the The-osophists at the time when he first came to Ascona, around 1907, was an enthusiastic admirer of Hartmann's Gita, as were many other Asconans. One of the founders of the sanatorium there, Ferdinand Brune, was a Theosophist (he went on to India) and so was Gustav Nagel, a *Wanderprediger*, a wandering preacher, who walked from one to another such settlement.

Another London group Gandhi was in sympathy with was called Ethical Culture or Ethical Religion. We don't know that he was acquainted with its leaders during this first period in London, but on later visits he certainly attended meetings, and his close friends in South Africa, Henry and Millie Polak, had been members before leaving England.

This movement had been founded in New York in 1876 by Felix Adler, an ex-Orthodox Jew. Theologically, it declared only that moral tenets should not be founded in dogma; but in social matters it was more positive and active and Tolstoyan. The members established a settlement house in 1886, and supported visiting nurses, camps for the young, legal aid, and model tenements. The three tenets governing members were sexual purity, intellectual development, and the giving of surplus income to the working class.

Adler's father was a rabbi; Felix studied at Heidelberg and took his moral philosophy from Kant. The tone of the meetings was intellectual, but at least in New York members of the movement attended Sunday services, and celebrated marriages and funerals. Many members were Jewish, many Unitarian by origin.

It was Stanton Coit, born in 1858, who brought Ethical Culture to London, and it was he whom Gandhi and Polak knew. He took his Ph.D. at Berlin University, and then went to London and lived for a year in the Toynbee Hall settlement house. He took over the South Place Chapel in 1888 and attracted an audience including Leslie Stephen, Henry Sidgwick, and J. A. Hobson. (The years of his engagement with this cause are those of the New Age: he joined the movement, in America, in 1880, and was minister in South Place 1888–91, the years Gandhi was in London.) Ramsay MacDonald edited the society's periodical for a time; so did J. A. Hobson, the author of *Imperialism*. Coit was an enthusiastic Fabian and feminist. He brought out a Tolstoy-like anthology of spiritual readings that included several passages from *The Kingdom of God Is Within You*, and many from Ruskin, but none from Marx; some Hindu and Buddhist texts; quite a bit of Shelley and Carpenter; George Eliot and Wordsworth; and a lot of Emerson.

The South Place Chapel (of which we shall hear more later) was served by another American minister before Coit—Moncure Conway. He was a comparative religionist, interested in the religions of the East, and especially India. Indeed, the South Place congregation had been addressed by traveling Hindu intellectuals, like Rammohan Roy and Keshav Chunder Sen, from early in the nineteenth century.

The South Place Chapel was a center of New Age ideas in the eighteenth-century New Age and right through the next century. It was a place where Annie Besant was heard speaking, from early in her career; and Moncure Conway introduced her to Charles Bradlaugh, initiating a famous alliance in the cause of atheism and religious freedom generally. Gandhi admired Bradlaugh, and attended his funeral, which occurred during Gandhi's first period in London.

Another interest at South Place was imperialism and the British Empire. In 1900 a book was published that incorporated seventy lectures given at South Place on that topic. J. A. Hobson, the economist, was a lecturer there for nearly forty years after 1899, and his friends were the main critics of empire. The influence of their ideas reached Gandhi in South Africa, probably via Henry Polak.

Hobson is a good example of certain qualities—severe moralism, emotional dryness, abstractness of style—that make the Ethical Culture movement seem the reverse of naïve and New Age. It certainly did not belong to the erotic New Age; but we must remember there was an ascetic and rationalist wing, too. In his autobiography, *Confessions of an Economic Heretic*, Hobson stresses his lifelong "heresy," and also makes a plea for a "free and fragmentary intercourse" as "a mode for the discovery and communication of truth." He says that "thinking is in itself a brief fragmentary process," and intellectual system is a form of self-aggrandizement: the great journalists, like Havelock Ellis and H. N. Brailsford, have often been more valuable than the scholars. Thus, at least in a theoretical way, Hobson set his face against theory, like a true New Ager.

The Ethical Culturists and their allies/rivals, the Positivists, were interested in teaching ethical values in schools, disentangled from all ecclesiastical and theological provenance. F. J. Gould, one of South Place's most prolific authors, and one of the founders of the Rationalist Press Association, went to India to lecture on this idea. He wrote biographies of great social revolutionaries, notably Tom Paine, H. M. Hyndman, the Marxist, and Auguste Comte, the Positivist. (We find references to Gould's work, and to many Ethical Culture activities, in Gandhi's *Indian Opinion*, and Gandhi corresponded for quite a long time with Florence Winterbottom, secretary to the society.)

Since Gandhi's friend, Edwin Arnold, was himself an Orientalist, we can guess that the Ethical Society's interest in India would be another attraction for him. Moncure Conway's major literary work, however, was a biography of Tom Paine, which, together with a Paine Exhibition, made everyone aware of that great—but up to then, scandalous—revolutionary.

Percy Chubb, who helped organize the Ethical Culture movement in England and then moved to America, declared later that Ethical Culture was a major precursor for socialism, which then displaced it as a secular religion. Chubb played a part in several manifestations of the New Age, including the Fellowship of the New Life in England, and somewhat peripheral offshoots like the play-way in education and the pageant movement, which brought artistic and spiritual values into schools and public life.

William Salter, in Chicago, wrote perhaps the best summary of Ethical Culture's position, *Ethical Religion*, which came out in 1905 and which Gandhi translated and summarized for *Indian Opinion* in South Africa. (Gandhi adopted the first eight out of its fourteen chapters.) It stressed the convergence of religion with contemporary philosophy and science, especially the idea of evolution. Coit's introduction said: "The Ethical Societies constitute the only organized religious movement which has come into existence and developed under the Darwinian method of viewing human events." In fact, its idea was creative rather than Darwinian evolution; it expounded not biological but moral evolution in man as a species. Salter himself said that the mistake of theology had been to conceive all our best thoughts in the form of a perfect other person. *We* are to become divine. This sort of proposition was very congenial to Gandhi.

Theosophy, Ethical Religion, and Vegetarianism were thus three of the intellectual institutions (though they were quite loosely instituted) of the New Age London of the 1880s and 1890s. But we should not neglect the nonintellectual, comic or crankish side of the New Age, for which also Gandhi had a strong appreciation. Chapter 22 of his autobiography is entitled "Narayan Hemchandra," and is about the traveling Hindu eccentric of that name.

"His dress was queer—a clumsy pair of trousers, a wrinkled, dirty, brown coat after the Parsee fashion, no necktie or collar, and a tasselled woolen cap. He grew a long beard. He was lightly built and short of stature. His round face was scarred with smallpox, and had a nose which was neither pointed nor blunt. With his hand he was constantly turning over his beard. Such a queer-looking and queerly dressed person was bound to be singled out in fashionable society."

It is unusual for Gandhi to give so much detail in describing a person. Clearly he is moved, in remembering the man, as he was in knowing him, by a fond appreciation, which is admiring as well as protective. Gandhi offered to teach the other man English, and they became "close friends." Hemchandra was innocent of grammar, but "was not to be baffled by his ignorance." He scorned Gandhi's instructions, saying that he himself had never felt the need of grammar. " 'Well, do you know Bengali? I know it. I have travelled in Bengal. It is I who have given Maharshi Devendranath Tagore's works to the Gujarati-speaking world. . . . And you know I am never literal in my translations. I always content myself with bringing out the spirit.' "

He was going on to France (he had heard there was a literature in French), Germany, and America for the same purpose. Gandhi is quite clear that the man's performance as a writer and intellectual was a joke, and says nothing of any spiritual or religious teaching, yet found his naïve originality, his courage in following his own line, impressive.

Gandhi asked where Hemchandra would find the money to do so much traveling. " 'What do I need money for? I am not a fashionable fellow like you. The minimum amount of food and the minimum amount of clothing suffice for me . . . I always travel third class.

While going to America also I shall travel on deck.' " By the time he was writing his autobiography, Gandhi was of course a Hemchandra himself, in his simplicity of dress, food, traveling, and so on. Even at the time, Gandhi says, there was "a considerable similarity between our thoughts and actions."

But when they first met, he had much to learn from Hemchandra. He tells us that they encountered each other at Miss Manning's National Indian Association, a regular social occasion in London, where Gandhi used to sit tongue-tied, never speaking except when spoken to—"Miss Manning knew that I could not make myself sociable." Hemchandra showed him how to shrug off such timidity, not by becoming polished but by a New Age indifference to the social game.

Gandhi gives us one striking example of that. John Burns's London Dock Strike had just ended, thanks in part to the intervention of Cardinal Manning, whose disinterested "simplicity" was held to have been politically effective. This prompted Hemchandra to visit "the sage" and congratulate him. Gandhi asked how he could get to see such a great man, but Hemchandra saw no difficulty. He had Gandhi write the Cardinal a letter saying Hemchandra was a traveling Indian author, and Gandhi was his translator. Their letter was politely acknowledged and they were invited to call. When they set out together, Hemchandra was wearing his usual shabby clothes, which embarrassed Gandhi; but his friend said, "You civilized fellows are all cowards," and in fact the interview with the Cardinal passed off perfectly well. The implication of the anecdote, and of much of Gandhi's later life story, is that he took this friend's lessons to heart.

Hemchandra came to Gandhi's lodgings one day in shirt and dhoti (which meant no trousers). This alarmed the landlady, who announced him to her tenant as "some kind of crazy man." Gandhi asked his friend if the children in the street hadn't shouted at him. "Well, they ran after me, but I did not mind them and they were quiet." Later, in America, he was even prosecuted for being indecently dressed. If he got to Germany, and stayed a few years, he may have reached Ascona, where there were often trouserless wanderers to be seen—who also were sometimes prosecuted by the Swiss authorities. Refusing trousers was like refusing meat, a gesture that made the Western world very uneasy, however serenely the gesture was performed.

Narayan Hemchandra exemplifies the comic side of the New Age that gets lost when we study it just as intellectual history and shows us Gandhi's attitude to that side, which is seriously as well as humorously appreciative. (Gandhi described himself as a crank, and encouraged people to laugh at him—it was one of his ways of making friends.) And he reminds us how often Indians were part of the New Age.

LEADERS GANDHI KNEW

Four of the New Age leaders who had especially interesting connections with Gandhi deserve some brief introduction. They are Henry Salt, Olive Schreiner, Edwin Arnold, and Annie Besant. Gandhi knew all of them personally, though it was via their writings that they made their biggest impact on him.

It was Henry Salt's pamphlet, "A Plea for Vegetarianism," that persuaded Gandhi of the wrongness of eating meat. Before reading Salt, Gandhi had abstained out of deference to his parents, but without rational conviction. That change we have seen to be a very important one, which initiated many others in his life. The pamphlet began with a quotation from Thoreau, and later Salt's little book about Thoreau introduced Gandhi to the American, in South Africa.

Salt was a long-term and close friend to George Bernard Shaw, though a much less brilliant figure. Shaw explained their friendship by saying that they had been Shelleyans and Humanitarians together. The love of Shelley was important to most New Agers then; he was the poet of idealism. For instance, Harold Monro was interested in horses, not books, up to about 1900. "Then, like most of us," says his friend, F. S. Flint, "he met Shelley, and his entire life was changed. He became a gloomily serious young man."

Salt's turn away from Tennyson toward Shelley announces his literary radicalism. In fact, his first book, of 1887, was a Shelley primer. As for humanitarianism, this was perhaps Salt's main cause. He founded the Humanitarian League, and edited the *Humanitarian Review*. The horror at vivisection, and the distrust of modern medicine this implied, as well as the reverence for animal life in general, was as important an item as vegetarianism in the humanitarian creed. The *Review* regularly attacked blood sports, corporal punishment, the death penalty, and the despoiling of the countryside. Shaw offered a sort of penitent tribute to Salt, and reproach to himself, saying: "My pastime has been writing sermons in plays, sermons preaching what Salt practiced."

Salt was the son of an Indian army officer who quarreled with his wife. The boy grew up—as Shaw did—unusually close to his mother and hostile to his father. (This pattern can be seen in the lives of many New Agers.) A brilliant student, Salt began a career as a teacher at Eton College, but wrote for progressive papers and journals like Hyndman's. He was a great friend of Jim Joynes, who also taught there but translated *Capital* and got arrested in Ireland for supporting Henry George, the economic radical. When Joynes was fired over this incident, Salt also resigned. (The headmaster of Eton put Salt's foolish gesture down not only to his socialism, but to his mixing that with vegetarianism.) He married Kate Joynes, Jim's sister. Salt seems to have played a subordinate role to his wife, as he did to his mother.

Salt's politics were what we would now call ecological, or New Age. Shaw called him a born revolutionist, but Salt himself said his profession was "looking for, and at, wild flowers." He loved Thoreau; to him, it has been said, *Walden* was as important as Whitman's *Leaves of Grass* was to Carpenter, and Butler's *Erewhon* was to Shaw. Carpenter was also an admirer of *Walden* and was sometimes called "The English Thoreau." Salt edited a later version of *Civilization: Its Cause and Cure*, as he did other New Age classics, like Godwin's *Political Justice*. Thus he served the New Age on several fronts. Gandhi remembered his old teacher gratefully, corresponded with him, and saw him on his last trip to England, in 1931.

Olive Schreiner, next, admired and supported Gandhi's New Age politics in her homeland, South Africa, and Gandhi referred to her as a friend. She was a central figure in the New Age, from certain points of view. In 1881, at the beginning of the period, she arrived in London to make her literary career. In 1883 she published her novel *The Story of an African Farm*, famous in its day for its realism about marriage, and in our day for opening fiction up to the experience of women in colonial society. (Elaine Showalter calls the heroine, Lyndall, the first wholly feminist heroine in English literature.)

In 1884 Schreiner made friends with Havelock Ellis, and, as we know, the two investigated sexual behavior and discussed all the current experiments in love and marriage. Their idea of sex was pre-Freudian, and was forgotten when Freud's more systematic idea triumphed. Their idea was unlike his because tied in to progressive and evolutionary sympathies; but in its day it was revolutionary, and it seems to have influenced Gandhi in his sexual experiments at the end of his life. Ellis and Schreiner belonged to the Men and Women Club, founded in 1885, where sexual problems were discussed. This club, of about twenty members, met from 1885 to 1889.

Schreiner also went with Ellis to meetings of the Progressive Association, and the Fellowship of the New Life, where Ellis met Edward Carpenter, who became a close friend of both. These were key institutions of the New Age.

Schreiner's book *Woman and Labor* came out in 1911, at the very end of this period. She was almost alone in seeing the race conflict in South Africa as part of the worldwide struggle between capital and labor. Nevertheless, she was a New Ager rather than a Marxist: though she was a close friend of Eleanor Marx, she never read Karl Marx's *Capital,* and very rarely joined organizations. In 1914 she took a pacifist position on the war, and scolded Gandhi for raising an Indian ambulance corps to support the British. Thereafter there was little connection between them.

The third of these personalities was Edwin Arnold, with whom Gandhi cooperated to found a new London branch of the Vegetarian Society. Arnold was born in 1832, and won the Newdigate Prize for poetry at Oxford with his *Feast of Belshazzar* in 1852. He became a chief interpreter of India to the West. In 1857 he was made principal of a government college in Poona, where he introduced Westernizing reforms—he reduced the amount of Sanskrit taught, introduced science and the English classics, and admitted non-Brahmin students. However, he also learned Sanskrit and Marathi, and became very interested in Indian culture.

In 1860, back in England, he became editorialist for the Liberal *Daily Telegraph,* where he remained an editor until 1889. This newspaper financed imperial expeditions, like Henry Stanley's three-year African journey from Zanzibar west to the mouth of the Congo. Arnold

GANDHI'S LONDON ■ 73

was much involved in promoting this journey, and Stanley named an African river after him. (In 1876 Stanley proposed building a railway from the Cape to Cairo, to make Africa a British continent.) The *Telegraph*'s imperialism led to a break between it and Gladstone; during the crisis of 1878, about the Russo-Turkish War, the newspaper went over to Disraeli and the Conservatives. Arnold was made a Companion of the Star of India in 1877 when Victoria was named Empress. He wrote passages of her Speech from the Throne in 1878.

However, there was another side to Arnold, which explains Gandhi's liking for him and their alliance. In 1879 he published *The Light of Asia*, a verse biography of the Buddha, which became very popular. It had appeared in thirty editions by 1885. (In the United States, where it appeared under Transcendentalist auspices, it was even more popular.) In 1885 he produced *The Song Celestial*, largely a translation of the Bhagavad Gita, in which version Gandhi first met that classic of Hinduism. In the 1890s he did some translations from the Koran, published as *Pearls of the Faith* and *The Gulistan;* but by then he was receiving rather contemptuous reviews both from scholars in religion and from literary critics. His work was seen as popularization, and his poetry was derived from Keats and Tennyson. He was, however, considered for the Poet Laureateship when Tennyson died, and Gandhi reported in *Indian Opinion* the rumor that he had been passed over because of his sympathy for Oriental culture.

All Arnold's work was in some ways ecumenical. *The Light of Asia* was said to be composed as a service to religious liberalism in England. Isabella Fyvie Mayo, the Tolstoyan, was a great admirer and knew Arnold personally. In 1868 Arnold married the daughter of his friend William H. Channing, minister at a Free Christian Church, an institution like the South Place Chapel, where Moncure Conway then preached. The Channings were a well-known New England Unitarian family; Emerson saw one of Arnold's children, named after him, in the cradle and gave him his blessing.

These affiliations made Arnold attractive to Gandhi, who cared little for fashions in poetics or for scholarly exactitude, and he did in fact remain long indebted to Arnold, recommending his Orientalist work to Indian as well as English friends and disciples. And the two men came together over vegetarianism, as noted. (Arnold was much influenced by Buddhism, giving up hunting as well as meat-eating.)

Finally, Annie Besant was born of Irish stock in 1847, married a curate in the Church of England in 1867, but left him in 1873, joining the National Secular Society the following year. She edited the society's publication, and made a close alliance with its leader, Charles Bradlaugh. (Gandhi much admired Bradlaugh, as one who stood alone against the world, and was himself a religious skeptic at this point.) She published *The Gospel of Atheism* in 1877, and was in consequence deprived of the custody of her daughter in 1878.

In the controversy surrounding this case, Bradlaugh made much reference to the precedent of Shelley, who was denied access to his children, as a result of a suit instituted by his father. We shall have occasion to return to that, and to the parallel case of Hanns and Otto Gross.

In 1885 Annie Besant joined the Fabian Society, and helped organize the strike of London's women matchmakers in 1888. But then she left the Fabians and joined the Theosophical Society in 1890. Gandhi was much impressed by Besant's lecture-account of this conversion, with its stress upon Truth as her only justification. For Gandhi, too, Truth was the supreme value. He and Besant were both New Age heroes, though in their later political careers, in India, they were rivals, and seem to have been temperamentally incompatible.

The founders of the Theosophical Society, Madame Blavatsky and Colonel Olcott, had gone to India in 1879, and by 1885 Theosophy had a hundred branches there, where it was practically a revivalist cult of Hinduism. In 1893 (the year Gandhi again left India) Besant went there, and discovered her earlier incarnations, which included two famous martyrs to truth, the Christian Hypatia and the Renaissance philosopher Giordano Bruno. (It is worth noting that Bruno, who was burned for heresy, was a hero to many New Agers then.) In 1895 Besant became the absolute head of the society. In London Gandhi was an associate member for a time. He had been asked by two Theosophists (an uncle and a nephew, so far as they can be identified) to help them read the Bhagavad Gita. It was the time when the literature of the East was acquiring great interest for the West, as we have seen. Anna Kingsford, the Theosophist, dramatized Arnold's *The Light of Asia.*

Among Englishmen, Theosophy signified a revolt against Protes-

tantism and patriotism and White Anglo-Saxon Protestant imperialism, toward spiritual values and especially those values associated
with India. It had also some of the elements of a revolt against mas-
culinism. It is notable how important women were among its leaders
(especially if one counts Esoteric Christianity as another branch of the
same tendency, since in that cult Anna Kingsford was dominant). It
is not accidental that Carpenter—a spokesman for Theosophy—was a
theorist of homosexuality. An interesting motif throughout Gandhi's
own life was his claim to speak for women, and even as a woman.
These were all signs of a revolt against patriarchy. Thus despite the
hostile rivalry between Besant and Gandhi later, the example she set
in the worlds of both thought and action was an important part of the
New Age that influenced him.

SOUTH AFRICA 1893–1914

In 1891 Gandhi went back to India, having acquired the law degree
for which he had gone to London. However, the practice of the law
was not his main concern, any more than the study of it had been; he
could not give it his best energies. He did not find a career or a family
role that satisfied him in his native land, and left it again in 1893 for
Natal, on the east coast of Southern Africa, to do legal work for some
of his countrymen there. There were Muslim merchants from his
hometown of Porbandar who had followed the indentured Indians
hired to cultivate the sugar plantations in Natal, and who had grown
rich in Durban and Pretoria in the Transvaal. Here he met other
manifestations of the New Age, first among Evangelical Christians,
then among Jews.

Here we should take note of a split within Gandhi, between his
New Age ideas and other kinds of activity, which—insofar as they
were radical at all—we might associate rather with the systematic
realism defined before. The main example of the second type of
activity is the professional legal work he was hired for by members of
the Muslim Indian merchant community, which developed into political work. At the end of twelve months he was ready to return to
India when the newspapers reported a proposal to disfranchise the
Indians of Natal. Gandhi exhorted his hosts and employers to resist
this, and they asked him to stay and lead such a resistance.

His first move was to organize a monster petition to halt the passage of the new legislation while the Indians organized themselves to fight it in a more permanent way. The major institution he founded was the Natal Indian Congress, and then he had to teach its members how to debate, to listen and speak in an orderly fashion, to keep records and balance accounts, to raise points of order, to amend movements and abide by votes, and so on—above all, how to persist in the parliamentary enterprise, and believe in themselves in this role, hitherto prescriptively English. This was the machinery of the free society, as it was understood by the British, and by other nations admiring of the British then.

Thus Gandhi's work of this kind, in his first decade or so in South Africa, though charged with optimism, was not New Age. Insofar as it was activist, it was primarily systematic; it was scarcely innovative enough to be called radical at all, if seen in an international perspective. It belonged to the major official tradition of the nineteenth century. Gandhi was merely inducting his countrymen into something that was well established in the West. He taught them the rituals and banners of parliamentary government, and embroidered upon those the official legends of English democratic history, invoking heroic names like John Hampden, John Bunyan, Cromwell, and so on.

At the same time, however, Gandhi was reading and talking of ideas that *were* New Age. He was official agent in South Africa for both the Vegetarian Society and the Esoteric Christian Union, an offshoot of Theosophy. In a letter to the *Natal Mercury* about the latter, in November 1894, he described Western civilization as inventing the most terrible weapons of destruction, and referred to the awful growth of anarchism, the frightful disputes between capital and labor, and the wanton and diabolical cruelty inflicted upon innocent, dumb, living animals. This very early formulation of his cultural radicalism clearly comes under New Age auspices. During his first year in South Africa, moreover, he read Tolstoy's *The Kingdom of God Is Within You*, sent out to Gandhi by a friend in England. This was to have a profound effect on Gandhi, and politically, too, when he reread it in 1906; but in 1894 the message he took from it was predominantly religious.

During the Boer War Gandhi continued to work to advance the Indian cause by making use of orthodox British ideas. He raised an ambulance unit of Indians to work with the British army, to demonstrate that his countrymen were loyal citizens of the Empire. But war was deeply repugnant to him (as to most New Agers) and his experience there, and in the Bambata Rebellion in 1906, seems to have driven him toward quite different and more "idealistic" forms of action, of which the most important was *satyagraha*, "firmness in truth," expressed in civil disobedience.

After the war, Gandhi returned to India, intending to stay, but was recalled after a year to lead his countrymen in resisting oppression. He then found it advisable to move from Durban to Johannesburg, where racism was at its worst. The active role he played in Transvaal politics then brought him into contact with Henry Polak, a young Anglo-Jew who came out to Natal to work as a journalist. Born in 1882 in Dover, England, his father was a member of the Port of London Immigration Board. Henry was educated partly in Switzerland, because of his health. He was already a New Ager, an admirer of Tolstoy and Ruskin, and a member of the South Place Ethical Society, where he had met the woman he was to marry. He met Gandhi in a vegetarian restaurant in Johannesburg (where Gandhi also made the acquaintance of another faithful English disciple, Albert West).

When they discussed vegetarianism at this first meeting, Polak said it was Tolstoy who had converted him. Gandhi replied that he had a shelf full of Tolstoy's books in his office, and Polak must come and look at them.

Thus theirs was a New Age union, cemented in the presence of New Age icons. In return, over the years, Polak gave Gandhi two New Age books that were important to him. One was Ruskin's *Unto This Last*, a book of political economy so radical that Ruskin's father feared it would ruin his reputation. (Mr. Ruskin thought his son would be lumped together with Robert Owen, an earlier New Age social theorist.) The book was in fact confidently dismissed by reviewers. In the first decade after it appeared, 1862–72, only nine hundred copies were sold. But by 1910—after thirty years of the New Age—a hundred thousand had been sold, and there had been pirated editions besides. Reading this inspired Gandhi to found his first ashram-commune, at Phoenix. The second of Polak's gifts was Thoreau's *Civil Disobedience*, which preaches a New Age politics like the one Gandhi developed.

Polak was also interested in the Nature Cure and diet experiments that were particularly advanced in Germany then. (He had gone to Switzerland, which had several Nature Cure sanatoria, partly for a cure.) Gandhi and Polak read books by Dr. Adolf Just and Dr. Louis Kuhne, and followed their recipes for bread, their vegetarian diets, and their mud and water therapies. At their first meeting, they discovered that both had read Just's *Return to Nature*, and neither had till then met a fellow enthusiast. This rebellion against scientific medicine was profoundly important for its symbolic rejection of elements of Western culture, of which most people were most proud.

One of the centers for this in Europe, as we know, was the Monte Verita sanatorium in Ascona. There is no proof that Polak visited Monte Verita, but it was famous in Switzerland among Nature Cure enthusiasts, and he may well have talked about it in South Africa. Certainly Gandhi's settlement at Phoenix and Monte Verita were two nodes on the international network of Nature Cure.

Another of Gandhi's Jewish friends in South Africa—also an enthusiast for both Tolstoy and the Nature Cure movement—was Hermann Kallenbach. Born in 1871, and growing up in East Prussia but of Russian origins, he studied architecture in Strelitz and Munich, and practiced it in Johannesburg. When he arrived in 1896 he brought with him New Age ideas in architecture—for instance, van de Velde's ideas, which were like those employed in Ascona for the sanatorium building. For himself and his brother he built a house composed of several of the round huts found in African villages—what was called the Rondaavals style—and had them built by native builders.

Kallenbach joined Gandhi in many of his diet experiments, and when Gandhi was ill, later, wanted him to go, at his expense, to Dr. Just's sanatorium in Germany. Kallenbach was also in touch with the Zionist movement, which was strong in South Africa, and which had New Age elements in some of its manifestations, such as those we associate with Martin Buber. Kallenbach's uncle was a friend of Leo Pinsker in Odessa, and bought land in Palestine; his daughter married Michael Halperin, who aroused the Jews to the need for self-defense. Kallenbach himself, however, was a follower of Tolstoy, and so unwilling to countenance violence.

He gave Gandhi's *satyagrahis* (his followers in civil disobedience) a refuge during the struggle, in 1910—land which he and Gandhi named Tolstoy Farm. We have seen that Tolstoy's death in 1910 was mourned at Monte Verita, and so it was at Tolstoy Farm. There were many forms of contact, personal and literary, between the various New Age institutions. We have met Dr. Skarvan, who spent time both at Ascona and at the Tolstoyan Brotherhood Church in Croydon, where people were planning another such colony. Harold Monro visited the Whiteway Colony in the Cotswolds, set up by the Croydon Tolstoyans. At much the same time, Gandhi also visited Whiteway.

All these groups were anti-imperialist. The people of Monte Verita were in rebellion against the new Germany, established as an empire under Bismarck's reactionary leadership in 1871; within that empire Prussia took the lead over other German states like Bavaria, which stood for quite a different idea of German-ness; within that empire, also, the power of regulation and bureaucratic control spread—the Iron Cage of which Max Weber wrote. The forming of the Union of South Africa in 1910, as a dominion within the British Empire, was a similar phenomenon from Gandhi's point of view. The New Age stood for smallness; that and nonviolence were its two main political ideas.

This was true of the Jewish movement, too. All Zionists had strong elements of idealism, and for many that idealism was of a pacific, simple-life, New Age kind. Someone Gandhi quite often referred to, as a spokesman for the Jews of England, was the novelist Israel Zangwill (1864–1916). Zangwill wrote an essay on Anglo-Jewry in the first number of the *Jewish Quarterly* in 1889, which led the Jewish Publication Society of America to invite him to write a novel about the Jews. This project resulted in his *Children of the Ghetto* of 1892, the beginning of Jewish literature in England. Theodor Herzl came to Zangwill in 1895 for help in rebuilding the Jewish state.

Zangwill did not think Judaism any longer a viable religion (a Jew is "like a mother clasping a dead child to her bosom"), but he cherished a nostalgic love for both the religion and the ghetto where it had been so humbly practiced. Zangwill wanted Zion to be a super-ghetto, an enclave within world society, which would preserve the best of Jewish pacifism and passivity. This was like Gandhi's vision of the international role of a free India. Thus both men embraced what seemed weakness in the world's eyes, and admired New Testament Christianity. "The history of the ghetto," Zangwill said, "is from more than one aspect the story of the longest and bravest experiment that has ever been made in practical Christianity." He also wanted a melting of Judaism into a religion of the future, together with Christianity, Hellenism, and Hebraism. In all this, Gandhi must have found much to admire, although his politics were more activist.

LONDON 1906, 1909, 1914

By 1906 Gandhi was acknowledged as the leader of the Hindus in Natal, and—less securely—of the Indian non-Hindus there. He was sent by his countrymen to London to make their case against the colonists to the imperial government. (The latter was the defender of the Indians; being piously if not practically committed to liberal principles, and also being concerned about the sensibilities of India—the jewel in the crown of the Empire.) Gandhi's political activities in London were radical in the political sense that he was pressuring the Empire to live up to its promises of recognizing brown-skinned citizens as having the same rights as whites; but they were in style and principle entirely orthodox. They were not revolutionary. He was much commended in the London papers for his parliamentary skill and hard work in presenting his case. But he also pursued New Age ideas, which were reaching a much wider public than before in England.

The general election of 1906 had returned a large Liberal majority to Parliament, which included a section of Nonconformists much larger than before. There was a striking number of members of Parliament who had never before been elected, and a goodly number of them were readers of Ruskin's *Unto This Last*, the radical tract which inspired Gandhi to found his settlement at Phoenix. (When he was given the book by Polak, it was to read on a long train journey, and Gandhi got off the train ready to buy land and put the idea into effect.)

Outside Parliament, moreover, Emmeline Pankhurst had persuaded the Women's Social and Political Union (which she had founded in 1903) to take up militant suffrage action. That happened in 1905, and in the same year H. G. Wells led a radical revolt inside the Fabian Society.

Finally, some Nonconformists were engaging in New Age political action in England. Objecting to the imposition in 1902 of local taxes that benefited Church of England schools, they were practicing civil disobedience by refusing to pay those taxes and were being arraigned or going to jail as a result. This was an inspiration to Gandhi, who got in touch with their leader, the Baptist minister Dr. Clifford, who had been taken to court several times for his actions. Gandhi asked him to serve as a judge for an essay competition on the topic of passive resistance in South Africa. (Clifford was a patron of Joseph Doke, the Baptist minister who befriended Gandhi in South Africa, and wrote the first biography of him.)

Gandhi was not quite fully a Tolstoyan at the time of this visit, though he was soon after; and Tolstoy and Tolstoyans were major sponsors of the New Life in England. John C. Kenworthy, whom we have met before in relation to Whiteway, was writing about Tolstoy. His book, *A Pilgrimage to Tolstoy*, was published in 1896 by the Brotherhood Publishing Company and written in the form of letters home from Russia.

Kenworthy had founded the Brotherhood Publishing Company together with Vladimir Chertkov. Gandhi corresponded with Chertkov and with the latter's friend Isabella Fyvie Mayo, and read the publications of the Brotherhood Press and its successor, the Free Age Press.

In 1894 Kenworthy came to be pastor of the Brotherhood Church in Croydon, which was closely linked to the Fellowship of the New Life and to Whiteway. In 1893 he had both joined the committee of the Fellowship and published his *Anatomy of Misery*, which Tolstoy read and admired. (All these groups were deeply concerned with social misery.)

Kenworthy was also a member of the Land Colonization Society, which encouraged and helped people to escape from the city to the country, in settlements much like Gandhi's Tolstoy Farm in South Africa, founded in 1910. Gandhi described his aim there as being "to implant the spirit of Tolstoy, and then of country life and of the way to make the best use of it." The Zionist movement had a strong infusion of these ideas.

Ebenezer Howard, the designer and founder of Letchworth and later Welwyn Garden City, was a member of the Fellowship of the

New Life, and many members went to live there. The Theosophical Society, of which Polak was an officer, later had a boarding school at the first Garden City, Letchworth. These were forms of practical idealism in the world of town planning and architecture.

In 1906 the New Age was making an impact on the world of journalism: besides those mentioned, there were the British magazines *The New Age* and *Commonweal*, and the newspaper *The Daily Chronicle;* and the famous journalists H. W. Massingham and W. T. Stead were Tolstoyans for a time. *The New Age* began in 1898 and *New Order* in 1899; the latter gave accounts of experimental communities; and the same function was performed by Joseph Edwards's *Labour Annual*, a publication Tolstoy read and prized.

When he returned to South Africa in 1906, Gandhi immediately began nonviolent but activist politics, burning the passes the Indians were required to carry and leading them into jail. He invented *satyagraha*, which became his major political tool and which can be considered the purest political manifestation of the New Age. In jail, and even in the courtrooms awaiting his sentence, he reread *The Kingdom of God Is Within You*. In 1907 he read *Civil Disobedience*.

British policy in South Africa after the war was aimed primarily at reconciling the Boers and uniting the four provinces of the Cape, Natal, the Transvaal, and the Orange Free State into another giant dominion of the Empire. This came to pass in 1910, much to the alarm of the Indian community, because the larger and more powerful that political unit, and the more independence it assumed, the more they would be at the mercy of the colonists. (The Boers, who soon took control in the new dominion, were less liberal than the English.)

For this reason, Gandhi, together with another delegate, was sent again to London in 1909 to make the voice of the Indians heard while there was still time. On this visit Gandhi was distressed, indeed disgusted, by London and England and Western civilization as a whole. He was ready to repudiate it, and to devise a radical New Age politics. At this point he reread the New Age thinkers, including Carpenter and his *Civilization: Its Cause and Cure*, the argument of which Gandhi now wholly accepted, demurring only that as an Englishman Carpenter was speculating theoretically, while an Indian knew whereof he spoke. Two articles by G. K. Chesterton also had a marked effect upon him, as we have seen.

Generally speaking, the ideas of the New Age were very current at this time in England. In 1907 A. R. Orage had taken over the editorship of the magazine *The New Age* and made it the leading left-wing journal of the day. It published controversies between Shaw and Wells, Chesterton and Belloc. Orage belonged to a more literary and philosophical side of the New Age than Gandhi, but his first public lectures were devoted to Theosophy, his first publications introduced Nietzsche to England, and he remained devoted to the Mahabharata all his life.

Orage's version of the New Age was, however, unlike Gandhi's. He took from Nietzche's *Also Sprach Zarathustra* three symbols of the spirit of man: the camel, the lion, and the child. The camel represented the slow and bureaucratic mind, which Orage saw operative around him. The lion represented the "ecstatic-destructive" mind, which could liberate man. And the child was the naïve mind, destined ultimately to triumph. It will be obvious that these symbols correspond to the three mentalities described at the start of this book. It will also be obvious that Nietzsche and Orage wanted the lion, the figure of power, to triumph in the short run. This was not what Gandhi wanted.

The political activity that most engaged Gandhi's attention on this visit to London was the violent protests of the Suffragists, whose courage he much admired, although he insisted that nonviolence was the better way.

Above all, however, he read Tolstoy's "Letter to a Hindu," which addressed the issue of how the Indians should resist the British Empire and gave both the diagnosis and the practical recommendations that Gandhi himself was independently coming to. While in London, Gandhi got in touch with Tolstoy, and also with Tolstoy's disciples Chertkov, Aylmer Maude, and Mayo.

Chertkov had established a Tolstoy community at Christchurch, outside Bournemouth, with a printing press, where he brought out the Free Press publications. Maude had begun a Tolstoy agricultural colony at Purleigh in Essex, also with a printing press, which brought out *The New Order*. These were strikingly like Gandhi's settlement at Phoenix, where he had the International Publishing Company, which published *Indian Opinion* and various short books.

The alternative publishing press is an important part of many New

Ages. Perhaps the most striking case in the nineteenth century was the Russian *Posrednik* ("The Intermediary") that Tolstoy set up—after publishing his long, elaborate, and beautiful novels with mainstream publishers—to serve a peasant readership with less leisure and education. He wrote, and solicited from other writers, simplifications, translations, abridgments.

He also compiled anthologies, almanacs, and Cycles of Readings, which assigned a paragraph or two, often of moral or spiritual reflection, each day of the calendar year. In *The Cycle of Reading*, published in English in 1911, January 1 had remarks on "The Passion of Reading" from Emerson, Thoreau, Locke, Seneca, and Schopenhauer. January 2 had Mazzini and Kant. January 3 had Ruskin. Chinese, Persian, and Talmudic sayings appeared, but also the words of contemporary New Agers like Henry George and Edward Carpenter. Each week had one longer reading, like a story by Victor Hugo.

The Free Press was the progeny and equivalent of *Posrednik* in England. Several of its pamphlets cost only a penny each, and it renounced all copyright. It announced that it wanted to spread "those deep convictions in which the noblest spirits of every age and race have united—that man's true aim and happiness is unity and reason and love." That language is Tolstoyan, and Tolstoy's works are described as the most *definite* expression of these *universal* aspirations. The publishers included a letter from Tolstoy, approving their books' appearance and (more important) their cheapness, which made them available to the great public, consisting of the working classes. Gandhi followed Tolstoy's example on a much smaller scale in South Africa, but his own writing took the form rather of weekly journalism.

On the boat on his way back to South Africa, inspired by Tolstoy and Carpenter, Gandhi wrote his major work of theory, *Hind Swaraj*, and then took up the struggle again. This time, however, he had Tolstoy Farm as a place of refuge for the families of *satyagrahis* who were arrested. Kallenbach, who gave the land, was personally devoted to Tolstoy. This act of tribute came at the very moment of Tolstoy's death; his last major letter was written to Gandhi. Tolstoy spoke of the antimilitary action of the Dukhobors as the resurrection of Christ; in the same sense, the foundation of the farm was the resurrection of Tolstoy.

In 1913 came Gandhi's triumph in South Africa, and he planned his return to India. But at the same moment, in 1914, came the outbreak of war. Gandhi arrived in London a few days after it broke out, on his way home to India. He felt it his duty to raise an ambulance corps again, but his attempts were much less successful than they had been in South Africa. He was unable to cure himself of various health problems—and such a failure always created a moral and philosophical crisis for him. Moreover, the conduct of a major war created a climate of opinion very unfavorable to the New Age. He felt defeated in England. But he took the New Age idea to a different locale, where it would have a heroic career ahead of it.

It is conceivable that during these months in London D. H. Lawrence may have been pointed out to Gandhi, or vice versa. They were both by then minor celebrities, Lawrence's *Sons and Lovers* having been published with a *succès d'estime* in the previous year. Both were suffering badly from the problems brought to them by the war—problems more complex for them than for their pacifist friends. Neither one could find a way to act in response to the war, simple denunciation being, for different reasons, impossible to both.

Lawrence was a child of the New Age, but a rebellious one. As a young man he had been much influenced by Carpenter, and then by Tolstoy, and had been a great admirer of Shelley. He had taught in Croydon while the Brotherhood Church was there. His novel *The Fox* might have been written about Whiteway's colonists; above all, since Otto Gross, spokesman and martyr of the New Age in Germany, had been Frieda Lawrence's teacher and lover, Lawrence had had to think hard about the New Age ideas.

In many ways Lawrence reacted against New Age enthusiasms. In *Twilight in Italy* he made veiled declarations against Gross, anarchism, and idealism. Lawrence declared himself on the side of hearty appetites, including meat-eating and the enjoyment of violence. He claimed a share of the man-of-power temperament, but in fact he was as incapable of violence as was Gandhi. And, trapped in England during the war, he spent most of his energies trying to organize a New Age community, which he called Rananim. On and off, indeed, this ambition remained with him all his life and was continued after his death by his friend and disciple John Middleton Murry. Though Lawrence's and Gandhi's paths never crossed, it is easy to see how frail and transparent were the membranes that kept them separate.

This was Gandhi's New Age experience, in London, from 1888 to 1891, then in 1906, 1909, and up to 1914. He did not spend long there after 1891, but he was in close touch with it via friends, as long as he was in South Africa. And when he turned his back on it, writing *Hind Swaraj*, it was because he was acting on its own message—that the heritage of the East, of India, must be called to life to counteract the destructive potential of the West.

CHAPTER FOUR

Then and Now

> [The New Ager] knows all about the aggressive militarism of you and your friends; he isn't quite sure of the necessity of an Army; he is quite sure that colonial expansion is nonsense. . . . I honestly believe that the average Englishman would faint if you told him it was lawful to use up human life for any purpose whatsoever. He believes that it has to be developed and made beautiful for the possessor.
>
> Rudyard Kipling, *Letters on Leave*

In this part I will discuss a dozen features of the nineteenth-century New Age, in England and Europe, moving from the political, via life-style and gender ideas, to the aesthetic—the last of them connecting with the first, aestheticism with imperialism. Along the way I will suggest which of today's phenomena seem to me comparable. In doing so, moreover, I will describe some of the ideas, persons, and events that were hostile to that New Age, because a movement can only be fully described if one names also what it opposes or seeks to change.

But first a word or two more of definition. Time and place, as we see, only go halfway toward fixing our idea. The English "New Age" of the nineteenth century was also, in terms of dates and location, "the Age of Kipling" (the cult of the Sahib, the cult of the Explorer, the Empire, the Royal Navy). It was also the age of "Sexual Anarchy" (Oscar Wilde, Aubrey Beardsley, all that Elaine Showalter covers in *Sexual Anarchy*). It was also "the Edwardian Age" (defined by George Orwell as an atmosphere of eating everlasting strawberry ices on green lawns to the tune of the Eton boating song).

Each of those three ideas acts like a sieve that (like "New Age" itself) selects from the general field a certain number of people, events, themes, values, of the 1880–1910 period, which selections are mutually exclusive with the "New Agers"—who are certainly not "Edwardians," nor yet "Decadents," nor "Kiplingites." The mutual exclusiveness is not sealed tight, however. There are interesting crossovers: an imperialist like Rider Haggard was also a New Age occultist, while a New Age socialist like Blatchford was also a celebrant of "Tommy Atkins" and the British army, like Kipling. Terms like "New Age" are useful just because they remind us how fluid history is.

Before any more refining of our terms, however, we need to stick a few flags in the intellectual map. Some particular cases, after all, are, or seem, straightforward. Let us therefore describe some of the striking features of the last century's New Age.

IMPERIALISM AND THE IRON CAGE

The old sense of reality against which the New Age rebelled was embodied in all sorts of institutions, from Parliament to the local police station, from individual factories to the Stock Exchange or the Royal Navy. In fact there are two kinds of reality to be distinguished here. When understood and contemplated in a common-sense way, these institutions were merely "facts," though large ones; when understood imaginatively and endorsed passionately, they were values that belonged above all to the authoritarian temperament and its sense of the real. It is as values that they concern us.

Two such features of the age were especially often discussed as rapidly growing powers: one was imperialism abroad, and the other was bureaucracy and industrialization at home. Because the latter was a case for grim realism, when the former declared itself romantic, the two often seemed to be in conflict; but in the work of the great proconsuls, like Cromer in Egypt, Milner in South Africa, and the viceroys in India, the two came together, and in Kipling's stories and poems about the imperial caste both the romantic and the realistic were celebrated and in some sense made to exchange character—the bureaucrats' systematic work was depicted as both infinitely dull and infinitely noble.

Looking at it from a less romantic point of view, Gandhi also saw the empire as the home of bureaucracy in South Africa. When the Transvaal was taken over by the British after the Boer War, its bureaucracy became much more rigid. "A good officer has not under the British Government as much scope for the exercise of his goodness as he had under the Boer regime." The British officers had to work like machines: "Their liberty of action is restricted by a system of progressive checks." This was system made concrete—the Iron Cage.

Imperialism was also spreading in other countries. In America, there was President Roosevelt and the Spanish-American War; and among European countries, the division of the spoils in Africa; the conflicts in the South Seas, involving Germany, Italy, France, Belgium; and the competition to inherit the estate when the old empires of China and Turkey should finally collapse.

As for today, we are, or have been, oppressed by a similar sense of reality: in our sense of the Communist "bloc" and the "Iron Curtain," but also in our sense of the FBI at home and the CIA abroad, the twin agencies of home-and-abroad imperialism. At least liberals and radicals have a strong sense of crimes committed secretly abroad, and of society at home as a gigantic prison for most people—at least those of disadvantaged groups—in which they are confined.

Thus we easily find American equivalents today of the imperial British institutions, in the Pentagon, the FBI, and the CIA; an equivalent for Kipling in Mailer; and an equivalent for John Buchan in Ian Fleming. There are differences between the members of each pair, but there is enough likeness to create a framework.

The second item, the Iron Cage, was first especially associated as a perception with Max Weber and so with Central Europe; seeing the unification and organization of Germany, Europeans were suddenly made aware that the organization of the modern state brought with it a great number of restrictions, regulations, and frustrations for the individual citizen. Max Weber saw these regulations and restrictions largely as something to be acknowledged, but to other people they were something to be protested.

For English writers and readers the two themes came together in the image of the little Londoner. Each man (this was typically a male image) was seen as identical with millions like him, all deprived of their manhood by their clerical work, and contrasted with splendid images of manhood in history or in the empire—whether white manhood or nonwhite. This image was given resonance by Kipling and Buchan, but also by writers on the other side politically, like Wells and E. M. Forster. In *Howards End*, for instance, Leonard Bast is described as underfed in mind and body, and craving better food; had he lived in "the brightly coloured civilizations of the past" he would have been better off.

New Age politics needed different images.

NEW AGE POLITICS

I have already mentioned major examples of New Age political action, such as Tolstoy's movement to support the Dukhobors, and Gandhi's *satyagraha* in South Africa. Another example of political idealism was Zionism, certain early varieties of which were scarcely political at all; all had some quality of religion. Those varieties can also be counted a New Age movement chronologically, for it was in the early 1880s that the Zionist organizations were founded: Rishon-le-Zion in 1882, and others in 1883 and 1884.

At that date the religious and idealistic element in the politics was especially clear, but it never died. As Conor Cruise O'Brien says, "The central mystery of Zionism, it seems to me, is the relation within it of religion to nationalism, with the suspicion, within the mystery, that religion and nationalism may ultimately be two words for the same thing." The same could be said of Tolstoy's and Gandhi's political initiatives.

Indeed, much early Zionism aimed primarily at reviving Jewish traditional culture (just as Gandhi intended to revive India's culture, rather than to win it political power). Jewish culture was seen as being corrupted by modern civilization. Thus in a pamphlet of 1912, *The Zionist Movement*, we are told that the Western Jews "have espoused modern education with enthusiasm: they have engaged in all trades and industries. . . . The consequences of the social and intellectual struggle has been disintegrating . . . it has undermined the Jewish national consciousness. The Western Jew has been slowly and subtly seduced from the beliefs and ideals of his ancestors; he has sold his birthright for a mess of pottage." Zionism was, for many of its adher-

ents, a New Age political venture, as *satyagraha* was, and the passage
just quoted could come from Gandhi's *Hind Swarij*—written only two
years earlier. And wherever radical religion becomes part of politics,
the scruple about violence—the hope of nonviolent action—is bound
to become a question.

For our purposes, it is most interesting to look at Zionism in South
Africa, where it came into contact with the first stages of Gandhi's
movement. There were only four thousand Jews in South Africa in
1880, but forty thousand more entered during the next thirty-five
years—the years of the New Age.

The Jews Gandhi himself knew (we have seen there were many
Jews in the Ethical Culture movement) saw being Jewish as a special
calling to a universal moral obligation. (They probably belonged to
what was called Liberal Judaism, as opposed to Zionism.) This idea
was quite widespread among Zionists at that time. Thus even Samuel
Goldreich (a leader of territorial Zionism in South Africa) said in 1911,
"The Jew was not preserved only to save himself. He was preserved
to save all the nations of the earth, even his enemies . . . to usher in
the Millennium, the Messianic era, to prepare the time of peace on
earth." Zionism must not be just nationalist but also Messianic.

Gandhi's disciple, Polak, who came from a rabbinical family, said
he had taken part in *satyagraha* because the Indian problem seemed to
him the Jewish problem all over again. At Gandhi's suggestion he
became a leader of South Africa's Indians, both inside that country
and even in India, which he visited as a spokesman for the Indians in
exile. (Such a transcending of nationalist loyalties was very New Age.)
He reproached his countrymen for failing to meet this challenge; in
1911, in *The Jewish Chronicle*, he complained that South African Jews,
as soon as they set foot upon South African soil, joined the hue and
cry raised against the disinherited residents of the subcontinent.

Two of the great Zionist idealists were Judah Magnes in America
and Martin Buber in Germany; they were also the spokesmen for
Zion who most admired Gandhi. Magnes began as a Reform rabbi,
and when he turned to Zionism, he preached the reform of Judaism
on a national basis—Zion as a nation-state. However, he did not want
Israel to be a military nation. He defended Britain's role in Palestine,
and wanted a binational state there, though that was unpopular.

Buber began to write in 1901 about what he called Zionism, by which term he then meant primarily individual and internal liberation and purification. (In just the same way, *Hind Swaraj* meant both individual self-control and political home rule to Gandhi.) In 1917–18, in *The Conquest of Palestine,* he declared his disbelief in the power of the sword. And in 1919: "We will succeed in keeping the country free from prevailing methods of Western politics, the prevailing system of Western economy, the prevailing styles of Western culture?" Western politics is about power, Western economics about profits, Western culture a public lie. The relation to the land is the true criterion of culture. And the Arabs must be included in Zion. Israel's attitude to Ishmael is the test of Zion.

For Zionism was not, said Buber, a nationalism like all those others, awakened by the French Revolution, but an adaptation of an age-old "reality"—the holy matrimony of a "holy" people and a "holy" land. "This is not sacerdotalism but what we find in tribes living close to Nature." This is the language of the New Age, and we are not surprised to find that Buber began as a post-Nietzschean, and that he was a close friend of Gustav Landauer, one of the intellectual patrons of Ascona.

The latter tried to put his ideas into practice in the Raeterepublik set up in Munich at the end of the world war, a regime of freedom, without magisterial compulsion. Landauer died when that regime collapsed, but Buber managed to carry some of his teaching to the idealistic Israeli kibbutzim, just as Gandhi, at much the same time, carried his idea to India. Both men were turning their backs on the war and Europe.

Gershom Scholem tells us that Landauer's *Aufruf zum Sozialismus* made a big impression on him when he was beginning to read about Zion. But Landauer's and Buber's influence seems to have gradually yielded to that of Walter Benjamin and his like, at least if Scholem's case was typical.

Walter Laqueur says that Buber was "dangerously close to the neighbourhood of the irrational, anti-liberal doctrines which infested European intellectual life during the decades before 1914." Buber did indeed refer to "the community of blood" and spoke often of *Volk* and *Voelkisch,* as did some of the culture theorists of Ascona. This language has been suspect since 1945, as a kind of pre-Nazism, but it is better understood as New Age thinking. For, as Laqueur admits, "Far from being an aggressive nationalist, Buber sympathized with pacifism and within the Zionist movement belonged to the minimalist trend, advocating a bi-national state."

There is thus a New Age link between Zionism and Ascona, as there is between *satyagraha* and Ascona. In 1915–16 Scholem saw much of Landauer, who was often asked to lecture to Zionists. And originally he and others were, like Buber, attracted to New Age anarchism—to Landauer, Bakunin, Kropotkin, Proudhon, and Reclus—rather than to socialism.

Laqueur says, "Through influential groups from Russia, the social and moral thought of anarchists like Tolstoy and Landauer has had an influence on the building of a new life in Eretz Israel that should not be underestimated." This was not altogether a good influence, in Laqueur's opinion; it tended to produce at best eccentricity and in-effectiveness of a New Age kind. "The pioneers of 1905 were the strangest workers the world had ever seen. Manual labor for them was not a necessary evil but an absolute moral value. . . . Living condi-tions were incredibly primitive even by eastern European standards."

Maurice Samuel described the same people more sympathetically. "They came of merchants, peddlers, scholars and rabbis. They were not handy at doing things. They had to learn to saw a piece of wood, drive in a nail, wield a spade and draw a furrow. All their lives they had been accustomed to the city and its conveniences. . . . Here they were in a wild country, semi-tropical climate, an isolated, forlorn patch of wilderness far from the world's highroads." This was what New Age political idealism meant.

One of the most eminent Tolstoyans among the early Zionists was A. D. Gordon (1856–1922), who went to Palestine in 1904. Like the Russian populists, he rejected urban culture and distrusted intellec-tualism. He wore a Russian tunic and a big beard, and based his religion on labor. He was the chief ideologist for the Hapoel Hatzair group. He wanted every tree and bush in Israel to be planted by pioneers. He was shocked by their predecessors, who had ceased to work with their hands. He and his friends refused to help found Hashomer, the defense organization. He spent eighteen years work-ing by day in the fields and citrus groves, and writing essays at night.

He did not believe in the class struggle or that socialism would put everything right. It is appropriate that Hermann Kallenbach, Gandhi's disciple turned Zionist, is buried beside Gordon.

NONVIOLENCE

Perhaps the most sharp-edged differentiation of the ascetic New Agers from other radicals was their engagement in nonviolent politics. The recourse to war, for no matter what end, was something they abjured absolutely, and they believed the analysis of a political problem should begin with that renunciation. As Kropotkin said in his 1880 essay, "Weary of these wars, weary of the miseries which they cause, society rushes to seek a new organization." Anarchists, at least those of Kropotkin's persuasion, believed in a peaceful dialectic. Of this nonviolence, the great theoretical teacher in the 1880s and 1890s was Tolstoy, and the great practical leader in the following decades was Gandhi.

Moreover, nonviolent political action was the clearest of all denials of the authoritarian or systematic sense of reality. Gandhi found his energy in reversing ordinary realism. He was a serious moral paradoxist. Sent to jail for the first time, he was dismayed, but then ashamed of that dismay, and reproached himself: "I, who had asked the people to consider the prisons as His Majesty's hotels, the suffering consequent upon disobeying the Black Act as perfect bliss, and the sacrifice of one's all and of life itself as consisting in supreme enjoyment!" This is a New Age in the most literal sense. "As a matter of fact, we have nothing to do with historical precedents. . . . Brute force has been the ruling force in the world for thousands of years, and mankind has been reaping its bitter harvest all along, as he who runs may read." We can change everything.

Tolstoy came of a military family, and had a stronger sense than most writers of the nobility and dignity of the soldier's life. However, at the beginning of the New Age, Tolstoy did renounce militarism. He encouraged young men to refuse military service (and suffer for doing so) and wrote pamphlets in their defense. Hence the welcome he gave to Francis Sedlak. He was recognized as the sponsor of such young men outside Russia as well as inside.

National conscription was newly becoming a regular practice among the European nations at the end of the nineteenth century. *The Kingdom of God Is Within You* ends with a denunciatory description of a conscript army and a plea against war. Tolstoy's admirers, like Isabella Fyvie Mayo, honored him above all for his public work against militarism.

Gandhi, on the other hand, came from a nonviolent family and in some sense a nonviolent culture. He wanted his *satyagrahis* to learn the soldier virtues—to be capable of nonviolence, one must first be capable of violence, he said. However, the major fact about Gandhi is that he led a nonviolent struggle by the Indians in South Africa, in protest against the white government's policies, which came to a successful conclusion in 1913, and he took the idea back to India. This and the resettlement of the Dukhobors are two examples of New Age politics on a large scale.

One of those who helped resettle the Dukhobors was Arthur St. John. He had been a captain in the Royal Irish Fusiliers in Burma, but journeying home on leave he read something by Tolstoy which so affected him that he threw up that career and took to nonviolent forms of action. He made his way to Russia to get from Tolstoy directions in his new career, and joined the Brotherhood Church in Croydon, where he managed the church store. This is not the only example of nonviolence recruiting from what would seem the most unlikely source. (St. John had been a pupil at the United Services College where Kipling studied—the school depicted in *Stalky and Co.*—indeed, he had known Kipling there.) Jack White was another professional soldier, from a military family, who took up the cause of peace. Some of Gandhi's bravest followers, too, were ex-soldiers.

It is worth noting the manifold interconnections between these individuals and groups. When Arthur St. John was in Russia with Tolstoy, he got an appeal from Nellie Shaw at Whiteway, and sent her the money to build herself a cottage there; more exactly, he sent her enough to buy the lumber, and Sedlak built it.

Nonviolence is the essence of religion from one point of view, because it denies the real world (it denies both "reality" in the philosophic sense and "the world" in the religious sense). It was an active cause in some of the Nonconformist churches and the Salvation Army.

The latter tried, like Tolstoy and Gandhi, to carry the military virtues in the sphere of nonviolent action. G. B. Shaw took an interest in the Salvation Army from that point of view notably in his play *Major Barbara*. In his preface to that play, Shaw said the Army was getting too big and too bureaucratized: "This has always happened sooner or later to great orders founded by saints."

In our own time we have seen a powerful antiwar movement during the Vietnam War; and perhaps even more similar action in opposition to nuclear arms—at its most striking, the women's Peace Camp outside the American air force base at Greenham Common in England. (This has something in common with the feminist suffragist movement in the nineteenth-century New Age.) This camp was set up in 1981 to demonstrate against the nuclear-powered Cruise missiles based there. The INF Treaty that America and Russia signed in December 1987, renouncing the Cruise missiles, might have seemed to remove the camp's function; but it has survived, and is now close to a decade old. (It has been suggested that its muddy huddle of polyethylene tents outside the multi-million dollar military installation speaks against the latter in many ways and on issues besides that of violence.) We could point also to those who invade testing grounds when weapons are to be tested, and those on the Greenpeace ship that was sunk in the Pacific. This is all current New Age nonviolence.

Two Kinds of the Simple Life

A number of interests, in diet, reformed clothing, nature cure, sunbathing, and so on—in opposition to city life and scientific medicine and factory production—came together to form a cult of nature and of simplicity. (Thomas Davidson's Fellowship of the New Life listed simplicity of living and manual labor as two of its first four aims.) They constituted a powerful symbol system, which I am calling the Simple Life.

One such symbol was the knitted wool clothing with which Dr. Gustave Jaeger promised to save his customers from physical degeneracy. He had cured his own ills (hemorrhoids and indigestion) by wearing these porous fabrics, made of natural materials like feathers and hair as well as wool, through which the body could breathe. Since dyes also were forbidden, these clothes (men wore a jacket, knee breeches, and stockings) were a reddish brown—at least in G. B. Shaw's case. Chesterton said the color matched Shaw's beard and eyebrows, and the suit was part of the animal.

Many other Fabians and New Agers bought Dr. Jaeger's clothing or attended his sanatoria. This was an example, like the shorts and tunics of Ascona, of the "reformed clothing" that released the body from its prison. This had its erotic implications. Shaw declared that his Jaeger suit made him irresistible to women; and Carpenter more seriously wrote about conventional dress that "the pure human heart grows feeble and weary in its isolation and imprisonment, the sexual parts degenerated and ashamed of themselves, the liver diseased, etc." The Simple Life was a crusade to rescue the body.

We have mentioned also the sandals that Carpenter made for his friends, on an Indian model. It was, of course, possible to go completely barefoot—as Francis Sedlak did—but even sandals stood in powerful contrast to leather boots or shoes. A book of 1901 by Ernest Crosby, an American Tolstoyan (his name appears frequently in the Free Age Press's list of authors), says that sandals free "the human foot from the stiff, impermeable leather boxes in which it is at present deformed and befouled." Writing about Carpenter, he says, "The boot is the symbol of the husks of which mankind must rid itself before it can attain to the human form divine, and blossom into the long awaited unity . . . when at last men's feet are shod with the winged sandals of Hermes which free and do not confine them." These sandals were the footwear worn by nearly everyone in the New Age, including Gertrude and Leo Stein, and Raymond and Isadora Duncan.

However, since we have already discussed Edward Carpenter, and that kind of pagan simple life, inspired by images of classical Greece and Italy, we might here examine a quite different kind, Nonconformist Christian and working class in its provenance. The two kinds perhaps correspond to two eye-catching sets of life-style dissenters in our own day, found among academic liberals—or their children—and nonwhite ethnic groups. These modern sets also practice the simple life in significantly different ways.

Wilfred Wellock wrote an autobiography entitled *Off the Beaten Track,* published by a Gandhian press in India in 1963, which is full of interesting detail of this different form of the simple life. Unlike

Carpenter, Wellock was born into the Nonconformist working class. This, I am suggesting, was the nearest equivalent, in England, of those peasant classes to which Tolstoy and Gandhi appealed, in Russia and India, and of Native Americans and Hispanics and Asian Americans today.

Wellock was born in 1879 in Nelson, a cotton-mill town in Lancashire, then with a population of about twenty thousand. There was no smoking or drinking in the family home, and Wilfred's recreation was a Saturday afternoon walk of ten or fifteen miles, and some carpentry or painting in the evenings; until, when he was ten, his parents bought a piano—which cost them forty-four pounds, a considerable sum.

For the decade 1892–1902 his Nonconformist church was the hub of Wellock's life. It had five hundred adult members and six hundred Sunday School children, plus a choir, a glee club, orchestra, hand-bell ringers, societies for humorists and for drama, and a Mutual Improvement Society. Because the Nonconformist churches had only one minister to four or five parishes, they relied on young helpers, and Wellock began to teach at fifteen and ran the Christian Endeavor Society at nineteen. At the age of twenty he was preaching every Sunday.

However, besides the Bible, he was also reading the sages of the New Age: Ruskin, Tolstoy, Carlyle, Kropotkin, Thoreau, Emerson, and Wordsworth. He was strongly influenced by Ruskin, and was later converted to socialism by the Independent Labor Party leaders Philip Snowdon and Keir Hardy. He preached against stock exchange gambling in cotton prices, which caused the unemployment from which his workmates suffered. (He was remonstrated with, but not silenced, for spreading these ideas.) He rejected the doctrine of sin, and came to see Jesus Christ as a man, not a god. His value system was henceforth oriented toward "life"; his aim was to be "rich in life."

Indians came to Nelson to study the cotton industry; Wellock met some students among them who were members of the Calcutta religious reform group, the Brahmo Samaj, and thus began to write for their *Modern Review* in Calcutta. His article of April 1913, "Modern Industrialism: Its Lessons for India," expressed the same ideas—

warning India against following England's path—as Gandhi's *Hind Swaraj* of 1910.

When the war broke out, in 1914, he became a conscientious objector. He had protested the Boer War before: "To me, the whole idea of war and military service was revolting and unthinkable." So he went to jail, taking with him a portrait of Tolstoy, and was not released until 1919.

On release, the first thing that struck him was the exposure of women's legs (the war had upset the old decorum of decency), and the second was the newspaper headlines—the propaganda methods of wartime were being continued into peacetime. In general he felt that England had turned away from idealism and become self-indulgent and pleasure seeking. The New Age was over.

In 1940, the Second World War having broken out, Wellock joined other belated New Agers, like John Middleton Murry and Max Plowman and Eric Gill, at the Adelphi Center in Essex. They brought out a weekly *Peace News*, and founded War Resisters International. None of these enterprises could be expected to thrive. After the war Wellock retired to his cottage, Orchard Lea, in the north of England, living the simple life and writing essays called *Orchard Lea Papers*.

Wellock's account confirms the chronology I suggested for the New Age. Born in 1879, he says everyone he knew before 1914 was an optimistic "idealist," seeing their enemies as only remnants of feudalism, and being inspired by a fine galaxy of poets. We can translate his term "idealist" into "New Ager" without qualification. But then, "As I reached middle life I began to notice that the idealists were declining in number . . . some years later came the biggest shock of all when I discovered that I had been swerved into a backwater. . . . People like me were relegated to the back stage." The New Age was over, and he was living in a social wilderness.

But if we look at how Wellock's story got published, we get a less gloomy picture. He had been pressed to write his story by the editor of the Gandhian Sarvodaya Press, and a foreword is contributed by J. P. Narayan, who became the greatest Gandhian political leader of the 1960s and 1970s. Narayan says he began to read Wellock's *Orchard Lea Papers* in 1954, and they had helped him to understand Western industrial society. In 1958 he went to meet him in his cottage home, and found the old man still living the simple life. He kept to a vegetarian life, kept his income below tax level, and so on. Narayan concludes that he hopes Wellock's book will find its way into the hands of every college student in India. Thus we see—as in Gandhi's own case—how New Age ideas, in some sense starved to death in England, after 1918, found their way to a more fertile soil and nourishment in India.

GARDEN CITIES

The Garden Cities conceived and even brought to birth in England in this period provided a congenial environment for lovers of the Simple Life. A typical citizen of the first of them, Letchworth, for instance, was vegetarian and Theosophist, had a photograph of Madame Blavatsky on the mantlepiece, and books by her, Morris, Tolstoy, and Wells on the shelves. (So we are told in "From a Letchworth Diary," in *Town and Country Planning*, in 1953.) These are the Socialists Stanley Pierson calls "Ethical Socialists." New Age summer schools were held in Letchworth. After the war, Howard organized another such city, Welwyn Garden City; and these cities were the models for the New Towns built on a large scale after the Second World War. After the First World War, the Theosophists ran a coeducational, vegetarian boarding school at Letchworth, to which Henry Polak sent his sons.

The Garden Cities are an example of the New Age mind at its mildest, its most practical, and compatible with ordinary respectable life. Ebenezer Howard produced a book called *Tomorrow* in 1898, which was used as the plan of the Garden City of Letchworth, founded in 1902. Howard was a long-term adherent of the South Place society, and sometimes led its Sunday excursions into Epping Forest, which took the place of church services. He also arranged for cooperative weekends at Letchworth. He was a friend of Shaw and of Sidney Webb, and influenced by Thomas Davidson of the Fellowship of the New Life. Members of the Fellowship, like J. Bruce Wallace, went to live in Letchworth.

Howard was a member of the Ethical Culture Society, and holiday weekends for that society, too, were held at Letchworth. As has been remarked, the same names turn up in the membership of each of these activities, and—more broadly—each group knew about the others. The New Age was a subculture of its own.

In matters of architecture and town planning, the Garden Cities were related to William Morris's Arts and Crafts movement, and their influence spread outside England. We find references in *Indian Opinion* in South Africa, which show that people there were aware of it. The most important architect in South Africa then, Herbert Baker, spread such ideas.

The Letchworth plan was for thirty thousand people to be settled on six thousand acres, and so to escape the ugliness of industrialism, to have easy access to the countryside and to grassy places within their city. Ernest Rhys, a director of the publishing firm Dents, had a printing press built there. The Everyman series of cheap classics were published by Dents—one of the valuable results of the extension of literacy. Rhys had been on the fringe of the Fellowship of the New Life.

Garden Cities were recognized as the enemy by the other mentalities. During the war John Buchan wrote a patriotic novel called *Mr. Standfast*, expressing the authoritarian temperament, in which he satirized the New Age people who live in a garden city. His hero, Hannay, in search of traitors, goes to live in disguise in the Garden City of Biggleswick. The house of Mr. and Mrs. Jimson, in which he lodges, is badly built and oddly furnished; the bed is too short, the windows do not fit, the doors do not stay shut. (This sort of entropic inefficiency was habitually attributed to New Age radicals.)

Hannay's hosts believe in the simple life, and grow herbs and sunflowers. Their friends are all laboring (like the objects of Kipling's satire) to "express their personalities." They talk of the good smell of the earth and getting close to nature, but are actually incapable of any such thing, being physically inept and feeble compared with the philistine Hannay. They wear sandals. Mr. Jimson wears, even in the city, loose dark-gray flannels, a soft collar, an orange tie, and a soft black hat. These are the "soft" clothes A. D. Orage wore, and—if we add knickerbockers—G. B. Shaw. Buchan, on the other hand, wore a uniform whenever he could, and when he couldn't a three-piece suit with a starched collar and buttonhole. New Age men also have longer hair than Buchan approves of.

Many of the people of Biggleswick are "artists," but they do not so much make things as sample new ideas. "A vast billowy creature was described as the leader of the new Orientalism in England." This suggests Madame Blavatsky. "It is one great laboratory of thought," said Mrs. Jimson, of the garden city. Her gushy language is intended by the author to condemn those who speak it, as well as the people praised. "It is glorious to feel that you are living among the eager vital people who are at the head of all the newest movements." Prominent among the population, of course, were academic pacifists and conscientious objectors.

The people of Biggleswick hadn't much use for books, especially the English classics, Buchan tells us. The only exception was some Russian novels—at that time regarded as both exotic and decadent. New Agers like Orage and Murry were particularly attached to Russian novelists, especially Dostoevsky. Buchan, of course, regarded the English classics as *his* party's property.

Novels are being written today in mockery of and warning against the commune culture of the sixties, quite like Buchan's. Of course, if we look around us now, there seems to be no contemporary equivalent to the Garden City phenomenon. But perhaps the universities were the crucial institutions of our New Age. (In the earlier period, universities like Oxford and Cambridge were *not* the main scene of New Age thinking or living.) If so, those set up precisely to perpetuate sixties radicalism are a kind of equivalent to garden cities. One such is Hampshire College in Massachusetts, founded in 1970, where meaningful assessments are given instead of grades, teachers do not get tenure, and all students are supposed to show that their studies have given them a sense of the Third World and its problems. Such institutions perhaps differ from ordinary universities in the way that garden cities differed from ordinary British cities.

ORIENTALISM

Passing from life-style to religion and philosophy, we come to the Orientalism and Theosophy so popular in Garden Cities. As in our own New Age, the people of the earlier one took a strong interest in the religions of the East, especially in Buddhism, Hinduism, and Taoism. We have mentioned Gusto Graeser's interest in Lao-tzu, and Hesse's in the Buddha, as well as the members of the Theosophical

Society. Edward Carpenter visited India, and wrote about it as the *gnana-bhuni*, the Wisdom-Land. In the careers of Annie Besant and Gandhi, we see that interest taking on a political dimension, in a major New Age enterprise.

But it is another example of what I called a crossover that Kipling's stories and poems were also a powerful force in interesting English readers in India, and in Indian religious ideas, via, for instance, the Lama in *Kim*. We have noted several connections between Anglo-Indians, especially military ones, and Orientalist ideas. Sir Francis Younghusband, for instance, arranged the 1936 World Congress of Faiths, at which D. T. Suzuki first drew large-scale attention to his version of Zen Buddhism. Alan Watts called Younghusband an ideal embodiment of Kipling's spiritual interests.

Among the Theosophical sects, the one with which Gandhi had most to do was Esoteric Christianity, founded by Edward Maitland and Anna Kingsford. Maitland was another Shelley-inspired New Ager, and a figure in several aspects of the Age. He was one of the founding members of Salt's Humanitarian League.

It is striking that Maitland subordinated himself almost completely to his female collaborator. This fits into a pattern we find in his life, and in the lives of several New Agers. He had been oppressed by his father and older brother, and was estranged from his son; but in compensation had the friendship of "several noble women." He wrote a biography of Kingsford, so that this time men might not be able to disregard "one of their Revelators and Saviors."

Kingsford had a number of talents (she dramatized Arnold's *The Light of Asia*) and was a strikingly good-looking woman and powerful personality. In 1870 she became a Roman Catholic and took the name Mary Magdalene, the harlot-saint having appeared to her in a number of visions. But she also owned and edited *The Lady's Own Paper*, and spoke and wrote as a feminist. Then in 1877 she took up medicine, which she studied in Paris. In 1890 she began to agitate against vivisection, a New Age cause to which she eventually converted Annie Besant. And she became head of the London Lodge of the Theosophical Society.

Maitland was declared a reincarnation of John the Baptist, as she was of Mary Magdalene. But she had been a man previously, and Christ had been a woman—such alternations of gender were a regular feature of Theosophists' sense of themselves. Quarreling with Blavatsky, they formed the Esoteric Christian Society. Gandhi was the agent of their society in South Africa, drawing attention to their work, and maintained an important correspondence with Maitland—one which seemed to Gandhi important to his development.

In 1890 the two authors published *The Perfect Way: or, The Finding of Christ*, which had considerable vogue, and also *The Perfect Way in Diet*. Both of these were praised by Gandhi, and one can see what would appeal to him in their teaching. For instance, Kingsford and Maitland said that Christian dogmas are the same as those of other religions, that true belief lies in the mind and heart, and that thus seen, Christianity is a *scientific* account of man's spiritual history.

They drew a good deal on the Cabala and the Gnostics. They said that Christ had probably been an adept of the religious science of Egypt and India. God is Twain in gender; He is the Life, and She is the Substance. Man, too, is a dual being, both man and woman, but woman is superior. "Once recognized, and her reality and superiority admitted, there is no height of goodness and knowledge to which she cannot raise him, if only he follow her lead and keep her face from defilement by Matter and Sense." All truths, such as the multiple rebirths of the ego, are discovered by intuition. Such Hermetic ideas obviously have much in common with the erotic and unconscious-life ideas of D. H. Lawrence and the Asconans. These conjunctions are signs of the New Age's kind of connection or convergence.

As for our own period, Harvey Cox's *Turning East* is a narrative and autobiographical investigation of our Orientalism. He began his investigation near his home, in Cambridge, Massachusetts, which he calls Benares-on-the-Charles, because of the number of Eastern religious sects flourishing there at the time of his writing. He counted some forty or fifty Eastern religious groups within twenty blocks of Harvard Square.

Cox presents himself on the whole as a representative of the Western academic mind, in its systematic and activist form, suspicious of inward-turning and socially passive New Age religions. In college he had fallen under the influence of Reinhold Niebuhr, and later Paul Tillich and Walter Rauschenbush were his heroes. He believed in a semipolitical and activist interpretation of piety. He was thus anti-Orientalist when he began his investigation, and still, at the time of writing the book, thought that Eastern detachment might combine with Western egotism quite dangerously. But he was able to find something of value for himself in this turn to the East.

OCCULTISM

The less specifically Oriental forms of the occult, New Age phenomena in the nineteenth century as in our own time, deserve separate treatment. But the two were connected. For instance, the word "occultism" seems to have been first used in 1881, by A. P. Sinnett, the Theosophist.

There have always been religious cults purveying mystery. For there is a tradition of radical dissent in Western thought unlike that which leads to revolutions. Some examples, among knowledge systems, are astrology and alchemy, magic and mystery; and among societies that transmit that knowledge, the Renaissance neo-platonic academies, the Rosicrucians, the Theosophists, the Freemasons. The last-named played a part in the New Age in Ascona; the Order of the Golden Dawn was instituted there, an Order which included some distinguished members, like W. B. Yeats.

Yeats is no doubt the great example of occultism among the literary members of the New Age of the English nineteenth century. He wrote, "Those learned men who are a terror to children and an ignominious sight in lovers' eyes, all those butts of a traditional humour where there is something of the wisdom of peasants, are mathematicians, theologians, lawyers, men of science of various kinds. [I have been calling them men of system.] They have followed some abstract reverie, which stirs the brain only and needs that only, and have therefore stood before the looking-glass without pleasure and never known those thoughts that shape the lines of the body for beauty or animation, and wake a desire for praise or for display.

As well as opposing the systematic mind, Yeats constituted himself an opposite, within the New Age, to the moralism of Tolstoy and Gandhi. He was perfectly clear about the connection between the imaginative virtues he sought for his poetry, and his "desire for praise or for display." Perhaps more clearly than anyone else, he shows us how a person's temperament can be changed by means of the Faustian bargain in our time. He did capture forces of personality for himself—at least as a poet—by studying the occult arts.

Yeats and Gandhi were both fringe theosophists, but they represented opposite sides of that movement; Gandhi eschewed the occultist side, precisely and consciously because he recognized it as a pursuit and a promise of personal power. He thought that that aspect was what had attracted Annie Besant to it.

Another aspect of the same thing is the cult of the relation of guru to chela (master to disciple) which attracts attention during New Ages. At least in the West, where the guru is not the semi-institutionalized figure he is in Indian religion and art, this relationship is essentially an invasion of the chela's psychic boundaries, a violation of his/her autonomy. The guru establishes a dominance that allows him sometimes—besides ordinary teaching—to release the other from uncontrollable inhibitions and compulsions. Obviously the effects can also be less beneficial. We think of cults in our own time like that of Jim Jones, with charismatic leaders, and brainwashed disciples.

The phenomenon in the New Age of the nineteenth century can be illustrated anecdotally in relation to one individual, the editor of *The New Age*. A. R. Orage was interested in a series of Slavic gurus, after having been a sort of guru himself to many young writers in London. There was R. A. Vran-Gavran, a Dostoevskyan holy sinner, who wrote for *The New Age*. Then came Dmitri Mitrinovic, who arrived in London in 1914 and established an occult influence over a series of Englishmen. And later came Gurdjieff.

Let us concentrate on the second. Mitrinovic was a Serbian who came to London attached to the Serbian embassy, a friend of both Kandinsky the painter and Mestrovic the sculptor, and knew people in all the arts. He was also a prophetic intellectual, who took Gnostic perspectives on world history. His gospel of world salvation was inspired by the perennial philosophy and Christian revelation.

In 1915, when his book on the Slav nations was unfavorably reviewed in *The New Age*, Mitrinovic came to see the reviewer, Paul Selver, who found him to be just like "the mystery man from the Near East" in popular novels: shaven head, swarthiness, dark garments, and hypnotic eyes. "Hardly had I shaken hands with him than I found myself so affected by his mere presence that I nearly lost consciousness. This had never before happened to me, nor did it ever happen again."

Philip Mairet (a friend of Orage and Coomaraswamy and others in the New Age) says that Mitrinovic set out to dominate others quite consciously. When he felt he had put himself in the wrong in a discussion, he immediately attacked at a point where the other had a bad conscience. He had the same "abundance of being" as Gurdjieff, who later played an even larger part in Orage's life. (When we add Rasputin to the list, we shall be struck by how many there were then of these Slavic "rascal-gurus," to use Alan Watts's terms.)

Alan Watts, who knew Mitrinovic in the 1930s, gives a similar account of him, both as rascal-guru and as philosopher. Mitrinovic saw mankind as one man, as Blake did, and organized an open conspiracy for Panhumanity. Like Blake, he called the soul of England Albion, and said that country had an angelic vocation for moral and political order, but was diabolic in its imperial arrogance and Pharisaism.

Mairet became his disciple in 1917 and—on Mitrinovic's prompting—began to write for Orage's *New Age* two years later. He wanted people in power to join his "open conspiracy." Later he sent disciples to learn the ideas and exercises of Gurdjieff's school. Nearly all the next decade Orage spent under Gurdjieff's dominance.

In the sixties, some of the radical leaders, especially the hippies, were gurus. In *The Armies of the Night*, Mailer tells us that a permit had been requested in 1967 to encircle the Pentagon with twelve hundred men in order to form a ring of exorcism sufficiently powerful to raise the Pentagon three hundred feet off the ground. The exhortation began, "We Freemen, of all colors of the spectrum, in the name of God, Ra, Jehovah, Anubis, Tlaloc, Quetzalcoatl, Thoth, Ptah, Allah, Krishna," and so on for another nineteen titles. This was a hippie occultist initiative, and one of those taking part was Ira Einhorn, a modern guru figure involved in murder. In his case, and others, the dominance of the guru over the chela was combined with the dominance of the male over the female.

FEMINISM

Gender is always a focus of anxiety and speculation in New Ages. At least at the level of theory, our own time is one of the great ages of feminism, as a visit to any serious bookstore will prove. Of course, insofar as it *becomes* theory, or system, it ceases to be New Age. But this is a major sign, however ambivalent, that ours is a New Age, as was the period from 1880 to 1910. That was the time of the New Woman, the symbol of a movement for the liberation of women, imaginatively as well as politically. She was depicted by women artists and writers like Olive Schreiner, but also by men like Shaw, Wells, Ibsen, and Hardy.

This was by a natural correspondence the period of the women's suffrage movement, led in England by Emmeline Pankhurst and her daughters. As we know, Gandhi was much impressed by the example set by the English women, though he disapproved of the violent methods they employed. The suffragist he knew and liked best was Charlotte Despard—whose love of liberty, it is worth noting, was first set ablaze by Shelley.

But there were a variety of ways in which women found freedom. The women of Ascona, for instance, included straightforward political feminists like Ida Hofmann and Margaret Faas-Hardegger; free women or hetaerae like Elly Lenz and Fanny zu Reventlow; and women of the arts like Mary Wigman, Marianne Werefkin, and Else Laske-Schuler. Wigman recalled that the last three were grouped together by the people of Ascona as "the three witches."

There were also, on the edge of Ascona and the edge of the New Age, women like Frieda Lawrence and Alma Mahler, who combined the refined style of the educated clan with the warmth and strength of peasant women. There were also mythical embodiments of woman-hood, in the Great Goddess and the Virgin Mary, whose cults were examined with fresh interest then. Like the others, however, they were living up to an idea of women as powerful.

Bachofen's theories of Mother-Right and prehistoric matriarchy influenced Ludwig Klages and D. H. Lawrence, and were taken up by Ida Hofmann at Monte Verita. These ideas, undermining the ideology of male chauvinism, are being pursued today under the slogan of the Goddess movement; and the space Bachofen occupied in the women's movement can also be compared with that of radical feminist theologians today, like Mary Daly.

Also at that time, the representatives of women began to intertwine their cause with that of the working classes and that of the colonized peoples in a modern way. Thus Olive Schreiner was a precursor for writers in our own day like Doris Lessing. The colonial woman writer's point of view has been the instrument of more than one radical analysis of English society. For instance, an important figure of Orage's *New Age* magazine was Beatrice Hastings, who came to London from South Africa; and Katherine Mansfield came from New Zealand.

The new woman appeared often in the arts, and often embodied ideas somewhat different from those of the suffrage movement. Famous women's movement novels of the time were written by women authors. But some of the best New Age fiction in England was written by men like D. H. Lawrence and E. M. Forster, whose divinizing of woman was seriously New Age, without being feminist in the suffragist sense.

A lot of fiction has been written with women similarly triumphant in today's New Age, but it is now written by women much more often than by men: Margaret Drabble and Doris Lessing, for example. Much of it seems to be meant specifically for feminist readers and women critics. For it is the elaboration of the critical and theoretical apparatus that marks the present feminism.

EROTIC LIBERATION

A great variety of attitudes toward eroticism can be called New Age; there is a range all the way from enthusiasm to rejection; but to qualify as New Age, the attitude must express some intensity of feeling. Both the other kinds of realism can often take life's sexual element for granted, at least more often than the New Age can. Because of the latter's assertively naïve and spontaneous values, anything that has as much as sex has the character of "unconscious" or "animal" truth is bound to seem to be of the utmost importance, whether as a manifestation of the inner life, or as an interruption of that life.

The years 1880–1910 were a period when marriage was under severe attack, usually in the name of erotic fulfillment. (In the teachings of Tolstoy and Gandhi it suffered an opposite rejection, the preferred state there being celibacy or renunciation.) It was depicted as a black hole of lovelessness or mutual hatred in novels and in the lives of novelists; see, for instance, the public misery of Tolstoy's marriage in this period. Lawrence was exceptional in his doctrine of (highly idealized) marriage.

Sexuality, however, became quite generally the object of great interest, moral and intellectual; that interest took on passion and dignity. Sexual fulfillment, sexual identity, sexual intelligence, and sexual adventure and exploration all became values in themselves or entwined with values, as they had not been before.

Havelock Ellis and Olive Schreiner were analysts of sexual problems in England. Freud and Jung and Otto Gross did the same more systematically in Germany. D. H. Lawrence became a great novelist of sex, in *Sons and Lovers*, in 1913, deriving some of his analytical ideas from Gross and Freud.

On the whole, Tolstoy and Gandhi were sharply separated from most other members of the New Age over this because of their asceticism. Writers like Lawrence and Carpenter were more attractive to even the morally serious readers of the New Age.

Perhaps the most striking aspect of this liberation of the sexual imagination was the defense of Uranian love, because it was there that the frontiers of sex were extended. The divisions between New Age eroticism and the "decadents" were in some cases blurred, but not as much as they are today. It seems fair in the earlier period to contrast both Lawrence and Carpenter with decadents like Wilde, since both of the former claim to identify the kind of sex they were interested in with health and nature (both the idea of the natural and the realm of birds, beasts, and flowers).

The institution of marriage has not been so much the object of attack in our own New Age, perhaps because it is so much feebler a social reality than it used to be. Feminism, on the other hand, has been an even more prominent feature of the scene, but predominantly an intellectual and literary feminism.

Gay liberation has recently taken the position of prominence, with a vehement aggression that subsumes both Wilde and Carpenter and goes much further than either. This is no doubt in part because of the disease of AIDS, but before that disease was written about, the work of Allen Ginsberg, William Burroughs, and James Baldwin had given descriptions of male homosexual suffering the accusatory ring that female marriage misery had had in the earlier New Age.

PSYCHOTHERAPY

In New Ages there are always bold experiments in the salvation of the individual, which correspond to the group movements in politics and economics. The "unconscious life" is, as was just said, very important to New Agers. Some of those experiments are connected *with* the group movements. Others are or became "sciences" (Freud and Jung are the greatest examples.) And yet others are connected with the gurus and shamans of the occult.

One of the most important figures in the history of the New Age idea in Europe was Otto Gross, who carried the ideal of individual liberation as far as it could go. He made powerful connections between sexual and political repression. His personal situation was extreme, both because his father embodied the patriarchal idea so forcefully, and because the son was so adept in translating experience into abstract ideas. As a result, Gross moved quickly away from the orthodox position of the ordinary medical man as servant of society, and toward the position of accuser of society (which sometimes meant the sick one's family) in the name of the patient. This was a New Age idea of medicine.

His life story will illuminate the general argument. Otto Gross was highly gifted and hypersensitive from his earliest days. He was passionately fond of animals and in sympathy with them, which was one reason why he would not eat meat. His empathy with animals and power over them is described in D. H. Lawrence's novel *Mr. Noon*.

After college Gross sailed as a ship's doctor to South America. He was then professionally interested in botany and drugs, and it seems to have been on this voyage that he became addicted to narcotics for the first time. His ship went all the way down the South American coast to Patagonia, and he often referred afterwards to the experience of standing at the very edge of the civilized world, at Punta Arenas, at the southernmost tip of Chile, looking south into the free land of Tierra del Fuego, literally lawless because not assimilated into any of the nation-states, a homeland for anarchists like himself, where everyone was free.

Back in Austria, Gross lived in Graz as long as his father was not there (he was away lecturing on the law) but left when his father returned in 1905. Otto then began to live in Ascona and Munich.

That same year Hanns Gross published an essay entitled "Degeneration and Deportation," arguing that Austro-Hungary must deport its
degenerates in order to save society. ("Degenerates" covered many
of Otto's patients, and Otto himself.)

Having gone into psychiatry, Otto Gross became an enthusiast for
Freud's teaching, and was—by general testimony—a very gifted an-
alyst. He worked in the Munich clinic of Emil Kraepelin, then a
leading psychiatrist who was suspicious of psychoanalysis as something allied to decadence. The two men were therefore mutually
hostile, and it seems clear that Otto saw a similarity between Kraeplin
and his father, Hanns. Both exemplified the systematic and patriarchal mentality of the "German professor."

Freud welcomed Otto Gross's support at first, but was soon alarmed
by his instability. He persuaded the young man to enter the Burghöl-
zli clinic for a cure, and to be analyzed by C. G. Jung. This experience was important in the development of Jung's psychological
theories, but Gross rebelled against the discipline and ran away from
the institution. He thereafter felt himself at odds with both Freud and
Jung. The former decided that Gross's ideas were in fact dangerous to
the psychoanalytical movement, and so excluded him from it. Indeed, it was often said that psychoanalytical doctors informed against
him to the police.

If Freud had saved Gross from the shadow of his father, who was to
save him from Freud? He himself declared that Frieda von Richthofen Weekley had done it, that she had "removed the shadow of
Freud" from his path. He described her as the woman of the future,
and the confirmation of his dreams. "My most paralyzing *doubts* about
mankind's future and my own striving" were over, thanks to her.
When she sent him a picture of herself, he replied, "Do you yourself
actually know *what* this picture reveals?—that you have been blessed
with a great gesture [*Gebaerde*] and an art that constantly recreates
beauty out of your own beauty."

Gebaerde, with its Nietzschean implications of splendor and mag-
nificence, was a key word in the Ascona vocabulary. We find it prominent in Rudolf von Laban's works on dance, and also in such fringe
Asconans as D. H. Lawrence and R. M. Rilke. It suggests the exaltation of the body to a larger than physical or psychological dignity; it
expresses a splendor of life that is at once sculptural (Rilke used the

word about Rodin's sculptures) and biological (see Rilke's and Lawrence's poems about animals).

In 1913, as we have heard, Hanns Gross had his son arrested, an event that caused an uproar among the members of the New Age in German-speaking Europe. It was a crisis, and, being followed by the outbreak of war, and of nationalist patriotism, a tragic end to New Age history, except that Otto Gross's memory was revived, because New Ages recur, as long as life goes on. In the years since 1960 we have heard of many doctors who have supported the patient against family or society. Probably R. D. Laing is the one most likely to remind the reader of Otto Gross.

ANTI-IDEALISM

If Gross's idealism was a feature of the New Age, so was anti-idealism, because some of the nineteenth century's accepted forms of accommodation to reality had to be rejected. This work was done above all by or in the name of Friedrich Nietzsche. In 1898 Hubert Bland gave a lecture on Nietzsche to the Fabian Society, recommending him as an antidote to current sentimentality. "We are all in danger of being done to death by Ethical Societies."

Nietzsche has some claims to be called the leading philosopher of the New Age, at least for the exuberant pole of that complex mentality.

The end of the century was the time of Nietzsche's greatest impact, when in England the variety of Nietzscheans ran from G. B. Shaw to D. H. Lawrence. One of the most ardent direct expounders of his doctrine was A. R. Orage, who published three books about the new German philosophy. When the Leeds Arts Club was founded, he delivered the first lecture, on Nietzsche.

Orage came to Nietzsche via Blake, but also via Theosophy. Both teachings, Nietzsche's and Blavatsky's, propounded the idea of Superman, a new mode of humanity; and Orage said it was man's task to define himself anew. The Theosophists spoke of five successive human races; both they and Nietzsche called for man to leave behind traditional limits and acquire new powers. In 1894 *Lucifer*, as the Theosophists' journal was then called, published a review of *Thus Spake Zarathustra*. Orage no doubt read R. D. Bucke's *Cosmic Con-*

sciousness of 1901, another book that announced the nearness of a New Humanity: "The future belongs not to man, but to superman, who is already born, and lives among us."

Orage's journal, *The New Age*, was also interested in eugenics from the start—another topic linked, together with "degeneration" and "sentimentality," to Nietzsche. This philosophy's love of the noble and the natural marks the split between the New Age's eroticism and "sexual anarchy," to use Showalter's term. Orage, for instance, always distanced himself from what he called the "Weirdsley" decadence of the 1890s.

Nietzsche's antidemocratic feelings were congenial to Orage and Wells and other New Agers, and were also linked to a kind of Orientalism. Section 57 of *Antichrist* is mostly "The Natural System of Ranks and Castes." He says, "*The arrangement of castes*, the highest, the cardinal law, is only the sanction of a natural arrangement." Yeats, of course, agreed, fearing that democracy would destroy the caste system, which had, he thought, saved the Indian intellect.

Almost everyone at Ascona was a Nietzschean; a major example is Rudolf von Laban, the founder of modern dance, and most of the theorists of that kind of dance (who were often its finest practitioners) had learned something from Nietzsche.

Laban was born in 1879, the same year as Graeser. And like Graeser, he says that for people of their generation, "The will and the wish to develop our instincts and powers is a part of our religious effort." Today we understand a good man to be someone who finds natural expression for the powers of his body; and so religion and art are today summed up in the dance. (Graeser himself was a dancer, of an eccentric kind.)

The supreme New Age art is dance—of the Isadora Duncan and Laban variety. All those interested in rituals, myths, and the Jungian archetypes are also interested in dance. Of course, those close to the Tolstoy and Gandhi pole of the New Age were not dancers, were not sensualists, and were suspicious of the great importance given to the arts in modern times. But gurus of the opposite pole were often devoted to dance, and it is notable how many New Age men of that kind married dancers: for instance, Ananda Coomaraswamy, Joseph Campbell, Erik Erikson, Gary Snyder.

Dance has been similarly important in our own New Age, and a characteristic feature of the 1960s was its intrusion into even religious services. This has never been ballroom dancing or ballet, but some kind of "modern" dance; at one pole, expressive and expressionist, at the other, oriented toward traditional and tribal dance, especially that of the American Indians. It has been an important theme of Gary Snyder's writing, and is part of the rituals devised by contemporary New Agers like Matthew Fox and Joanna Macy.

However, among contemporary Nietzscheans, perhaps the most striking group is rather different: Jacques Derrida and the other post-structuralists, like Deleuze and Guattari. They too want to go beyond "man," but their debt is not so much a matter of the ethical heresy (the anti-Christianism) that made Nietzsche notorious in his lifetime as the epistemology, his emptying of the substance out of our substantives—his substitutions of the verb for the noun. In matters of cognition, it is Nietzsche the poststructuralists all acknowledge as their master.

AESTHETICISM

The arts—compared with other forms of activity, like politics, commerce, or even science—always have a New Age tendency to favor spontaneity and enthusiasm.

But when art itself constitutes a counter-world, and includes all other realities in itself, it separates itself from the rest of life and makes its spontaneity and playfulness purely aesthetic. It then runs counter to New Age values. Joyce's *Ulysses*, for instance, is a gigantic act of play, but, as Joyce said, it asks the readers to give it *all* their attention: no doubt they must put in their hours earning a living, and campaigning for their candidate, but their enthusiasm is reserved for art. Thus their spontaneous life-play is crystallized into predominantly aesthetic form. One must in some sense study *Ulysses*. (Writers like E. M. Forster and D. H. Lawrence wrote New Age fiction in that both their styles and themes derived from a spontaneous, intuitive, naïve sense of truth.)

The years 1880–1910, however, were a time when many artists did constitute such a counterworld. Art made itself important in culture, and asserted its freedom from old moral constraints. Coming to this idea, we are at the furthest extreme from Tolstoy and Gandhi, for we have come full circle, and the aestheticism of 1800–1910 was closely linked to the imperialism with which we began. There was a split, at best a dialectic, within that New Age, as there is in our own, between the two drives, the ascetic and the aesthetic.

That was an age of empire, and one way for art to respond to the pressure empire brought with it was to become imperial itself, to create a purely aesthetic empire. (We shall see how that happened before, in the equivalent period at the end of the eighteenth century.) In terms of literature in England, this was the Age of Kipling. Kipling and Stevenson and Barrie made a cult of play in art. In Europe it was the period of Diaghilev and Proust and Mann. In America, the period of the great Boston aesthetes—James and Adams, Santayana and Berenson. In all such writers art tended to become monumental, as it did in modernists like Joyce also. (This monumentality did not have to be literally large and elaborate in all cases—the highly polished epigram or haiku could breathe the same aestheticism as *Ulysses*, and fragmentation was a method for T. S. Eliot.) Such art appealed to the systematic mind.

Modernism developed out of aestheticism, by contradiction. The large-scale public splendor of the aestheticism at the end of the nineteenth century (whether in the Ballets Russes de Sergei Diaghilev or in *A la Recherche du Temps Perdu*) was compromisingly like the great public squares and theaters of the capital cities of Europe. In order to remain true to its most spiritual inspiration, this aestheticism had to develop into Modernism, which differed by embodying a defiance of all that empire signifies. (We could point to "The Waste Land" as an example; and analytically, using the terms of art, point to fragmentation, irony, ellipsis, and all those other defiances of the bourgeois art-lover.)

From our present point of view, nevertheless, the dramatic change from the Age of Kipling to Modernism is not so important as the continuity. Following up the clue of names like Kipling and Barrie will lead us quickly to contemporary writers like Salman Rushdie, Günter Grass, Gabriel García Márquez—to Magic Realism. It is striking how much more these writers (proclaimed as anti-imperialist) owe to Kipling than to a truly liberal novelist like E. M. Forster.

The only effective alternative is the New Age art of the Northwest American coast, California, Oregon, and Washington. The crucial opposition runs between Rushdie and his like, the rootless, and the West Coast prophets of rootedness. One thinks above all of Gary Snyder and his allies. Perhaps more strikingly, the crack of mutual opposition runs also between contemporary theory (implicitly in alliance with the rootless writers) and the Northwest writers. But of that more later.

CHAPTER FIVE

Tom Paine's Philadelphia

Hey for the New Jerusalem! The millennium! And peace
and eternal beatitude to the soul of Thomas Paine.

Thomas Holcroft to William Godwin,
on reading *The Rights of Man* in 1789

The idea of the New Age amounts to a sieve, which selects some
aspects of the intellectual life of the 1775–1805 period and blocks
others out. And thus if we imagine ourselves in the mind of the
fifteen-year-old William Hazlitt, as he walked the streets of London
in 1793, a radically minded student at the Hackney Dissenting
Academy—if we look around us with Hazlitt's eyes, we shall see a city
that belonged to the New Age radicals of that time, to Tom Paine and
Mary Wollstonecraft, as much as the London of the 1890s belonged to
George Bernard Shaw and Annie Besant. Paine's red nose will replace
Shaw's ginger beard; the powdered hair and fichu of Wollstonecraft
will replace the sad prettiness and propriety of Besant.

This was of course an imaginative, and paradoxical, belonging, as is
proper to New Agers. In the more literal sense London belonged to
the opposite party. What Hazlitt saw, in the literal sense, was the
Palace of Westminster, with seats filled by "representatives" of the
rotten boroughs; St. Paul's Cathedral, with tombs commemorating
generals, admirals, and bishops; the royal parks, where the army was
drilled; and the prisons, where radicals were punished. In matters of
commerce, he saw the port of London, with its African and Indian

sailors and their mixed-race children, and the East End with its poor Jewish and Huguenot minorities, and in the city the rich merchants' mansions, the Bank of England and the East India Company. He saw all this, and blocked it out, with the energy that constitutes vision.

So the big buildings were denied by Hazlitt, and by Godwin, Blake, and Wollstonecraft, as not being their city. What did they acknowledge as their own? In terms of London's past, the little Dissenting chapels and academies; and the burying ground in Bunhill Fields, where many of the famous Dissenters—Bunyan, Milton, Defoe—lay, the heroes of freedom. Of contemporary London, perhaps they acknowledged the Revolution Society's annual banquets, dedicated to keeping alive the tradition of 1688 and the Glorious Bloodless Revolution—the source of England's proud but incomplete liberties. And of future events, their own small, spied-on, dangerous meetings and discussions.

For their New Age was an age of revolution—a revolution accomplished in America, triumphant in France, and threatening or promising in England. This made for certain differences between it and the nineteenth century New Age, and between it and our 1990s. In times of revolution, militancy is felt (by radicals) to be required, and so the question of violence (is it ever allowable? if so, when and where?) is in the air. This question separates groups and ideas from each other. The ascetic New Age radicals—more reluctant to use violence than any other kind of radical—sooner or later get separated from the authoritarian and the systematic ones, and even from their former comrades. Burke became Paine's enemy; Godwin became Thelwall's enemy.

TOM PAINE

The similarity between Paine and Gandhi is, of course, a functional and not an intrinsic one. Their ideas were dissimilar in many ways, but the men were similar in the way they served their respective New Ages. Wherever in each one's New Age the moral leaven was fermenting, there he was. They were to be found at a great number of the crucial places on the ideological map, and both became representative names. And then both did embody the key New Age credo, that the single individual, together with other single individuals, could say no to tyranny and could begin to build a new society, simply by taking thought.

Intellectually, Paine was devoted to reason and not imagination (if the latter term implies "subconscious" powers). But then the same was true of Gandhi and the late Tolstoy. Usually such men are not poets, or any other kind of "creative" writer. Such a man is likely to make his contribution to myth by the life he leads, to inspire poetry rather than to write it. Hazlitt and his fellow students at Hackney wrote poems about Paine. Blake made him into a character, in his "America," and in his antimonarchical allegory, "Gwin."

Physically, Paine had a rosy country complexion (even before his face reddened with drink) and—according to his friend Clio Rickman—a full, brilliant, and singularly piercing eye. A recent biographer asked us to imagine him busily walking the town of Lewes (where he was exciseman, 1768–74, before going to America) with his cane marked out with numbers and his ink bottle hanging from his buttonhole, ready to measure quantities and give receipts. He frequented the White Hart there, and its Bowling Green Club, where he was known as an obstinate arguer.

Royall Taylor, who knew him in 1790, presented him as a socially insecure conversationalist in his novel *The Algerine Captive*. "If encouraged by success or the applause of the company, his countenance was animated by an expression of feature, which, on ordinary occasion one would look for in vain [though one would expect it] in a man so celebrated for acuteness of thought; but if interrupted by an extraneous observation, by the inattention of his auditory, or, in an irritable moment, even by the accidental fall of the poker, he would retire into himself and no persuasion could induce him to proceed, on [even] the most familiar subject."

In personal relations Paine seems to have been both insecure and lacking in what is needed for warm intimacy. His personality did not lack fire, but his was a passion directed toward his political cause, and toward the group that fought for that cause. Everything in his life ranged itself around that center, that source of value, and anything else that could not or would not do that was ignored or carelessly indulged. He gave and took offense readily, and lost friends by the legion over his lifetime. Compared with both Gandhi and Snyder, he was not a "natural" leader, and was not regularly surrounded, as they were/are, by a settlement of followers.

Nevertheless, he was a hero, an inspiration, to many. Benjamin Franklin had said, "Where Liberty is, there is my country"; Paine improved upon him radically: "Where is not Liberty, there is mine." Like Che Guevara and other revolutionary heroes of the 1960s, Paine and Lafayette carried the torch of rebellion across the Atlantic into lands not their own, and back again. In the seventh *American Crisis* pamphlet, Paine wrote "My principle is universal. My attachment is to all the world." He set the pattern of bookman-turned-liberator that was followed by Shelley in Ireland and Byron in Greece.

So we will take Paine to be our guide through the 1775–1805 period, as Gandhi was our guide for the later New Age. As emblem, the Englishman's large-nosed face, in later years often red with drink, can replace the broad-cheeked Gujarati's. Gandhi was nineteen when he left India for London, in 1888. Paine was thirty-seven, and a failure, when he sailed from London for America in 1774. He was discharged, for the second time, from his job as an exciseman, separated from his second wife, and armed only with a letter of recommendation from Benjamin Franklin. But Franklin's letter said he would make a good clerk, assistant tutor, or assistant surveyor; and he had an aptitude, and some training, in both oral and written debate— the consecrated weapons of freedom.

He settled in Philadelphia, the Quaker city, then containing nearly forty thousand inhabitants, and the rich ones quite fashionable. Paine was part Quaker on his father's side, though his mother, the more dominant of the parents and superior in social status, was a member of the Church of England. Our Paine was, however, hostile to the American Quakers when he mentioned them, because their nonviolence was a disadvantage to those who were starting a revolution in America. (Here the unlikeness to Gandhi is clear, but the latter, too, had to exhort his passive fellow countrymen to become active.) In some ways, however, Paine exhibited Quaker traits in morals and politics; he disapproved of profanity, and was remarkably chaste; and his early articles in the *Pennsylvania Magazine* were critical of Establishment culture—of things like dueling, titles, and cruelty to animals. Indeed, even when he said that he did not believe in churches, that his own mind was his church, and that he was hostile to priests and scriptures, in all this he was only taking traditional dissent to a logical extreme.

Paine must have recognized other kinds of New Age symbolism in their new home. Before and during the Revolution, patriotic Americans wore homespun clothes instead of imported English cloth, because they seemed to them natural and wholesome, as well as politically symbolic. There were spinning bees and home weaving, and tea was made from raspberry leaves, to avoid using imported goods. All this was to be echoed in India a century and a half later, when Gandhi made the spinning wheel the emblem of the nationalist movement there.

In 1776 the New Age began in earnest, with the Declaration of Independence; and Paine produced two famous pamphlets: *Common Sense*, and *American Crisis I*. *Common Sense* carried the cult of freedom to the verge of anarchism. It set up a series of oppositions between society and government, such as are often attractive to the New Age mentality. Society is produced by our wants, government by our wickedness, society promotes our happiness positively, government negatively; society is a blessing, government a necessary evil. Thus simple governments are best, and kings are to be distrusted. George III is presented as "the hardened and sullen-tempered Pharaoh of England."

We see in Paine's work an eminent example of the way one kind of New Age writing aspires to the very simple and clear in matters of style. He wanted to give the title "Plain Truth" to what was finally called "Common Sense." He wrote philosophy and moral theory for the common reader, declaring that he himself found even Locke, far from the most professional or academic of philosophers, too heavy and tedious (in other words, too systematic). The pamphlet was perhaps the literary form at which Paine excelled. He criticized, just for being too complex, the British constitution, at that time so much admired, by foreigners as well as the English. This love of simplicity is not merely a matter of personal preference, or of communicative efficiency. It is a part of Paine's New Age ideology, for simplicity enables the common man to understand political issues and to act on them.

Indeed, this tradition persisted and persists. Edward Thompson says that the tradition of Paine's thinking and his rhetoric were still alive in the nineteenth-century New Age, and could be found in the journalism of Robert Blatchford and in the popular appeal of David Lloyd George. In our own New Age Father Thomas Berry quotes him. Paine is very quotable; thus in 1990 we find a quotation from *American Crisis XIII*, written in 1783, displayed as a slogan on the front cover of one of the New Age giveaway magazines: ". . . to exhibit on the theater of the universe a character hitherto unknown, and to have a new creation entrusted to our hands." New and unknown, these are the characters inscribed in every New Age's aspirations.

But this is not just a matter of style. Paine's ideas and life story have made him a hero to New Age movements of many kinds and dates. The Theosophists, for instance, cited him as one of their forebears. So did the secularists and rationalists of the nineteenth century. Paine and Voltaire were read aloud at Sunday meetings of the Ethical Society. Eric Hobsbawm, in his *Labouring Men* of 1964, describes Paine as a hero of all subsequent working-class movements, and says that he reflected the rainbow light of an age "in which everything may be looked for."

However, though his writings made Paine a hero of the American Revolution in public, in private he was from the start anathema to Americans like John Adams, men with the authoritative temperament. They saw his cult of freedom as leading to anarchy as well as anarchism. Even Franklin, though he called Paine his adoptive son in politics, does not seem to have seen a great deal of him apart from politics.

Franklin and Paine were, however, both interested in science and designed gadgets (Paine sent the other man his smokeless candle), and that aptitude and interest seem to have been often the link between Paine and the Americans he was friends with, men like Benjamin Rush, David Rittenhouse, Benjamin Franklin, Joel Barlow, George Washington, and Thomas Jefferson. Paine proposed to Jefferson the idea of an engine to be powered by a succession of gunpowder explosions. He and Washington experimented together with inflammable gases which bubbled up through a stream. In 1785 he designed a single-arch bridge, which was in adapted form built in England, and had a considerable influence on later British bridge-building in iron. (Hobsbawm says this was the most popular single structure of the industrial revolution, to judge by its innumerable depictions on pottery.) Unexpectedly, perhaps, this love of home-made technology can often be found allied to New Age political enthusiasms—in Gandhi, for instance, working at improving the spinning wheel.

LONDON AND PARIS

In 1787 Paine went to France with the plans for this bridge, hoping for and getting the approval of the Académie des Sciences, and was caught up in the beginnings of the French Revolution. In 1788 he went to England and met some of the leading Whigs, like Burke and Lansdowne. He set up his model bridge on the grounds of the "Yorkshire Stingo" in Lisson Grove, near Paddington. Edmund Burke, Paine's great antagonist-to-be, was eight years his elder. He had been a founding member of Dr. Johnson's Literary Club, which we can think of as the sort of institution Paine did *not* belong to. But the two men were friends for a time—Burke thought of himself as a liberal—and Paine wrote Burke his enthusiastic "liberal" interpretation of the events in France. Burke accepted it—until those events became too violent for him to stomach.

On July 14, 1789, came the successful attack on the Bastille prison in Paris by French revolutionary forces. Lafayette, whom Paine had known in America, later gave Paine the key to the main gate of the Bastille, for him to present to President Washington. (Paine was, of course, a very prominent figure in his New Age; much more so than Gandhi was in England in the equivalent period.) On November 4, Dr. Price gave his sermon to the Revolution Society banquet, in praise of the French events, and hoping for similar reforms in England. (On the same date in 1791 Paine proposed as a toast to the Revolution Society, "Gentlemen, I give you the Revolution of the World.") Edmund Burke announced that he would make a hostile reply to Price, and Paine determined to answer whatever Burke said. Such arguments and counterarguments constituted a great political debate. Because Burke took eight months to produce his *Reflections on the Revolution in France*, Paine had to wait, before he could write his *The Rights of Man*.

During this time, Paine met William Godwin, as fellow members of a New Age circle around the bookseller Joseph Johnson—a group that was the opposite equivalent for the conservative circle that had formed around Samuel Johnson. Indeed, that second Johnson can be regarded as in opposition to all these men—there was no trace of New Age optimism about him. Godwin wrote to his patron, Thomas Wedgwood: "Allow me to recommend to you a very cautious admission of the moral apothegms of Dr. Johnson. He had an unprecedented tendency to dwell on the dark and unamiable side of our nature."

This circle also included William Blake, and one story has it that it was Blake who brought Paine warning of the danger that he would be arrested, in 1792, so that he could escape to France in time. (Paine, and Paine's friends, were spied on by the government's agents.) St. Paul's Churchyard, the street where Joseph Johnson had his bookshop, is the London Street we most especially associate with Blake and the other radicals. At number 72, Joseph Johnson invited all his authors to dine with him at four o'clock on Monday afternoons.

St. Paul's Cathedral itself was very alien to them; its cold and ceremonious spaces belonged to the state and the court, to England's great soldiers and great statesmen—to the Established Church. But in the Churchyard, around Joseph Johnson's bookshop, were found the small shops and the sharp minds and the strong talk of London dissent denying the great world of the Establishment. It was here that Johnson was surrounded by Blake, William Godwin, Mary Wollstonecraft, Dr. Priestley, Henry Fuseli, Horne Tooke, and many of the leading spirits of the Society for Constitutional Information. And when Johnson in his turn went to Newgate for six months in February 1798, for his politics, he continued to give his dinners there.

Thomas Holcroft, the radical playwright, was probably not present at many of Johnson's dinners, but he was a great friend of Godwin's, and spoke on behalf of Godwinian gradualism and pacifism in the London Corresponding Society, when pressure built up in that society for more immediate and more militant action. This was the political society which the government considered the most dangerous. It was founded by Thomas Hardy in 1792, and was reputed to have thirty thousand members across the country before its suppression in 1797. In 1794 Hardy was put in the Tower, charged with high treason. He and Holcroft, Horne Tooke, John Thelwall, and others were committed for trial with him, and Godwin came to their defense with a powerful letter to the press.

Joseph Johnson (1738–1809) is an interesting enigma in the social complex of radical intelligentsia then. Mary Wollstonecraft spoke of him being the father and brother nature had denied her, and he looked after her, finding her lodgings, putting her up in his own house, dealing with tradesmen for her, finding her work, and nursing her through the writing of, for instance, her reply to Burke, *Vindication of the Rights of Man*. When Tom Paine, equally unworldly, had to be moved to new lodgings for his safety, Johnson found them for him, and picked up Paine and his belongings, and transported them to the new address and installed him.

Johnson was born into a Baptist family in Everton, Liverpool, and came to London at the age of fourteen. At twenty-two he took a bookshop, and when that burned down in 1772, he took this more famous shop in St. Paul's Churchyard. According to Alexander Gilchrist, he was a man of plain tastes and strict probity, who lived in his shop and for it, as well as by it. He seems to have made no demands, and engaged in no adventures, for himself. His style, in behavior as in language, had no heroic dimensions; Wollstonecraft refers to him as "Little Johnson" on occasion.

His authors, however, were all on the rebellious left, or Evangelical-Dissenting, wing of British intellectual life—the New Age. In 1772 he began to publish Anna Letitia Barbauld, the writer for children, and Joseph Priestley, the scientist and theologian. He also brought out the works of Maria Edgeworth and Horne Tooke, the friend of John Wilkes, a radical of rather a different kind.

There were at least three centers of interest to the range of books Johnson published: the scientific, especially books on medicine and surgery; the politically radical; and the educational. Mary Wollstonecraft worked eventually on both the second and third types, but initially on the third—one of her children's books being illustrated by Blake. Johnson brought out both works by Paine and (at least it got as far as proof) the only book by Blake ever published in this ordinary way—*The French Revolution*. But Johnson, like Tolstoy and Gandhi later, wanted cheap books and wide circulation for his authors; he was an enemy to the "typographical luxury" that became the vogue among booksellers and publishers around 1780. This presumably cut down his employment of Blake.

Via Johnson, his authors acted on each other, and not only in dinner conversations. Between 1788 and 1799 he brought out a magazine, *The Analytical Review*, for which all his friends wrote, and in which they commented on each other. (The conservative equivalent was *The Critical Review*, edited by Smollett, to which Samuel Johnson and Goldsmith had contributed.) He also passed the manuscripts of one of his authors around among the others for comments. Thus Fuseli was asked to read that part of Cowper's translation of *The Iliad* that the poet sent in as a sample. Fuseli made many criticisms, which Cowper followed, and in fact the Swiss artist was consulted throughout the work. Bonnycastle, the mathematician, read Paine's *The Rights of Man*; Wollstonecraft read many submitted manuscripts, and wrote letters of advice to their authors.

Several of Johnson's habitual guests made their living doing hackwork for him. Wollstonecraft translated political pamphlets from the French, and reviewed for the magazine. Holcroft also translated from the French (his greatest coup was the pirating of Beaumarchais's play *Figaro*, by memorizing it in the Paris theater where it was being played) and later from the German. Godwin began his literary career with novelettes, summaries of the year's events, and even indexing. This was a Grub Street radicalism. Nearly all the guests were later imprisoned or arrested on political charges. When Johnson's own turn came (he was jailed for selling a subversive pamphlet), he continued to give his dinners—in the marshal's house of the King's Bench prison.

The Rights of Man, Part I, came out in 1791, its arguments greatly influenced by Rousseau. Johnson recalled the copies on sale on the day of publication, when he was told that it contained seditious material and so he might be prosecuted. He had already published without trouble answers to Burke by Wollstonecraft, and two others, and had assumed that Paine's book would make no more scandal; in the event, the pamphlet was published by another bookseller, J. S. Jordan, without any changes. (Both booksellers stocked the even more radical *Rights of Man*, Part II.) Paine had gone away to write a new preface, and Thomas Hollis, Holcroft, and Godwin undertook to see the manuscript through the press.

By the end of the decade, the atmosphere of hope was blighted, and the government was taking severe repressive measures. *The Rights of Man* was banned, and the London Corresponding Society was outlawed. This and the societies in other cities with which it exchanged news spread Paine's ideas among the working class, and so attracted the hostile attention of the government. In May 1794 some of the leaders, as mentioned, were arrested, taken before the Privy Council, and tried for high treason. The trial was a social event that brought together many New Agers. In the courtroom, watching the proceedings, were many people of radical sympathies: Samuel Taylor Coleridge was one; another was Amelia Alderson, a radical woman of letters, who married John Opie, the painter of the best-known portrait of Mary Wollstonecraft.

The release of the prisoners was a radical triumph, and in the short run inspired those released to bolder efforts. John Thelwall, a journalist and teacher of elocution, would not be silenced; he went around the country lecturing, still a prominent radical. He began to correspond with Coleridge in 1796, and visited the latter and Wordsworth near Bristol in the following year. Thelwall was himself a poet; Wordsworth used the idea of his 1793 poem *The Peripatetic* as a framework for his own *The Excursion*. But it was as a man of politics that these new friends valued him. Coleridge called Thelwall "intrepid, eloquent and honest" in a letter of 1796, and said, "If the day of darkness and tempest should come, it is most probable that the influence of Thelwall would be great upon the lower classes."

If we follow the figures of Thelwall and Coleridge, we shall be led a little distance away from Paine, but we shall meet other important leaders of his New Age, and discover some of its range and complexity, just as we followed the idea of Nature Cure and the Simple Life away from Gandhi, toward Ascona and Gusto Graeser.

THE LAKE DISTRICT

John Thelwall was, says Edward P. Thompson, the outstanding leader of the English jacobins. For this reason, no doubt, Wordsworth and Coleridge and their friends were, like Paine, spied on by government agents during Thelwall's visit, and after. Thelwall and Coleridge addressed each other, defiantly, in revolutionary fashion—as Citizen John and Citizen Sam.

The younger men and their friend Robert Southey had long been sympathizers with the Revolution. Even Southey, so soon to turn conservative, was expelled from his school for an article attacking corporal punishment. He wrote of those times, "Old things seemed passing away and nothing was dreamt of but the regeneration of the human race."

Coleridge had read Godwin's *Enquiry Concerning Political Justice* when it came out in 1793, and was eager to found a new community, far from England. His friends at Cambridge included Quakers, like Charles Lloyd and Robert Lovell. The latter knew about Dr. Joseph Priestley's purchase of land on the banks of the Susquehanna, in America. Coleridge was told by an American land agent that twelve men could easily clear three hundred acres in four or five months, working only three hours a day, and that even "literary characters" could become economically self-sufficient there.

However, it was not, of course, an economic but a moral and political enthusiasm that inspired the group. Their bywords were "pantisocracy," meaning equal government by all, and "aspheterism," meaning the "generalizing" of private property. There would be no servants, and marriage would probably be dissolvable at will. They planned to embark in April 1795, twelve persons of each sex. Each person need bring only £125. Southey was then twenty-one, Coleridge twenty-three. Southey said that Godwin, Holcroft, and Joseph Gerrald (deported to Botany Bay) had approved of the scheme. It was after all part of a great tradition. Perhaps they recalled that in the seventeenth century Cromwell and some of his friends had planned to leave England and set up a new and better society in America. At the end of the nineteenth century, Davidson's Fellowship of the New Life was felt to be a revival of pantisocracy.

By the time Thelwall paid his visit, however, the enthusiasm of the poets had turned toward the idea of practicing the simple life in England, and toward the practice of poetry in that setting. This was of course politically unrevolutionary; but it was very New Age, because it was something that could be done peacefully, immediately, and individually. William and Dorothy Wordsworth had rented a house in a solitary place near Lyme Regis. William wrote, "We plant cabbages, and if retirement, in its full perfection, be as powerful in working transformations as one of Ovid's gods, you may expect that into cabbages we shall be transformed." All provision had to be brought from seven miles away, so their diet and comfort must have been simple, as was their regimen: they gardened, walked, and read, apparently without employing any servant. Wordsworth had of course lived much of his life out-of-doors. Sounding like the Asconans—they made the same jokes—he said, "I have lately been living upon air and the essence of carrots, cabbages, turnips."

After a visit to Germany, they settled in Grasmere, in the Wordsworths' home country; but the house they lived in, later called Dove Cottage, was also a center of the simple life. The place fetched a rent of only eight pounds a year, and had three rooms downstairs and three up. Dorothy was in charge of all the cooking and cleaning, William of digging the garden, cleaning the well, collecting firewood. They ate mostly porridge, with occasionally some mutton, and took long walks, morning and evening. A woman, Molly Fisher, came in to help by the day. They lived among, and in much the same style as, cottage weavers and spinners who wore clogs and homespun. William drank water at home, though he would accept ale outside.

A recent biographer described the Wordsworths and the friends who gathered round them in Grasmere as "dropouts" from the middle-class world they had been born into, and the phrase helps us to make the connection to our own New Age. Coleridge's wife found them eccentric, ungenteel, uncivilized. But through their work and the legend of their lives, a mild version of the simple life was installed in the educated English mind, as a sort of alternative life-style, throughout the nineteenth century.

SOUTH PLACE

Another group of people who were not among Paine's friends but are important to understanding him and his heritage were the founders of the South Place Chapel. The Reverend Elhanan Winchester, who brought the Universalist teaching of a Christianity without eternal punishment from Boston to England, established a church in London in 1793. He was politically conservative, and wrote another of the rejoinders to *The Age of Reason*. But his successor was a Unitarian, and the next minister at South Place was a political radical, W. J. Fox. All through the nineteenth century advanced ideas could be heard at the chapel, and it was attended by Harriet Martineau, John Stuart Mill and his wife, Browning, and so on. The cult of Shelley, his radicalism and his martyrdom, was maintained there. At the end of the century, as we know, Moncure Conway was the minister there and wrote a long and vindicatory life of Paine. Another American, Stanton Coit, succeeded Conway. The link to America (essentially, to Transcendentalist America) is significant.

South Place, and the Ethical Culture movement that found its first home in London there, was an important part of a loosely organized tendency toward secularism and rationalism. Susan Budd, in her *Varieties of Unbelief*, says that this tendency can only be understood as part of the radical tradition of English urban working-class life. Though they were not linked organizationally, what ties various movements together, including Ethical Culture, she says, is their attack on supernatural religion and their faith in reason over authority.

The Rationalist Press Association, with its publisher Watts, aimed to serve this whole tendency, bringing out cheap editions of pamphlets and abridgments of books. It was closely associated with the Ethical Society. Paine's name comes up, as the founder of rationalism, over and over in Budd's pages, and so does Robert Owen's. Owenism and moral-force Chartism (so named to distinguish it from the physical-force variety) were major precursors for secularism, Budd says, and when they lost impetus, their members joined the later movement. In his autobiography, Hobson speaks of that fuller rationalism of Paine, Godwin, and Owen, as a challenge that the Rationalist Press should have met more fully.

When William Archer died, in 1924, his friend J. M. Robertson edited a collection of his essays, *William Archer as Rationalist*, published by Watts. Robertson wrote like a New Age radical himself, saying that Archer had been as much a rationalist as a drama critic or translator, but "This could not be guessed from any word in the *Times* obituary notice. . . . It is one of the functions of such journals to keep the deeper issues of modern thought out of sight." Archer was interested in a range of New Age issues, from spelling reform via spiritualism to racial harmony.

Connected with the Rationalist Press were the Halls of Science, working-class institutions that held lectures on orthodox science but also on mesmerism, phrenology, astrology, and uncooked food—New Age science. The Halls of Science were places where people heard Bradlaugh and Besant speak. South Place was a sort of university for those who had matriculated at the Halls of Science. As a high-level focus for these ideas and activities, therefore, South Place is of the greatest interest to students of New Ages.

PAINE IN PARIS

To return to Paine himself: Going to Paris in 1789, he wrote gleefully, "A share in two revolutions is living to some purpose." And indeed he hoped to share in a third—a revolution in England. In Paris he was friend to Condorcet, Brissot de Warville, and other Girondins. Part II of *The Rights of Man*, published in 1793, was a more radical and risky work in which he declared that monarchy and aristocracy would not last another seven years in Europe. They would be swept away before the symbolic centenary year arrived. Paine had to leave England—indeed, he had been elected a member of the French National Assembly—and in his absence was found guilty of treason to his native country. He and Anacharsis Cloots (a Belgian noble who called himself a citizen of the world) were then the only foreigners in the National Assembly.

But Paine's days of immediate effectiveness were over. In France he was not trusted by the Jacobins, one reason being that he voted against the execution of Louis XVI. Another reason was his ignorance of the French language, and of the historical and geographical provenance of French politics. His habitual simplification of issues in the direction of moral and "international" decisions here ran into the swamp of geographical and historical complexities and special interests, and was blocked by the opposition of French nationalist solidarity.

Thus he was not able to accomplish much in French politics, and indeed spent quite a long time there in prison. This was partly because of the hostility of the American political establishment. The American minister to France, hostile to Paine as were so many Americans by then, declined to claim him as an American citizen and so to secure his release.

However, Paine did play a role in the intellectual history of the French Revolution, in part as the living symbol of the American Revolution and of international revolutionism. It was at his house in Paris that Mary Wollstonecraft met M. and Mme. Roland and other

Girondins during her visit in 1792. He was a great hero of the Irish in Ireland, and of the Irish émigrés in Paris. He was also a friend of Francisco de Miranda, famous among radicals for his plan to spread the revolution to the Spanish colonies in the Americas. (Godwin sent a copy of his *Political Justice* to Paris, as a gift for "General" Miranda.) He and Joel Barlow were the living symbols in Paris of the link between the American and the French Revolutions, but Paine was essentially a private citizen and spectator of public events. He led a kind of politically posthumous existence.

Paine had been called to life by the coming of an age of revolution, like Tolstoy in Russia in 1880. As he wrote, in Part II of *The Rights of Man*, "It appears to general observation that revolutions create genius and talents." But like others he disapproved—was horrified by—the way revolution developed in France. And when the life of revolution was cut off from him, in prison or in hiding, he lapsed back into inertia and frequent drunkenness. The last twenty years of his life demonstrated the death of a New Age's heroism as vividly as the previous twenty years had demonstrated its life.

As tirelessly as Calvin himself, he had reduced all the complexities of cultural tradition to simple alternatives, with an equally simple choice to be made between them. His schematic analysis turned all history and all experience into transparent streams of tendency, each making its moral character clearly legible within it. But, at the end of a New Age, to do that seemed both crude and dangerous, morally as well as practically.

GODWIN AND BLAKE TEXTS

We took two texts to be of central importance for the nineteenth century period: Tolstoy's *The Kingdom of God Is Within You* and Carpenter's *Civilization: Its Cause and Cure*. We might suggest Blake's *Prophetic Books*, and Godwin's *Enquiry Concerning Political Justice*, which were both finished in 1793, as the equivalents for this earlier period. (Blake was less read in his time than Tolstoy, but he is a powerful presence to us, looking back.)

Political Justice, to use the common abbreviation, was begun in September 1791—in effect, it was another of the many replies to Burke, whose *Reflections* appeared in 1790—and took Godwin sixteen months to write. William St. Clair says it was conceived in an age of enlightenment—Godwin being England's leading *philosophe*—but born in an age of revolution. The title of Godwin's book, it has often been pointed out, is rather misleading, because its main concern is with what is usually called ethics rather than politics. Hence its extreme and politically infeasible individualism; it proposes that people should always strive to be able to do without one another. Godwin distrusted all collective action and all bureaucratized or institutionalized virtue. He thought that cooperation, cohabitation, and even marriage must always be held secondary in value to the primary freedom of the individual.

His philosophy was certainly not identical with that of Gandhi and Tolstoy. But some important idealistic turns of phrase in his discourse will nevertheless remind us of their thinking, as when he says that "a nation has only to wish to be free in order to be so." Or, men have no rights, only duties. Or, as H. N. Brailsford quotes it, "An earnest desire will in some degree generate capacity." Brailsford comments, "There Godwin opened a profoundly interesting and stimulating line of thought." This is the creative evolution that, in Brailsford's time, Shaw was to play with in *Back to Methuselah*. The same idea is to be found in Gandhi and Tolstoy, and in some sense it must be implicit, whether or not it is explicit, in any New Age thinker.

Godwin's writing had a somewhat systematic character, but his political philosophy was anarchism, which must always be New Age. Indeed, his appearance of containing everything in a system was mostly achieved by ruthless simplification and excision. But despite his idealism, he took a keen interest in politics, and intervened effectively on occasion, as in his 1794 pamphlet/letter to the press entitled "Cursory Strictures," which is usually credited with defeating the government's attack upon the leading radicals. If these men (those mentioned before) had been condemned, dozens more would have been arrested, so Godwin's protest was very important.

On the other hand his pamphlet, "Considerations on Lord Grenville's and Mr. Pitt's Bills," because it censured John Thelwall and the London Corresponding Society for their violence, offended the militant radicals. And the three editions of *Political Justice* (in 1793, 1796, and 1798) grew progressively more conservative, politically and even ethically. Godwin came, for instance, to allot progressively more importance to the private affections, in a commonsense way. In the course of Godwin's development we see the intellectual effects of increasing government repression fairly simply reflected.

However, Godwin remained in some ways a leader of radical thought. Like Shelley later, he was a great patron of rebellious youth, often aiding even schoolchildren to throw off the bonds imposed by tyrannical teachers and fathers. In Godwin's case, it was boys and young men he aided; in Shelley's case, typically, it was young girls, from Harriet Westbrook to Emilia Vivaldi. And this radicalism was not just a matter of personal temperament; Godwin's philosophy, too, though quite impersonal, was extremist and idealist. Every relationship, private as well as public, must be made dissolvable at will.

William St. Clair draws our attention to the connection between Godwin and William Blake, when he says that a single lyric by Blake, "London," makes all the "connections" Godwin spoke of in his philosophy. The streets of London, the chartered Thames, the winding sheet, the sexual blight on the marriage bed, the marks of weakness and woe—all are seen by the poet as connected, in just the way the philosopher saw them.

The Prophetic Books are perhaps most striking for their interest in revolutionary energy as a force to be found in various forms and social places, outside politics as well as inside, and most notably in the erotic life and in art. This conception of Blake's is something alien to Paine (never mind Tolstoy and Gandhi), but it radically expanded the idea of art and the artist, for everyone coming after. It was for this, above all, that W. B. Yeats revered Blake, and a similar faith in what gives a New Age character to so much modern literature, even when written by otherwise conservative authors. We see again how various are the ideas propounded by the New Age mentality.

Paradoxical as it may seem, Blake's thought was a development of the New Age aspect of Dissenting Christianity, developing that heritage in new directions. He hated eighteenth-century rationalism, writing "Mock on! mock on! Voltaire! Rousseau!" On the other hand, he sometimes saw the rationalist Tom Paine as a figure comparable with Jesus Christ. Paine's *Agrarian Justice* pamphlet, which laid out plans for social justice as a whole, not unlike Henry George's in the next New Age, made Blake class him with Jesus, as a worker of miracles. And when the Anglican Bishop Watson of Llandaff wrote an

Apology for the Bible, in answer to Paine's *Age of Reason,* Blake wrote in his copy, "It appears to me Now that Tom Paine is a better Christian than the Bishop. I have read this Book with attention and find that the Bishop has only hurt Paine's heel while Paine has broken his head." This congeniality of Paine and Blake is hard to explain, if we are studying their ideas, but if we think of the New Age mentality, the two have quite a lot in common.

Even more strikingly, Blake was ready to reverse the conventional moral terms, and to see Hell, being the abode of energy, as divine. This paradox, of course, involved a fundamental transvaluation of erotic experience.

Thus in *The Marriage of Heaven and Hell,* he says:

> The pride of the peacock is the glory of God.
> The lust of the goat is the bounty of God.
> The wrath of the lion is the wisdom of God.
> The nakedness of woman is the work of God.

Above all, it was system Blake hated, and in this matter he was the most vehement spokesman for the New Age's antagonism toward the systematic temperament. Priesthood began when a system was formed, he said. Jesus was all virtue and acted from impulse, not from rules. He said he himself went mad as a refuge from unbelief—meaning by that term the great theorists, Bacon, Newton, and Locke.

It is Blake more than any other of those eighteenth-century radicals who has interested the literary reader of later New Ages, both our own and that of the nineteenth century. He has remained modern, and—for those who love him—has maintained the alliance between literature and the New Age mentality. When A. R. Orage presented Nietzsche to English readers, he pointed out the likeness between him and Blake. I have already cited Yeats. And in the 1960s, I was much struck by a likeness between him and Norman Mailer.

PAINE'S FRIENDS AND ACQUAINTANCES

In "Gandhi's London" I also introduced semi-biographically Henry Salt, Olive Schreiner, Edwin Arnold, and Annie Besant, as four important personalities in that nineteenth-century New Age, personally known to Gandhi. Looking for equivalents for them in this earlier period we can take William Godwin and Mary Wollstonecraft in England, Nicolas and Margaret de Bonneville in France and America. These were not all his intimate friends, but people well-known to Paine, and representing some of the forces of the times.

Born in 1756, Godwin was the son and grandson of Dissenting ministers, and there were close connections between Dissent and political radicalism in the eighteenth century, as we noted in reference to Blake, and as the careers of Dr. Price and Dr. Priestley show. While a student at Hoxton Dissenting Academy, moreover, he had come under the influence of the American Calvinist Jonathan Edwards, and his own writing has sometimes an Edwards-like mixture of logical stringency and emotional fervor.

As a child Godwin read such books as *The Pilgrim's Progress*, his uncle's poem "The Death Bed," and James Janeway's *Token for Children*, about the conversion, lives, and joyful deaths of several young children. Its readers were urged to pray and weep over such stories. (Gandhi's childhood reading, with its stress on death and sacrifice and penitence, which seems to us almost incredibly severe and depressive, was not without its Western equivalents.)

Among the Dissenters were to be found many of the intellectual and moral leaders of Enlightenment England. It was appropriate that Burke's *Reflections on the French Revolution*, which led the reaction against Enlightenment ideas, should have been addressed to Richard Price, the Dissenting minister, while *The Rights of Man*, which led the resistance to Burke, was written by an ex-Quaker, and welcomed enthusiastically by ex-Dissenters like Godwin and Holcroft. Holcroft wrote Godwin about it, "I have read the pamphlet once through and am absolutely in an extacy with the acute the profound the divine author." Godwin wrote Paine, "It is perhaps impossible to arise from perusing it, without feeling oneself both wiser and better."

Godwin began life as a Sandemanian, espousing a creed whose character was defined by the saying that after the Calvinists had allowed one out of ten Christians to be saved, the Sandemanians allowed one out of ten Calvinists. This faith held the communism preached and depicted in the Acts of the Apostles to be normative for modern Christians. He came to London in 1782, and gradually detached himself from his religious origins, becoming a man of letters and working for Joseph Johnson. This seemed like a permanent change, away from religious fervor toward a life of contemplation.

Under the stimulus of an age of revolution, however, Godwin's heritage expressed itself in a heroic and idealistic posture. Like Rousseau in his Calvinist phase, Godwin was easily intoxicated with abstract nouns, and wrote pages that promised a nobility of behavior he knew in soberer moments he was unlikely to deliver. Both of them had, in these phases of their lives, images of Spartan, Roman, and Genevan virtue glowing on their mental screens. This fervor brought popular success in the short run; Godwin got the enormous sum of a thousand guineas for *Political Justice*.

The woman to whom Godwin was briefly married, Mary Wollstonecraft, was born into the Church of England, had an unhappy childhood, oppressed by an unstable father, and supported herself as a companion and governess from a very early age. Having generally radical sympathies, she made the fate of women especially her concern. She rescued her sister Eliza from an unhappy marriage, and settled with her in 1782 in Newington Green, where Dr. Richard Price lived and preached. This was the Price who gave the address on the French Revolution in 1789. The year before—on the actual centenary of the English Revolution—that annual address had been given by Andrew Kippis, who had been Godwin's tutor at Hoxton Academy.

The circle of Price's friends (which included Kippis, Franklin, Hume, and Priestley) believed that England's Glorious Bloodless Revolution of 1688 had been left incomplete, for instance because it favored the established Church of England over the other Christian sects. It left intact the Test and Corporation Acts (of 1661 and 1673), which penalized the Dissenters and reduced them to second-class citizens. The Revolution Society that Price addressed kept alive the hope of further reform, and saw the revolutionary events in France as parallel.

Setting Paine among these four friends, we see the pattern of the New Age's features already studied begin to appear in their lives. We can begin with feminism and Wollstonecraft. At the outset of her career as a woman of letters, she was already concerned with the position of women. She was much indebted to the protection of Joseph Johnson, and she was almost the only woman at his dinners, because most of the intellectual women of London were too conservative, in various ways, to enjoy the company. She was conscious of being a risky innovator. "I am then going to be the first in a new genus," she wrote her sister. "I must be independent. . . . You know I was not born to tread the beaten track, the peculiar bent of my nature pushes me on."

She made a career in letters, beginning a translation of Campe's version of *Robinson Crusoe*, as well as of Lavater. Her *Original Stories from Real Life*, 1788, had three editions by 1800, and three more plus a translation into German. But her great opportunities were offered her by the Revolution, and the enthusiasm it aroused in England, which led her on to feminism. She wrote *A Vindication of the Rights of Man*, and then *A Vindication of the Rights of Woman*. In this last, she was able to outpace some of her old masters—for instance, she chastised Rousseau for what we would call his male chauvinism in *Emile*.

It was a period of wild experiment in all modes of behavior and sensibility. Blake and his wife are said to have received their friends in their garden nude one day; and though that anecdote has been questioned, his friend Holcroft certainly practiced nudity. And Wollstonecraft's feminism gave an extra intensity to all of these ideas. Blake had a theoretical belief in polygamy, and proposed to add a concubine to his own household. But Mary Wollstonecraft actually proposed herself to the wife of the Swiss artist Henry Fuseli as a new inmate to *her* household. She avowed that the idea "arises from the sincere affection which I have for your husband, for I find that I cannot live without the satisfaction of seeing and conversing with him daily."

Thus Wollstonecraft took part in the erotic liberation of the times. Then in 1792 she and Johnson, and Fuseli and his wife, set out for France together to be exultantly present at the Revolution. In France, she wrote on education for the National Assembly's Committee on Public Instruction, of which Condorcet was a member. She watched the French king go to his death with a thrill of revolutionary guilt, expressed in Gothic-novel terms; and she herself was penalized by the violent disorder of the times in her love relationships.

The father of Wollstonecraft's first child, the American "Captain" Gilbert Imlay, was a land agent for the Scioto company, which sold land in the Ohio Valley, but which collapsed. (Joel Barlow was another such agent, and his wife, Ruth Barlow, became a good friend of

Wollstonecraft.) He was something of a writer; he published a *Topographical Description of the Western Territories* in 1792 and a novel, *The Emigrants*, in 1793—obviously both of them "American" in subject.

Imlay was forty-one in 1793, and presented himself as a Kentucky frontier adventurer; but there was much that was shady about his adventures. He was a fugitive from the Kentucky courts between 1786 and 1799. He was also involved in a scheme to win back for France the colonies held by Spain in North America—a scheme that the American government did not approve. And his love affairs with women seem to have caused them a lot of grief. His unhappy relations with Wollstonecraft drove her to two suicide attempts in London. Imlay is thus a very modern figure, a phenomenon of an age of revolution.

Although Paine knew both Mary Wollstonecraft and Godwin, he did not know the former as "Mrs. Godwin," and the marital link between those two personalities was of minor importance to him (and others). Wollstonecraft was a respected thinker and writer, famous quite apart from her relation to Godwin. In the next case we come to, Paine's friendship with M. and Mme. de Bonneville, that link was all-important at first, but Madame de Bonneville herself came to play a considerable part in Paine's life.

Paine went to live with Nicolas and Margaret de Bonneville in Paris in 1797, and became a part of their family. Nicolas de Bonneville was then thirty-seven, and had been married three years. He had published a translation of Paine's *Rights of Man*, Part II, in 1792, and many other things by Paine after that. He spoke excellent English, and Holcroft had stayed with the de Bonnevilles when he came to Paris to listen to *Figaro* and transcribe it piratically.

At the same time, de Bonneville was more than a mere publisher. He was a journalist and man of ideas, in the Masonic line. He had been converted to "Illuminism" in 1787 by Christian Bode, a friend of Adam Weishaupt, the German inventor of that purified form of the Masonic mysteries; and in his turn de Bonneville tried to convert Condorcet to that belief. (The Illuminists thought the ordinary Masons had been infiltrated and corrupted by the Jesuits.) This was an interest he communicated to or shared with Paine. De Bonneville was also one of the translators of German literature into French, including the early Sturm und Drang Romantics.

Above all, he was one of the founding fathers of the modern revolutionary tradition, according to James H. Billington. The latter's *Fire in the Minds of Men* has a chapter on how the fourth estate in France, the press, replaced the first estate, the priesthood. This transition is surely a crucial phenomenon in the history of revolution, and Billington's chapter is suggestively entitled, "Nicholas Bonneville and Oracular Journalism."

De Bonneville looked to the republic of letters to provide the direct means of political deliverance, or at least to provide slogans as weapons, which made Paine his natural hero since he was such a skilled sloganeer. De Bonneville himself first issued the famous cry *"Aux armes, citoyens"* in print, and first addressed the king with the familiar pronoun "tu." Paine was the first to refer to the king of France as "Louis Capet," implicitly stripping him of his titles. De Bonneville was hostile to the moderates, and promised the revolution a "voice of iron"—the name he gave a new journal that he brought out in 1790–91. He invented a new language, rich in neologisms, Billington says.

He also edited *Le Tribun du Peuple*, and then *Le Bien Informé*, from within the Palais Royal. The most secret inner circle in that hatching ground of revolution, says Billington, was Bonneville's Social Circle, which combined the form of the Masonic lodge with Rousseau's idea of a social contract. Christian Bode was the first to use the word "circle" to mean such an organization—one which made both individual moral demands on its members and universal ideological claims.

Freemasonry had been powerful among the patriots in the American Revolution: it is said that all the American generals but one were Masons, and it is certain that fifty-two out of fifty-six signatories of the Declaration of Independence were. In 1783 Captain George Smith's *Use and Abuse of Masonry* appeared in London; it praised the Masons' teaching, employing the traditional association of reason and truth and the sun. (Smith, and Paine, derived Masonry from the Druid priests of the sun.) The scientific culture that acknowledged Newton as its great master, and which was politically liberal, often found mystical expression via Masonry.

Thus de Bonneville contributed something to the organization of the revolution, and partly as a result of his interest in Illuminism—in the occult. Moreover, Bode's blueprint for political Illuminism was called *Pythagoras*, making use of numerical and geometrical symbol-

ism associated with the Greek mathematician, and both de Bonneville and Paine were in that sense Pythagoreans. This ideology made
a hero of the exiled intellectual who helps build a new order, and
Paine saw himself in those terms.

On the other hand, de Bonneville and Paine were not Jacobins.
They wanted to abolish the monarchy but, like Paine, de Bonneville
voted against the execution of the king, and deplored the dictatorship
of Robespiere. De Bonneville suffered for his dissent. He was sent to
jail, and then kept under surveillance. But he charged his wife to
escape by herself to America, the land of liberty, taking their sons
with her. Paine had lodged with the family in France from 1797 to
1802, and in America lived, on and off, with Madame de Bonneville
for the rest of his days.

The intellectual career of these radicals, Godwin as much as Paine,
were promoted by the Revolution. To a striking degree, indeed, this
was true of Blake, too, and most of the others we have named. Perhaps
all radicals need the impelling and compelling stimulus of a New Age,
and if possible a period when revolution is in the air. Ages of conformity
reinforce the authoritarian and systematic tendencies in us. But it
seems likely that the age of revolution released in Godwin and Paine
a strain of intellectual heroism that otherwise would *never* have found
expression. Once that excitement passed, as we saw, Godwin reverted
to his previous pattern of quite narrowly literary and speculative interests, and Paine relapsed into periodic self-indulgence.

In Paris he did write his defense of Deism, *The Age of Reason*, in
1793, but then was imprisoned in Luxembourg and released only
when a newly appointed American minister certified him to be an
American citizen. Part II of *The Age of Reason* came out in 1795, and
then his *Agrarian Justice* pamphlet (which aroused Blake's enthusiasm). Napoleon called on him to discuss how to construct gunboats
for the invasion of England—a scheme in which Paine got quite
involved.

But Napoleon's France was no place for Paine. He went back to
John Adams's America, which was also no place for him, and where he
died, not only exiled from his native country but rejected and dis-
honored by that adoptive country he had helped create. In bad shape,
physically and mentally, and mocked by his neighbors, he was looked
after by his fellow exile, Margaret de Bonneville.

We do not know as much about her as about Mary Wollstonecraft, but Margaret Brazier de Bonneville was a woman of education, and she, too, apparently defined herself in nondomestic terms. She earned her living in America as a teacher and governess, and was unwilling— according to Paine in one of their quarrels—to do any cooking, even for her children. He left nearly all his estate to the de Bonnevilles, and she arranged his burial to give it some public dignity—to express, as she put it, the gratitude of America, and that of France, to this great benefactor.

Paine had secured a place at West Point for one of her sons, who engaged in adventures in the Far West, and was made famous as Captain Bonneville, in a book by Washington Irving. At the beginning of that book we get a glimpse of Nicolas de Bonneville, passing his old age in New York. Paine was dead, and so was the revolutionary mood. Irving presents de Bonneville as a great reader—not of revolutionary manuals, but of Latin and Greek, of Voltaire and Racine, and of Shakespeare. In summer weather he could be seen sitting under a tree on the Battery, or in a church portico, his hat by his side, his bald head uncovered, his eyes riveted on the page, unconscious of the passing hours and the passing throng. The image can stand for many other former activists at the end of their age of revolution.

Then and Now

> Godwin's leading idea when he comes to sketch a shadowy
> constitution is an extreme dislike of overgrown national
> states. Political speculation in his day idealised the city re-
> public of antiquity. . . . Tolstoy, going back to the village
> community as the only possible scene of a natural and virtu-
> ous life, exhibits the same tendency.
>
> H. N. Brailsford, *Shelley, Godwin, and Their Circle*

In chapter 5 we looked mostly for likenesses between Tom Paine's
New Age and Gandhi's. Here we shall begin by looking for likenesses
between Paine's London and the London and New York of the 1960s.
But it should be said that these are more tentatively offered than
those of the earlier "Then and Now" chapter, because I could not
find such rich sources of data. We need a scholar who will do for the
eighteenth-century New Age what E. P. Thompson had done for the
working-class movements of that time.

LONDON AND LITERATURE

Some fairly obvious and striking likenesses happen to be fictional:
that is, a scene from novels of the later period resembles a scene from
life of the earlier one. Doris Lessing's *The Golden Notebook*, for instance, depicts a domestic world very like that of Godwin and his
family. We see that likeness in the large part played in the early lives
of Lessing's Anna and Molly by an idealism about revolution, in the
threat they feel of direct or indirect punishment by society, and in the
radicals' own gathering skepticism as time goes by. Moreover, Less-

ing's female characters and their friends find many parallels in the social milieu in which the Godwins moved. For instance, besides Mary Wollstonecraft and Mary Hays and Helen Maria Williams, and other free women/women of letters, Godwin knew Elizabeth Inchbald and Perdita Robinson, both of whom were successful as actresses before they became novelists, both beautiful women with a succession of suitors, some rich and powerful, some men of ideas. They were New Age figures.

Perhaps the London of *The Four-Gated City* reminds us even more of that eighteenth-century London than *The Golden Notebook* scene does. Certainly the genealogical jigsaw puzzle of the Godwin-Shelley household looks like the picture Lessing draws of the Coleridges in *The Four-Gated City*. When Shelley began to visit Godwin, the household of the latter included Mary, Godwin's daughter by Mary Wollstonecraft; Fanny, Mary Wollstonecraft's daughter by Gilbert Imlay; and Jane Clairmont, the second Mrs. Godwin's daughter by a former husband. At the Coleridges', in Lessing's novel, one met the strange triangle of Mark, Lynda, and Martha, as well as Francis, the son of Mark and Lynda; Paul, the son of Mark's brother Colin (himself an exile in Russia); Jill and Gwen, daughters of another brother; and Graham, son of John Patton, now married to Margaret, mother of the brothers. These New Age family patterns and displaced relationships corresponded to ideological and emotional contrasts and promoted conflicts, as they did in the case of the Godwin-Shelleys.

To return to *The Golden Notebook*, Anna Wulf's unhappy affairs with Paul/Michael and with Saul Green fit into a pattern like that of Mary Wollstonecraft's affair with Gilbert Imlay. Imlay had had an affair in Paris before he met Mary with Helen Maria Williams, the novelist and poet of radical sympathies who made her home in Paris, during the Revolution, and wrote about it for British publications. Imlay had other mistresses after Mary, and as we know her unhappiness drove her to attempt suicide more than once.

Moreover, Imlay, too, was something of an intellectual, a novelist, a radical. Thus his Don Juan career had its ideological aspect, defying the institution and the commitments of marriage. He was a friend of Joel Barlow, the American poet, diplomatist, and revolutionary, who acted something of the same social role. They were both friends of Paine and of Jefferson. In Lessing's London novels, figures similar in their international provenance and political significance appear and disappear. In his relation with Wollstonecraft, one might compare Imlay with Saul Green in *The Golden Notebook*, in his relations with Anna Wulf.

Thus, despite the impression given by the novels of Jane Austen, there was in her time (which was almost exactly contemporaneous with the New Age) an international bohemia of the left wing quite like the one portrayed in Lessing's books, who behaved not dissimilarly in their personal relations. Mary Hay, another novelist, proposed marriage to Godwin herself, and then helped persuade Wollstonecraft to marry him. The difference is that Jane Austen was *not* a New Ager, and that the period's most serious novels did not depict this behavior. Modern novels forward just the sides of life that were then omitted.

However, there was one genre then widely read, though of doubtful literary prestige, that was closer to our own fiction, in relevant ways. This genre, the Gothic, could combine melodrama with serious material, and that combination is well-represented by Godwin's Gothic-cum-social-problem novel, *Caleb Williams*. This is a puzzling and clumsy performance in many ways, but a fascinating experiment in consciousness. The author was plainly in touch with the hidden workings of his mind and personality, and his knowledge of unconscious psychology, his speculations about is own "self," are at the source of his politics and philosophy. Reading him, one can think of modern novelists, or of Rousseau, as comparable. Neither Paine, among the radicals, nor Austen or Scott among the conservatives, could have written such a novel; it comes out of a different eighteenth century—a New Age. The Gothic terror novel of flight and pursuit, of suspense and revelations, linked with apocalyptic social analysis (Mary Shelley's *Frankenstein* is another example) would have developed into one of the great literary forms of radicalism, if the whole movement had not been suppressed. That was a New Age genre.

In our own day, a phenomenon one might call parallel has been the pornography-cum-social-problem novel, in which elaborated sexual excitement takes the place held by terror before, and—in the hands of some brilliant American writers—that crude interest is allied with morally serious and sometimes apocalyptic social criticism. In the 1960–1990 period we had *An American Dream, Lolita, Portnoy's Com-*

plaint, *Couples*, *Catch-22*, and *Myra Breckenridge*. The most recent that has reached a wide readership was Tom Wolfe's *Bonfire of the Vanities*.

The Marquis de Sade was formulating the theory of such fiction in Godwin's time, and introduced into the form sexual material of the kind the modern practitioners use—a kind of material that Godwin could not have handled. But not until our own age of revolution had the radicalization of the intellect and the imagination gone far enough to produce a series of books that actually exploit the possibilities of such an idea.

To return to Doris Lessing's novels: another striking coincidence in theme or motif between Paine's London and the world of *The Golden Notebook* is the suicide attempt of Molly's son, Tommy. This theme expresses a concern that runs through all Doris Lessing's work, a concern for the children of the emancipated women and divorced radicals she describes, a guilt before their sullen accusations and their mute maladjustments.

The actual event finds a striking parallel in the suicides of Harriet Westbrook Shelley and Fanny Imlay (the one following on the other in 1816) and even more in the death of Thomas Holcroft's son. Harriet killed herself, having lost Shelley; Fanny took laudanum, believing herself to be of no use to anyone, after her two stepsisters eloped together with Shelley. The second case makes an even more tragic story, for the boy, who was sixteen and trying to run away to sea, shot himself just when he heard his father's footsteps approach his hiding place on the ship.

One could also cite the painful relations between Godwin and his protégé Thomas Cooper. And the tangles of neurotic sexual involvement we can sum up in the names of Harriet Westbrook and Shelley, and Claire Clairmont and Byron, are very like those of Lessing's characters. In both cases, sex and revolution are intertwined, behind the private life stands the public, and the betrayed promise of Russia in the one parallels the betrayed promise of France in the other. America was the homeland of Saul Green as well as of Gilbert Imlay— the two hero/villains of the stories, fictional and nonfictional. Their Americas were separated by a hundred and fifty years, and so were very different, but it may not be too fanciful to suggest that both men were seen by those who knew them as charged with a more than English energy, just by virtue of being American.

HISTORICAL PARALLELS

Turning away from novels, we would find it easy to parallel the lists of arrests and imprisonments of the 1790s among American radicals in the 1960s, all the way from Dr. Spock and Norman Mailer to Eldridge Cleaver and LeRoi Jones. It was a time—as New Ages tend to be—when going to court and going to jail were crucial qualifications for men and women of conscience, and occasions of pride and congratulation.

Such contradictions of ordinary social honor come, at least in theory, easily and regularly to ascetic New Agers. This was certainly true of Gandhi and his close comrades, for instance, who entered and left jail beaming. They were delighted to be arrested, disappointed not to be jailed, emotionally exalted by the whole enterprise. Gandhi said they were to regard the jails as His Majesty's hotels; to regard suffering as happiness and self-sacrifice as supreme bliss. Their actions, their whole lives, were to be New—innovative; i.e., predicated on behavioral paradox.

On intellectuals of a different type, however, on non–New Agers, physical punishment and social dishonor can have radically disabling effects. Their sense of reality owing more to the authoritarian or systematic mentality, they cannot shrug off social punishments. (In their writings, Pope and Swift make jocular references to their enemies' disgrace—such as Defoe being put in the stocks—and take for granted that such disgrace disproves the victim's claims to moral or intellectual authority.) Certainly the repressive measures taken by the various British authorities in the 1790s did disable some of the intellectuals, as we have seen.

As everyone knows, the period from 1775 to 1805 was first a time of unparalleled hope—"Bliss was it in that dawn to be alive, But to be young was very Heaven!"—and then a time of savage repression, by law and by mob action, by government and by society. The New Age sense of reality first bloomed and spread across much of thinking society, but then was so sternly punished as to be replaced by the authoritarian alternative. In terms of personal experience, Paine's last years are a vivid example of that punishment. In this it was more like the period beginning in the 1960s than like either the nineteenth-century New Age in England or the one beginning in the 1990s, so far as we can foresee the latter. There were the same changes from bold gaiety to pathos. Life endings like that of Abbie Hoffman were as saddening as the last years and death of Thomas Paine.

The nearest equivalent for William Godwin in the New York of the 1960s may have been Paul Goodman, whose anarchist ideas we find discussed in Snyder's circle much later. Born in 1911, and like Godwin born into a family outside the world of letters, Goodman largely educated himself. Also like Godwin, he came to profess himself an anarchist and friend of youth (this by the 1940s, already). He had much the same range of interests and of activities as Godwin, from literature to politics. There was the same vein of pedantry in the style of both, combined with a wild innovativeness. This paradoxicality was a matter of concepts as well as verbal style; Goodman's *The New Reformation* is subtitled "Notes of a Neolithic Conservative." And he seems to have belonged as completely and exclusively to his metropolis as Godwin did to his.

Goodman took the same practical interest as Godwin in liberating young people from oppressive parents and teachers; and if this idealism was tainted with the scandal of his flaunted bisexual seductions—something unimaginable in Godwin—this perhaps only made him a more proper spokesman for our hyper-erotic times. His most famous title was *Growing Up Absurd,* published at the very beginning of the 1960s, and the charter of freedom for many young people in that decade. The other book of his which now seems likely to survive is *Communitas,* originally published in 1947 but revised in 1960. It is interesting to note how that book continues other nineteenth-century New Age themes, containing essays on the Garden Cities designed by Ebenezer Howard, Patrick Geddes, and Raymond Unwin.

As for Blake, reading him in the 1960s I was much struck by a likeness I saw between him and Norman Mailer. Like the latter, Blake acquired an extraordinary faith in himself by means of a spiritual bargain that repudiated the ordinary cultural bargain, the ordinary social identity assigned him. The Mother of his Mortal Part, he says, with cruelty did mould his heart, and with false, self-deceiving tears did bind his nostrils, eyes, and ears. Just so Mailer, in his account of the march on the Pentagon, repudiated his role as a mother's son and a modest, ironic, humorous Jew. Both defied the limits set by com-

mon sense and common decency, and the forms of established philosophy, religion, and morality.

We see this mental freedom of Blake's, this self-creativity, in his
speculative dealings with occult philosophy and in his quite modernist sexual theories, as well as in his visions, his angels, and his
voices. What he learned from Swedenborg, and Boehme, and Para-
celsus, put him in touch with that stream of forbidden knowledge
flowing underground through European culture and occasionally
coming to the surface in the work of artists. Blake managed to combine that imaginative tradition with evangelical Christian piety.
Mailer's dealings with the occult and with sexual mysticism are obviously parallel. Both men were precursors to Gary Snyder and drew
on what he calls the great subculture, the underground tradition of
shamanism.

Then Blake was, like Mailer, very much a man, and a writer, of his
city. His imagination received its education there, and—more
important—he deliberately possessed the city, incorporated it into
himself:

> Loud sounds the Hammer of Los and loud his Bellows is heard
> Before London to Hampsted's breadths and Highgate's Heights,
> To Stratford and old Bow and across to the gardens of Kensington
> On Tyburn's Brook; loud groans Thames beneath the iron Forge
> Of Rintrah and Palamabron, of Theotorm and Bromion, to force the
> instruments
> Of Harvest, the Plow and Harrow to pass over the Nations.

This reminded me of Mailer's treatment of New York in *An American
Dream*. Both writers seem to recite the place names of the city in an
incantation, to make it become what they want. The poet as shaman
is forcing his own and our imaginations.

Just so, in his commentary on *Why Are We in Vietnam?*, Mailer says
he was trying to ward off certain dangers to America by imagining
them in fictional form. Mailer describes himself as a shaman, fash-
ioning a totem as much as an aesthetic, and the same could surely be
said of Blake. Like Mailer, Blake tried to teach his fellow citizens
saving truths, and he, too, had a vivid sense of himself as a prophet,

though for lack of recognition he became—opposite to Mailer—long one of the most overlooked figures in English literature.

But it was perhaps perverse to put Mailer rather than Ginsberg in conjunction with Blake. It was Allen Ginsberg who, among the people of the American 1960s, most clearly asked to be associated with Blake. In the period 1948–49, living in Spanish Harlem, he had a series of visions of Blake that determined his poetic life, and that led him, like Blake himself, to be treated as crazy.

Born in 1926, in Paterson, New Jersey, Ginsberg was brought up in a home divided between the literary interests of his father, a high school English teacher, and the radical political enthusiasms of his mentally ill mother. For him, the heroic traditions of radical politics seem to have taken the place of Blake's Dissenting sect traditions. But then, as a student at Columbia, he shared an apartment with Jack Kerouac and William Burroughs, who educated him in new ideas—an education that had an overwhelming effect, partly because it involved his acknowledgment of a new sexual identity, a recognition of himself as homosexual.

Having begun as a poet under the influence of William Carlos Williams, Ginsberg was liberated by Blake's influence to trust what he called his "romantic inspiration—Hebraic-Melvillean bardic breath." Writing in this vein, he produced *Howl*, which he declaimed at a famous reading in San Francisco in 1955, where he made an alliance with Snyder, Kerouac, and the others who became known as the Beat poets. The idea of Zen-lunacy, very similar to the idea of the holy fool, was acted out by them at public readings, and attracted a lot of attention. The publication of *Howl*, moreover, led to a trial for obscenity, and a lot more publicity. This book was Ginsberg's equivalent for the *Prophetic Books*, but it brought him much more recognition. By 1961 he was an internationally famous poet.

He traveled in India, where Buddhism became more important to him, replacing Blake and the heretical-Christian vein of inspiration. His Orientalism was therefore more traditional than Snyder's, inasmuch as it focused on India; but in his combining of Buddhism with the heresy of homosexuality, it was more radical than Snyder's. In the 1960s age of revolution, Ginsberg was semi-institutionally the embodiment of that mode of freedom. In 1965 he was crowned King of the May, Kral Majales, by the young people of Czechoslovakia, a lord of misrule in the brief Prague Spring—and was soon expelled from that country.

ASPECTS OF THE AGE

More or less all the dozen features of the New Ages we have already studied, occurring in the nineteenth and twentieth centuries, are also to be recognized in the history of the thirty years after 1775. However, the comparison is much more profitable in some cases than in others, and some new categories should replace the old ones.

First of all, empire was felt as a pressure then too: one of the substantial books of recent years about Blake is entitled *Prophet Against Empire*. The capitalization of the abstract noun, which follows Blake's own practice, and the omission of either a qualifying adjective like French or British, or even a definite or indefinite article, is typical of New Age feelings even today. Snyder uses the word the same way, and so does Matthew Fox.

The eighteenth century had been a time of triumph for the British Empire abroad, as for middle-class freedom at home. The journeys of Captain Cook were triumphs of adventure and experiment, which resulted in the acquisition of Australia; Clive drove the French out of India and left that enormous and ancient civilization apparently doomed to fall into British hands; the wars against France had driven that country's forces out of Canada.

The defeat of the British in America by the colonists was, of course, a defeat for the government and for some parts of the ruling class. Thus as far as the Dissenters and much of the middle class of England went, that defeat could seem like another triumph for the idea of liberty and the claims of the British—as a people, not as a nation-state—to have appropriated that idea, or at least defined it for the rest of the world. For them, Empire was usually the mark of an enemy.

This was true of many liberals; the great achievement of Burke's famous book was precisely his devising of a new rhetoric in which to speak for Empire—a mild rich voice for men of power. All the more, therefore, was the British (and also the French) Empire held in contempt, or at the least in question, by most of the New Age radicals of the time.

For although France did not become literally an empire till the end of this period, Napoleon's conquests—and indeed Robespierre's Terror before that—vividly reinforced everyone's sense of what was meant by Empire.

As in the 1960s, government spying was also a feature of the eighteenth-century New Age, as we saw in the case of Paine and the anecdotes about Wordsworth and Coleridge. There was the same awareness (whether shocked or sympathetic) of British citizens going to live with the national enemy—in that case, France. (In our day, we think of American radicals visiting Vietnam, later China, and then Central America.) Wollstonecraft and her friends, as well as Paine himself, went to observe and delight in the revolution in France. St. Clair says that Helen Maria Williams, living in Paris, was probably paid by the British government to send it information about events there, despite her radical sympathies. The Englishman she lived with, John Hurford Stone, also a writer, was probably subsidized by the French government. This will remind us of the 1960s in America.

There was also an intellectual pressure toward science and systematization, like that which we associate with later New Ages, and a similar resistance to that pressure. Tom Paine, we saw, refused to read Locke, who was far from the most elaborate philosopher of society. And on the opposite political side, Burke spoke from the point of view of the authoritarian temperament. He complained that the age of chivalry was gone, the general imagination ruled by sophisters, economists, and calculators.

Perhaps the biggest example of system then was political economy. Adam Smith's *Wealth of Nations* came out in 1776, and was one of the most important books of the century. The "dismal science" of Smith, Ricardo, and Malthus exemplified the oppressive character of systematic knowledge generally, and was in conscious conflict with New Age thinking. Malthus's *Essay on the Principle of Population* was directed against "Godwin, Condorcet, and other writers," as the subtitle says in so many words. There was a similar set of ideas about educational methods. The Lancaster and Bell societies for education, which Godwin objected to, were said to be triumphant moral and intellectual equivalents of steam engines. In the field of education, however, there were other, radically liberal and "creative" ideas—New Age ideas, which followed the experiments of Rousseau and his disciples.

Nonviolence, as a slogan, does not seem to have been as important a feature of the political scene then as it was in later New Ages. On the other hand, Godwin's anarchism, which was implicitly nonviolent, was the subject of much discussion. Godwin spoke against political revolution just on the grounds that it was bloody.

It is notable how often Brailsford, in his 1913 book, *Shelley, Godwin, and Their Circle*, compares Godwin with Tolstoy, the great anarchist of the nineteenth-century New Age. He says that Godwin and Holcroft were natural Quakers, and they preached nonresistance before Tolstoy did. Godwin indeed only approved of the use of force—and then reluctantly—when it was needed to restrain someone actually engaged in violence. (Brailsford cited Godwin again when he wrote about Gandhi some thirty-six years later.)

As we saw, Godwin believed—as did Paine—in what was later called creative evolution: the power of the human race, via individuals, to radically improve its own nature by making moral efforts, such improvements being passed on by inheritance. This idea was taken up in the next New Age, by Bernard Shaw in *Back to Methuselah*, and by Aldous Huxley.

Shaw's preface to *Back to Methuselah* says, "Creative Evolution is already a religion, and is now unmistakably the religion of the twentieth century." He wrote his play to provide that religion with legends and parables. Huxley's novel *Island* is another such legend. Huxley's letters in the 1940s have several affirmations of New Age faith in small marginal groups and in the "spiritual" alternatives to both direct political action and aestheticism.

Godwin's is the most important English name in the theory of nonviolent anarchism, followed by that of his son-in-law, Shelley. Both writers were revived in the nineteenth-century New Age as Brailsford's work on Godwin and Salt's on Shelley. The Ethical Culture movement and its friends also reinstated Tom Paine in historical respectability in America. Henry Salt brought out an abridged version of Godwin, and Moncure Conway wrote a full-scale rehabilitation of Paine.

Thus anarchism was in the air in the nineteenth-century New Age, as well as the eighteenth. Gross and Landauer were professed anarchists in the German branch. In the 1960s and later, Gary Snyder professed the faith, and there were many who were judged to be anarchists by their friends or enemies. The people of Ascona, and the people of the communes in California and elsewhere have been anarchists in one sense or another.

If Godwin was the theorist of nonviolence, he was also the patron of the simple life. Henry Salt saw the simple-life enthusiasm of his own day as an effect of the influence of Godwin—whom he calls "In many ways a true prophet." The simple life was also connected to Shelley. "The Poet-Pioneer," Chapter 7 of Salt's autobiography, is devoted to Shelley, a hero of free thought, socialism, sexual freedom, and food reform. (Shelley added a note to *Queen Mab*, condemning Prometheus for teaching men to cook meat—"the source of all our woe.")

Vegetarianism was practiced by some other of Godwin's friends, like Richard Phillips, Joseph Ritson, the medieval scholar and antiquary, and John Frank Newton, whose pamphlet *Return to Nature* (1811) converted Shelley to that practice. Newton recommended a diet of water and vegetables; Phillips allowed tea and lemonade. John "Walking" Stewart (he walked through much of India, Persia, Ethiopia, and North America) lived on bread and milk. Stewart was a friend of Paine, who saw much of him in his 1791–9 period in London. From Rousseau's time on, some people had played with the idea of vegetarianism, which usually went with a love of animals, and sometimes with more radical propositions, like nudism. John Frank Newton's sister-in-law, Mrs. de Boinville, practiced "nakedism."

In the eighteenth century, these ideas seem to have been regarded by most people, even radicals, as so eccentric as to deserve no serious response, and that is why they have been overlooked by historians. But they were part of the Simple Life, which was also followed by Rousseau and by the Lake Poets; and these last were socially very influential in the long run. The Lake Poets understood the idea more in the moderate style of Carpenter and his friends than in the extremist fashion of Graeser and Gross at Ascona, but it was still the Simple Life. And thanks principally to Wordsworth's enormous prestige as a nineteenth-century poet, this was the aspect of the New Age that had the greatest cultural effect on England in the age to come.

The Simple Life was also influential at a more theoretical level, moreover, in aesthetics and in morals. At that level, it has to be understood as a revolt against cities, polished rhetoric, elaborate manners, and *civilisation* in the French sense. This revolt was strong in both England and Germany. The Simple Life allied itself to those "organic" ideas of culture and the people that we associate with Herder. And Wordsworth in the *Lyrical Ballads* (1798), claimed to use the language of men speaking to men.

Then this 1775–1805 period was a time when hallucinogenic drugs became a prominent fact in the intellectual life in England, famous cases being Coleridge and, later, de Quincey. One of the popular favorites in the treasuries of English verse in the nineteenth century, Coleridge's "Xanadu," was popularly supposed to be drug-inspired.

Drugs have a morally lurid reputation as addictive and self-destructive, but they are also agents of innovative experiment, which have a special affinity for New Ages in that they cause immediate changes of consciousness and changes of life. In our examination of the nineteenth century we associated drugs especially with Otto Gross. Of course, Freud, too, experimented with the use of cocaine, and so did many others. But in Gross's life various drugs played a major tragic part. And besides Gross, other Asconans took them. Drugs were a part of the Asconan scene.

The mushroom drugs used by the American Indians played an especially important part in the last two New Ages, in England as well as America. Havelock Ellis, Carpenter's friend, tried peyote in the spring of 1897 (a year after the American doctor S. Weir Mitchell) and gave some to W. B. Yeats. Ellis wrote an article about the experience the drugs caused in the *Contemporary Review* for January 1898—an article which brought down the rebuke of the *British Medical Journal.* In 1914 Mabel Dodge took some in a ritual modeled on Kiowan Indian ceremonies, and described the occasion in her autobiography, a whole chapter of which is entitled "Peyote." Some of the fascination of the Pueblo Indian culture of Taos for her was the idea of the Indian use of drugs.

The same has been true for many members of our own New Age. In *Turning East,* Harvey Cox described the experience of taking peyote with the Huichole Indians in Mexico in 1974. Most of the neo-Oriental religions forbid drugs, he says, but a lot of their disciples told him that their drug experience had made Western religion nonviable for them, so it had been one of the motives behind their "turn East."

Certainly it has been part of the New Age experience as a whole.

Drugs have generally been associated with New Age enthusiasms. It was rumored among Jungians that the great man had secretly taken peyote in the 1920s; and the same rumor was spread about D. H. Lawrence. Both of these men were associated with Ascona, as I have said. Ascona ceased to be a center of radical life experiment at the end of that New Age, but for the next half century it was the site of the Eranos Conferences, at which Jung or Jungian disciples were a dominant presence. Gary Snyder has suggested a "karmic connection" between Jung's peyote and the later discovery of LSD and its alarming effects—a discovery which also took place in Switzerland, though at a large chemical firm. In the 1960s LSD seemed like a major threat to official American culture—a dissolvent of officialdom. Some radicals talked of "turning on" a whole city by tampering with the municipal water supply.

In the 1930s Jung visited Taos, which was, under Mabel Dodge's influence, in some ways the nearest thing to Ascona in America then. But it was Haight-Ashbury in the 1960s that really replayed the more reckless and drug-related aspects of Ascona.

As far as the ecological movement goes, and its equivalent in the eighteenth century, the word *ecology* seems not to have been used before 1866, and it was a hundred years more before it became part of the general language. However, there were some important events in the history or prehistory of ecology in the thirty-year period that concerns us. The subject might be said to have been born then.

Gilbert White's *Natural History of Selborne* was published in 1789, and just ten years before that the books and papers of Linnaeus were bought and brought to England. These two naturalists are usually considered the founding fathers of the ecological movement, in its twin but divergent streams, sometimes called the arcadian and the imperial. (These are also called the biocentric and the technocentric forms of environmentalism.)

Gilbert White was the curate of a Church of England parish, fifty miles southwest of London, where he had in fact been born. His study of nature escaped ordinary scientific limits by being much involved with his religious feelings, and by his intention to be "useful."

It was also much involved with his reading of the Latin poets, Virgil and Horace, and their love of nature.

White's great achievement was to see the interdependence of the life forms he studied. He wrote down his observations of all the natural life around him in his parish of Selborne (at a time when most scientists were collecting exotica) in the form of frequent letters to Daines Barrington, a Welsh barrister and judge, and Thomas Pennant, a zoologist. These letters he was then persuaded to publish in the form of a book. Donald Worster draws a likeness between White's work and Rachel Carson's and even Barry Commoner's, in our own New Age.

Worster's chapter on Linnaeus, on the other hand, is entitled "The Empire of Reason," and he presents Linnaeus as taking his place in a line of natural philosophers begun by Francis Bacon: that Lord Chancellor of England who wrote that the aim of science was "the enlargement of the bounds of Human Empire, to the effecting of all things possible. . . . The world is made for man, not man for the world." Carl Linne or Linnaeus rose from rural poverty to nobility and a place in Sweden's royal councils. He, too, was notably pious, but his religion was more anthropocentric than White's. He thought nature was a machine, the interworking of whose parts could be separated out and studied to man's profit. So though he, too, analyzed and celebrated the elaborate systems of nature with a range and scope they had not known before, he was less the New Age ecologist.

Neither White's work nor Linnaeus's was related to the New Age of Godwin and Paine, except insofar as individuals who were interested in the new science were often also interested in the new politics. (I have quoted Wollstonecraft calling herself the first of a new *genus*.) And in the years after his death even White's work served only the least revolutionary (in effect, conservative) kind of New Age interest, promoting a pastoral quietism. Looking back from later New Ages, however, we see some of the sources of later ideas that, though they did not interact and reinforce each other, did run side by side.

Garden Cities were not a social entity in the eighteenth-century New Age; but the experimental communities begun, or even only planned then, constituted part of the tradition on which Ebenezer Howard drew later. One instance already mentioned is the Pantisocracy scheme of Coleridge and Southey. Rather differently, the cotton manufacturer Robert Owen had a great success from 1800 to 1816 with his technically and socially reformist cotton mills in New Lanark, near the Falls of Clyde. He later tried to create an experimental community at Orbiston; and then lived in America (where he founded the New Harmony colony) between 1825 and 1829.

When Owen took over the New Lanark mills, they were recruiting their labor from the orphanages of Edinburgh—most of them illegitimate children—and working them eighteen hours a day, without making a profit. He made the mills profitable, and gave the workers better wages, housing, and education than they got elsewhere. Owen met Godwin in January 1813, and the two men saw a lot of each other for a time. St. Clair says that Owen's book is permeated with Godwinian sentiment.

Owen publicly declared in 1816 that he knew how to design a society so that it would function without crime, poverty, or misery. This was a New Age aspiration, but much of the effort that went into realizing it was systematic in character. Owen's project was essentially aimed at disciplining the poor, remoralizing the Lower Orders, as he said; and so was resented by William Cobbett, a different kind of radical, who described New Lanark as "parallelograms of paupers." (Owen liked buildings and institutions to have geometrical forms.)

Agreeing with Cobbett's judgment on the whole, E. P. Thompson says that Owen was not really a nineteenth-century socialist, speaking for the working class, but rather the last of the eighteenth-century rationalists—was another Godwin, claiming the chairmanship of the Directors of the Industrial Revolution. In our terms, Owen represented a blend of the very systematic with the very naïve. Others at the time, in fact, compared him with Joanna Southcott, the religious visionary. But many were moved by his tone of joy and exultation, and even Engels spoke of Owen's "almost sublimely child-like simplicity of character." This is the generous, and condescending, tone of the systematic radical toward the naïve.

In *Crochet Castle*, Thomas Love Peacock's *roman à clef* satirizing various contemporary ideologues, the reader was told that the Owen figure "will have neither fighting nor praying; but wants to parcel out the world into squares like a chess-board, with a community on each, raising everything for one another, with a great steam-engine to serve them in common." This is the *conservative* mind's view of the matter.

But the New Agers of South Place, as we have seen, saw Owen as the true founder of Secularism and Rationalism and other causes they lived by throughout the nineteenth century.

Owen's *New View of Society* (1818) attracted a great deal of attention, much of it favorable. As Hazlitt said, this was ironic. Very similar ideas had already been circulated to wide applause in 1793, when they "got into the hearts of poets and the brains of metaphysicians, took possession of the fancies of boys and women, and turned the heads of almost the whole kingdom." For that reason, when the years of repression came, all such ideas were denounced. Now, with the Tories secure in power, said Hazlitt, many of the latter again declared themselves delighted with Owen's reforms and theories. However, let Owen make as many disciplines as Godwin did, said Hazlitt, and we shall see that the tide will turn against him, too.

A notable group among Owen's early supporters were Quakers— until the moment came when they were scared off by his religious skepticism. Such New Age ideas about experimental communities had been circulating among that sect for a long time. The early Quaker John Bellers, born in 1754, produced his "Proposals for Raising a College of Industry" in 1795. (Owen acknowledged his debt to Bellers; even Marx acknowledged him.) He declared that the poor could raise provisions and manufactures that would bring England as much treasure as the mines brought Spain. He saw that it was the multitude of people in England that made the land there worth more than American land was—and made Dutch land worth more than Irish: "regular people, of all living creatures, being the life and perfection of treasure, the strength of nations and the glory of princes." A college of three hundred people would provide a surplus of the work of one hundred, worth one thousand dollars a year. Bellers's ideas were rediscovered and redescribed by Godwin's radical friend Francis Place in the eighteenth-century's New Age.

In Bellers's time, the Quakers were exemplary New Agers, carrying their Gospel far and wide. Mary Fisher, a servant girl, exhorted the Sultan at the Sublime Porte; John Perrot went to Rome, to speak before the Pope and all his cardinals (he was jailed for three years); and in 1661 a small party set out to evangelize the Celestial Empire of China, though it was turned back in the countries beyond the Holy Land.

Passing from Quakers to Jews, a variety of idealistic Zionism came to life in this eighteenth-century period, precursive to the Zionism examined before. Napoleon took an interest in the Jewish question, and briefly considered setting up a Jewish state in Palestine. This scheme was in fact an echo of a native, seventeenth-century Zionism. Sabbatai Zevi, born in 1626 in Smyrna, had decided that a New Age would begin for Jews in Palestine in 1666; and he was aware of similar speculations among radical Christians like the Fifth Monarchy Men. (He therefore fits into the chronological period that included the Quakers in England.)

Sabbatai Zevi went to Jerusalem in 1663, to await events, which did not, of course, transpire. Later he went to the court of the Sultan in Istanbul, a dangerous place for a Jew, and in 1676 became a Muslim, to save his life.

Within the Judaic tradition, Sabbatai Zevi took his stand doctrinally on the speculative Cabala, which he pitted against the legalistic Talmud—a typical New Age preference. There was even a component of erotic and aesthetic mysticism to his doctrine, which will remind us of later New Ages. We are told that he was a singer, and his ballads had erotic lyrics, to which he attached esoteric meanings. His followers said that he showed them the way to a more adventurous, less guilt-ridden life.

In fact the eighteenth-century New Age was the time when the Jews came out of the ghettos of Western Europe into social freedom, but by and large they seem to have chosen to assimilate themselves to Enlightenment ideas rather than to engage in radical experimentalism. Napoleon convened a so-called Sanhedrin in Paris in 1807 to offer them the chance of "assimilating," meaning that the only thing that would thereafter distinguish the Jews from their fellow citizens, in whatever country they chose to live in, should be their religion. This was the policy Reform Judaism accepted in the nineteenth century, against which Zionism rebelled.

Orientalist learning, so notable in later New Ages as a source of new ideas, had its beginnings in this period, thanks in part to England's imperial contacts with India. Sir William Jones, a poet as well as scholar, went out to India and became the great founder of Sanskrit studies in the West. The German scholars in particular learned much from him in the 1790s. This knowledge of the East affected the major

Romantic poets of all Europe, but in England they wrote mostly "Oriental" romances: Southey's *The Curse of Kehama*; Shelley's *The Revolt of Islam*; Byron's *Lara*.

Shelley at least seems to have been strongly influenced by what he understood of Hindu philosophy, and Wordsworth and Coleridge by what the German philosophers made of it. In the realm of myth, there was a tradition that the Druids of England—great figures of lost wisdom—were somehow connected to the Brahmins of India. Blake played with that idea in his poetry. Godwin, too, produced an early pastoral romance, *Imogen*, the original of which was alleged to be written by a Druid.

However, this Orientalism does not seem to have had much to do with the New Age enterprises at the end of the eighteenth century, if it is measured against the Orientalism of the Theosophists and the translators of Lao-tzu in the next New Age (though let us note that the revolutionary London Corresponding Society sang or recited one of Jones's Odes as an anthem of freedom). The Romantics' Oriental tales are based on melodramatic legends, notably revenge stories, and are not the most impressive part of their literary work.

On the other hand, we should not entirely discount, even in the eighteenth century, the challenge to ordinary English realism conveyed by Orientalist studies. James Lawrence—a friend of the English vegetarians mentioned—did write about the Nair caste in South India, saying that the women there were sexually free and indeed dominant, and Godwin seems to have followed up this interest in discussions with Sir Joseph Banks. We also hear of Englishmen in India inviting others to join them in practicing Brahmin asceticism, though that phenomenon seems to have no established connection to those in England who were living out the ideas of revolution.

Occultism, on the other hand, was very important to Blake, and I have pointed to some parallels between his use of occult imagery and Mailer's and Ginsberg's ways of presenting America. I could also have quoted Gary Snyder. When he defines the idea of the yogi, he says, "The alchemical, occult, neo-platonist, and various sorts of Gnostic traditions of what might be called occidental counter-philosophy are strongly yogic." (He is there using the idea of the yogi as an option alternative to both the philosopher and the priest.)

Nietzsche, for obvious reasons, cannot be considered an influence on this period, but the cult of energy and the scorn for pity which we find in Blake are very similar. As we saw, when Orage presented Nietzsche to England, in his three little books in the first decade of the twentieth century, he described him as another Blake. And Yeats's enthusiasm for Blake was an extension of his response to the Nietzschean ideas in the air in the nineteenth-century New Age.

It was importantly an age of feminism, in which the principal name as far as theory goes was Mary Wollstonecraft, to whom we can compare Betty Friedan and Germaine Greer in the twentieth century, and Olive Schreiner and Emmeline Pankhurst in the nineteenth. Actresses seem to have played an important part, as did actresses like Vanessa Redgrave in the twentieth century.

This was particularly true in France. Olympe de Gouges was a French actress in melodramas who in 1791 wrote a *Rights of Woman*, like Wollstonecraft. She, like Paine and Bonneville, defended Louis XVI against the proposed sentence of death, and as a result was herself guillotined in 1793. The ex-queen, Marie Antoinette, was guillotined on October 16 of that year; and she was followed by Charlotte Corday (the assassin of Marat), de Gouges, and Madame Roland, the Girondiste, by November 8. David's realistic sketch of the aging ex-queen going to her execution is opposite in aesthetic style to his nude male warrior heroes, who glorify the nation. The revolution was glorified by being associated with *men*. Billington suggests that the male leaders of the Revolution were haunted by the fear of a women's revenge after these executions.

That it was an age of erotic liberation in the modern sense, the anecdotes about both Blake and Wollstonecraft have shown. And this was not limited to intellectuals. The relation of the New Agers' ideas to the more general behavior of the day is suggested by the likeness between the transparent costumes Blake gave to some of his female figures and the Directoire styles actually worn in Paris and copied in London. There was a similar erotic self-flaunting among the male dandies; two famous instances are Pushkin and Byron. There were extravagances of dance at the same time. It seemed to conservatives at the time that every kind of decency and self-restraint had been abandoned.

As in other New Ages, erotic experiment figured as another among the many radical ideas, and was to be found conjoined with revolutionary politics and serious poetry. A lot of the rumored scandals about Byron and Shelley had to do with erotic matters. Horne Tooke treasured the memory of a gathering (around 1790) at which he sat with Tom Paine on one side, and a famous transvestite, the Chevalier d'Eon, on the other—certainly a New Age grouping. This was a small-scale equivalent of the great achievements of gay liberation in the New Age of the 1960s and later, like the huge parades through Manhattan, and the occupation of whole districts of San Francisco.

The cult of libertarian psychoanalysis that we associated with Otto Gross in the nineteenth century and with R. D. Laing in the sixties has been compared with the work of Lavater and phrenology in the eighteenth-century New Age. Phrenology had been developed in Europe by Gall and Spurzheim, and as St. Clair says, it attracted the kind of attention in England that psychoanalysis would a hundred years later. It promised to reveal hidden truths and forces in the individual psyche. Mary Wollstonecraft and Holcroft spent months working on a translation of Lavater's *Essays in Physiognomy*. Fuseli was a friend of Lavater, and himself a phrenologist, and through him Blake became enthusiastic about such ideas. In New Ages, people are especially ready to believe that there are forms of knowledge and power that have been hidden from them by vested interests in the past. Another interest of a related kind was the enthusiasm for animal magnetism. Cagliostro, perhaps the most famous name associated with that magnetism, was a figure to whom people compared Laban later, in Ascona. Naming these names, we stand on the verge of the topic of gurus again.

The last of our categories was aestheticism: the tendency of an age of empire to create an aesthetic alternative to political action, when the latter comes to seem too dangerous, confusing, or hopeless. This takes a number of quite different forms in different personalities—for instance in Coleridge and in Blake. The efforts or ambitions of both men to transfer into the arts all the powers traditionally associated with religion and philosophy have in fact gone on bearing fruit ever since.

But besides them, Goethe, Scott, and Wordsworth, in various ways, all diffused or diverted their audience's political energies in safer directions. Scott is no doubt the most striking case of immediate effectiveness. He invented a new literary form that became enormously popular (not just in his home country, and not just with conservatives) by deploying a number of the apparently revolutionary ideas of romanticism to conservative effect.

But Scott was consciously, and demonstrably, the honored servant of the British Empire, and his conservative aesthetics is perhaps too blatant to be generally representative. However, while Goethe made apparently an opposite choice, by going to live in a political backwater, the small dukedom of Weimar, he too made culturally responsible art an alternative to revolutionary action. And Wordsworth and Coleridge, though profoundly dissatisfied with Scott, both ended in forms of quietism significantly allied to conservatism. The turn of Godwin toward Coleridge and literature is a vivid case of the change, in one of the leaders of the New Age.

It is already clear that as well as being diffused, when a New Age ends, its energy is also conserved, in the form of aesthetic achievements. But there are still many questions to ask about the total cultural effect of the translation.

CHAPTER SEVEN

Beginning and End of Hope

> "What is this Government? Who wants it?". . . He [an Italian anarchist] waited patiently, looking at me. But I did not want him to go on: I did not want to answer. I could feel a new spirit in him, something strange and pure and slightly frightening. And my soul was somewhere in tears, crying helplessly like an infant in the night. I could not respond: I could not answer. He seemed to look at me, me, an Englishman, an educated man, for corroboration. But I could not corroborate him. I knew the purity and new struggling towards birth of a true star-like spirit. But I could not confirm him in his utterance: my soul could not respond. I did not believe in the perfectibility of man. I did not believe in infinite harmony among men. And this was his star, this belief.
>
> D. H. Lawrence, *Twilight in Italy*

The way each New Age begins and ends is not only interesting in itself, but illustrates the inner workings of all such periods. As for beginnings, New Age energies reach a self-sustaining level of interaction when the preceding cultural consensus is shown up to be shabby as a whole, and people find each other looking for something new. But that transcendent-sounding change may occur when something empirical and quite external, like an unpopular war or a judiciary scandal, arouses indignation. In the 1770s there was the War of Independence of the American colonies, in the 1960s the war in Vietnam.

As for endings, the energies of New Ages then pass over into new cultural enterprises, sometimes of an opposite character. This section will deal principally with the end of the nineteenth-century New Age. When war broke out in 1914, old patterns of behavior revived—authoritarian patterns of militarism and patriotism—and many people reverted to the authoritarian sense of reality.

War was not the only check to that New Age movement, as we shall see. But wars are very important in this matter. The New Age periods of the eighteenth and nineteenth centuries were alike (despite the difference between an age of revolution and a comparatively pacific New Age) because both saw the breaking out of a great patriotic war—against revolutionary and then Napoleonic France in the one case, against imperial Germany in the other. Such a situation (whether the war is popular or not) is peculiarly unfavorable to New Age enterprises, as Gandhi discovered again in India during the Second World War. (Even he was unable in war circumstances to find an effective form of nonviolent action for the Gandhi movement to engage in; the movement indeed slipped out of his control temporarily.) However, the two periods, the nineteenth and the eighteenth centuries, differed because in the second the national enemy, Robespierre's France, seemed to be a hideous incarnation of the New Age's earlier aspirations—of, say, Tom Paine's political ideas. That meant that the New Agers were more bitterly blamed—by themselves too— and more brutally punished.

THE END OF THE EIGHTEENTH-CENTURY NEW AGE

The punishments imposed by the British government on radical activists in the 1790s turned many people's attention away from politics toward literature. Godwin, for instance, began writing books of history, and then, in 1805, books for children, using noms de plume because of the ill repute attaching to his own name.

His series was called the Juvenile Library, and round it collected the scattered remnants of Joseph Johnson's old group, now no longer essaying political themes or major literary genres, but doing the humble and innocuous caretaking tasks of culture. There was, besides the work of Godwin himself and his second wife, Hazlitt's *English Grammar*, which was based on the philological theories of Horne-Tooke, and Lamb's *Tales from Shakespeare*, which was illustrated by William Blake. The radical tradition ran underground, as far as adult literature was concerned.

But this political retreat was not all prudential in character; it was in part principled and the result of a conversion. Godwin said that a "great epocha" in his life began in 1799 when he discovered the old English writers. But this was also the moment when Coleridge became a big influence on his intellectual life, as he did, gradually, on many other people's. (In an act of dramatic submission, Godwin considered writing the latter's biography, though Coleridge was much the younger man.) At the same time Coleridge's friend, Charles Lamb, also became a close friend of Godwin's; they shared a taste for book-collecting.

The effect this influence had was to move Godwin in the direction of aesthetic mysticism, toward belief in the mysterious "organic" unity of a work of art. Like a tree or like a human being, Coleridge said, a poem grows and lives according to "biological" and not "rational" laws. He taught Godwin that one could no more alter a word in Shakespeare's plays than one could remove a stone from the pyramids, without causing irreparable damage to those magnificent structures, both the architectural and the literary. This philosophy transforms art into an autonomous realm worthy of profound and humble study, and not to be subsumed in politics or criticized by political criteria—it becomes a field of action, and an alternative to revolution. As we know, Coleridge had gone through the same intellectual development himself, from radical politics to conservative aesthetics.

Thus we find that between 1800 and 1803 Godwin worked on a *Life of Chaucer*, which celebrated the imagination as a moral force. In it he says that Chaucer nearly ruined his genius by practicing as a lawyer. A poet must not subdue his heart and his mind to external laws and systems; he must keep them both ever free. Godwin's *Bible Stories*, which he brought out in 1802, also celebrated the poetic imagination.

Even in this phase of his work, he was—though anonymously—part of a powerful movement. Godwin wrote several works of history under the name of Edward Baldwin, and it happens that one of them, on classical myths, was read with enthusiasm by John Keats while a schoolboy. Since the classical myths became an important part of Keats's poetic, both theory and practice, Godwin thus had an influence on a poet who was very important for the century to come. For many nineteenth-century English poets, Keats's aestheticism became a major alternative to the New Age idealism of Shelley—the earlier Godwin's principal disciple.

For that early New Age, Godwin did have important disciples. Even in 1815, at the height of the repression, it could be seen that writers like Hazlitt and Shelley were forming a second New Age generation who would receive and hand down the radical tradition. In

1811 Shelley had "discovered" that Godwin was still alive—so dead was the general hero worship offered him in 1793—and wrote to him and visited him. A few years later, he married Godwin's daughter, even as he had already married his theories. (Shelley was also devoted to Paine's memory, but Paine was indeed dead.)

There were marked differences between the personalities of Godwin and Shelley, their modes of behavior and emotion in social and ultimate relations, and even in the world of ideas. Shelley allotted a big place in his scheme of things to romantic love, and to the young hero figure, both of them highly sexual, in however ambiguous a manner, and both related to himself. Socially, Godwin—no human skylark he—seemed to most people a dull, clumsy, routine-bound pedant.

But if we are considering strictly intellectual temperament, we see a likeness. Indeed, we have already noted the similarity between Godwin and Puritans like Jonathan Edwards, and we see a similar syndrome of qualities—stringency, fervor, and idealism—strikingly developed in Shelley, and in him related to Godwin's New Age position. The two men have the same disembodied energy, and their ideas have the same independence of experience, the same enthusiastic intellectuality. Both men had rebelled against their fathers very bitterly, and they seem to have rejected, along with the father figure, all the "given" character of traditional wisdom, even in matters of personal experience. They had the New Age sense of reality. *Everything*, they felt, could be changed. *Nothing* need be accepted as a necessary limitation.

It is known that Shelley reread *Political Justice*, after meeting its author, in 1812, in 1816, and in 1820. Its profound influence on him is one of the classic cases of how intellectual temperament can be inherited, and how it can overpower differences in "natural" endowment and experience. And Godwin's thought reached later readers insofar as Shelley's poetry reached the anthologies, where it lay, latent in periods of conservatism, but potentially explosive.

A good example of the Victorian consensus establishing itself by mocking the preceding New Age is to be found in Dickens, especially early work like *Sketches by Boz* (1836). (Victoria came to the throne in 1837.) Dickens was not thinking in historical terms anything like my own—he was setting out to amuse—but one soon notices a recurrent mockery of "the poet" or "the poetical young gentleman," who writes verse, we are told, in the biting, semi-atheistical, demoniac style (obviously pretentious nonsense). Who would such a young poet, in the 1830s, be imitating? Shelley, for one.

One notices, too, Dickens's heavy stress on gender and family orthodoxy, implicitly hostile to New Age experimentalism. At the heart of his stories is often a gentlemanly young man of eighteen to twenty-five—one who will kiss a pretty girl and knock down a rough fellow as soon as look at them—who falls in love with a beautiful and blushing girl of sixteen to nineteen. And flanking those two figures we see the pathos of brutalized children and the quaintness of old bachelors. A halo surrounds the holy family. But as far as love goes, for women, life after nineteen is a desert. And all of them are deemed to be aiming at love in matrimony—anything like Wollstonecraft's experiments in gender and marriage are out of the question. While antislavery societies, church charities, philanthropy, all group attempts to change the world in a New Age way, are turned into farce.

Dickens also gives his readers some nonhumorous, melodramatic warnings against the eighteenth-century New Age. (I quote a few lines as an epigraph to this book.) *Barnaby Rudge* and *A Tale of Two Cities*—in both the plot begins in that fatal year, 1775—express the horror of violence in a revolutionary age, and the imperative need to restore order. But humor, in its less obtrusive way, is just as effective in establishing cultural hegemony.

THE DISPLACEMENT OF THE NAÏVE

Something similar is likely to occur at the end of every New Age. D. H. Lawrence had *his* meeting with anarchism in 1913; it was part of his curiously indirect encounter with Otto Gross. He rejected the New Age invitation, painfully, as we see in the passage quoted as an epigraph to this chapter, but turned that rejection into works of literature, inside which the invitation lay latent.

The same rejection of the radical happens in religion as well as in literature. Gary Snyder, expressing his disappointment with the social inactivity of Zen Buddhists in Japan, says, "They got the message, but they didn't open the envelope." The same thing has been said often enough about the Christian churches by the radically religious. And politics has parallel phenomena.

Lawrence was in step with his age, for if we turn now to the political manifestations of the nineteenth century, one of the most striking events in 1914 was the behavior of the various European labor and socialist parties which had professed skepticism about "capitalist wars" right up to the point of conflict, but which then acted like Frenchmen or Germans rather than like Socialists or proletarians. This marked the end of the New Age even before the governments could begin their repressive measures, and before the social xenophobia and bully-boy patriotism—women handing white feathers to civilians who should be in the trenches.

However, if we look to the history of India after 1915, we will see the Gandhi movement there as an enactment of New Age ideas. These were paradoxical ideas, in the eyes of Indians as much as Europeans, which had amazing and large-scale results that defied probability. Not that Gandhi simply succeeded: indeed, at the end of his life he declared that he had failed. But he achieved as much as other political leaders did, including the most realistic, and he made "incredible" things happen. People in the West by and large could scarcely believe in what they saw happening in India. Perhaps the most similar political paradox occurred at the same time in the Near East—the founding of a Jewish state in Palestine, which was inspired in part by the New Age ideas of Buber and Magnes.

Another case, which can be studied in the history of America, was of a convergence of different kinds of radicalism in the years before 1914, followed by their dispersal afterwards. These were notably the IWW political radicalism of the labor movement, and the aesthetic radicalism of the new art, displayed in the Armory Show of 1913, which seemed to coincide and express the same spirit. The guns of 1914 did not sound so loudly in New York as in London, but it was nevertheless clear, long before 1917, that the generally radical mood was fading in America soon after the anti-Communist reaction brought J. Edgar Hoover and the FBI to power for the first time.

After the 1914–18 war there was, in America and elsewhere, a period of frivolity and revulsion from anything "too serious," "too real," which accompanied the reaction against political radicalism, and its suppression in the Red Scare. Feminism, along with all the more serious causes that flourished before 1914, lost energy. This was a cynical frivolity, which flouted reality rather than creating a new reality sense of its own.

One thing that survived was the IWW tradition in the Pacific Northwest, and southwards from there, on which Gary Snyder's early imagination was nourished. He is a descendant of Wobblies, the grandson of a soapbox orator. The legend of the Everett massacre of Wobblies in 1916 appears in his verse, and he more than once cites the IWW slogan, "Forming the new society within the shell of the old," and speaks of a cultural tradition—"with some lovely stories handed down of free love"—preserved in San Francisco, where poets and gurus were attending meetings of the "Anarchist Circle"—old Italians and Finns—into the 1940s.

In fact, Jerome Rothenberg has described Snyder's poetry as being a kind of Wobbly Modernism: regional and specific, gritty and colloquial, because Wobbly, but comparable with the Modernist work of Duchamp and Breton as an exploration of the mind. This, Rothenberg thinks, Snyder achieved in poetic terms before and independent of his encounter with Zen.

THE SYSTEMATIC MIND

The attempts to assimilate the experience of 1914–18 (the part of that experience that *was* absorbed and rationalized by the most serious-minded) were invested in the great intellectual systems. The most important examples were the Roman Catholic Church and the Communist Party; we see those attempts in Evelyn Waugh and Graham Greene and T. S. Eliot, in John Strachey and Bertolt Brecht and Raymond Williams, and so on. Alternatively, intellectuals looked to Marx, Freud, and Weber, the founders of social science. (This is what usually happens after a revolution or a war; the claim to seriousness shifts from the authoritarian mind to the systematic.) These were the sources of the sense of reality that was for us the equivalent of the Victorians' consensus faith in Christianity, democracy, and so on.

Thus, after the Second World War, Lionel Trilling praised Freud for his sense of tragedy, his reintroduction of the dimension of weight and substance into modern experience. Edmund Wilson, in *To the Finland Station*, implicitly makes the same claim for Marx and Lenin, as opposed to the Utopian Socialists. Weber believed in *der Wahrheitssadismus der Wissenschaft*, the truth-cruelty of science—that nothing important can be known without suffering pain, indeed, without taking pleasure in that pain. These are three important ways of saluting older, harsher reality principles, intellectually. All these forms of reverence for weight, hardness, and force are reactions against the naïve temperament.

The realism of the New Age often seems to contrast with other kinds of realism, the way topology contrasts with geometry within the larger field of mathematics. Geometry measures solids, and its angles and lengths are unalterable. Topology deals with angles and lengths that stretch and implicitly deny the solidity of the subject.

Weber's essay on the morality of science in 1920, at the end of his life, was paralleled by Eliot's essays like "Tradition and the Individual Talent," asserting the need for poetry to be difficult and obscure. Modernism can, in such cases, be an equivalent for system in the aesthetic world. These are all triumphs over Shelley and Gross and other heroes of the New Age, whose work seems wordy, windy, gushy.

In most Western countries, therefore, the New Age was in defeat in the period after 1914, and ideas implicitly hostile to it developed. Indeed, Orage began attacks on social and literary "decadence" as early as 1895 in *The Labour Leader*, and continued them in *The New Age*. He associated decadence with modern commercialism, which he felt corrupts our standards of criticism. New Agers would not have to disagree with such ideas, but they must find uncongenial the implication of staying loyal to a critical tradition inherited from a hierarchical society.

Because of the moral function of art, Orage said, literary critics must be severe. Artists should not touch diseased or ugly subjects. This idea linked up with Orage's Orientalism, for he often cited the Mahabharata as an example of nobility that the modern writer should consult. "The rediscovery of ancient Indian culture will give us the Europe of tomorrow. Nothing else will." He insisted that art has nothing to do with emotions or ideas, and analyzed style without attention to the meaning of its statements. This enabled him to insist on aristocratic values in art without feeling undemocratic in politics. The same was true of F. R. Leavis, in many ways Orage's heir.

HUMOR AND CULTURE

Another phenomenon of the defeat of New Ages is the spread of a sense of humor that is hostile to idealism. (We have already glanced at Dickens' work, as an example of an earlier period.) This negativeness, of course, relates to the political and social repression already discussed; a sense of humor is always a function of the larger sense of reality. But it does not seem right to treat this as just a function, because the humor is sometimes so lively and natural, so genuine. Nevertheless, even when it is lively, nothing is sadder to read or hear than the humorous accounts of bold experiments, given by participants after the experiment has failed, as if they had always been self-evidently absurd.

Nellie Shaw's account of Whiteway, the one account we have of that colony in the Cotswolds, is in its concrete details full of jokes, the same kind of jokes as we find in Betty Macdonald's *The Egg and I*. The simple life has become the object of derision. The general mood is of warm remembering, but it is all nostalgia, and implicitly hopeless. The same is true of Emil Szittya's account of Ascona, and of the accounts I know of the California communes. Many of the events made funny in the books mentioned *were* funny at the time, but presumably in a different way. Presumably then the actors and the observers were, fundamentally, allied against the outside world, and the joke bounced off that shared vocation. In the book, written long after, the writer makes alliance with the reader against all divergences from the normal. It is implied from the beginning that this was mostly foolish.

It was an important failure in Wells and Shaw that, even during the New Age, they joined in this humorousness, despite their interest in the ideas of the time. In novels like *Kipps* and *Mr. Polly* and plays like *Candida*, the writer invites the reader to join him in irony at the expense of the life-experimenter. It is essentially safe and conservative figures—often women, like Shaw's Candida or Wells's Ann—who represent wisdom and happiness.

And when, as happened in England after 1910, New Age enthusiasm becomes a major object of humor, its subject becomes the dandy: that is, the reader sees things from a dandy's point of view. He or she laughs *with* the dandy protagonists of Waugh and Wodehouse stories, and the English detective story. The dandy is always the opposite of the simple-lifer or enthusiast. In Dorothy Sayers's *Gaudy Night*, for instance, we are told that "fancy religions" always go along with bad syntax—and badly cut frocks—and untidy hair. These phrases are an implicit call for tighter moral corsets. And when, in *Clouds of Witness*, Lord Peter Wimsey visits the Soviet Club in Soho (in historical fact a New Age institution), he finds it has that *curious* amateur air that pervades the worldly institutions planned by unworldly people; the staff are sketchily trained and the cutlery is *curiously* unequal.

Clearly this antagonism has something to do with specifically literary form, with the inner laws of literature, which is so often—at least, the humorous branches thereof—a conservative institution. More generally, surely we can say that it has to do with high culture. "Culture" is predisposed to laugh at idealism; that is a proviso of its constitution. This is because culture, holding the ring in which the three temperaments wrestle together, has a bias against the naïve when that stands alone. The idea of the holy fool, or the Zen lunatic, is thus simply dismissed, unless it has some forceful anticultural animus; hence the grossness of Beat behavior at poetry readings.

We can take an example of this culture snobbery from George Orwell—certainly not the worst of culture snobs. He gives a satirical characterization of 1930s New Agers in *The Road to Wigan Pier* that has often been quoted. "One sometimes gets the impression that the mere words 'Socialist' and 'Communist' draw towards them with magnetic force every fruit-juice drinker, nudist, sandal-wearer, sex-maniac, Quaker, 'Nature-Cure' quack, pacifist and feminist in England." One might notice how hard it would be to fully understand that list without knowing the history of the New Age. He goes on to add "the outer-suburban creeping Jesus, a hangover from the William Morris period, who proposes to level the working class up"—by means of hygiene, fruit juice, birth control, and poetry.

In the same passage, Orwell describes being on a bus in Letchworth when two men in shorts got on. The man sitting next to Orwell looked at him and murmured, "Socialists!" Orwell's contention was that socialism could not survive in England as long as it was associated with crankishness. As we know, Gandhi often referred to himself as a crank and a quack, and his follower, Arthur St. John, ran a magazine defiantly called *The Crank*. But is is more important to ask why Orwell himself was on a bus in Letchworth. He had just told us that the Independent Labor Party was holding its summer school there, and it's ten to one he was there to attend it—just like the other two men—who were his brothers in the spirit.

Of course, that fact or supposition does not invalidate Orwell's argument, but it does remind us of its element of self-betrayal— betrayal of his own tenderest and most vulnerable hopes. The same is true of the next example I will offer, from Muriel Spark's *The Prime of Miss Jean Brodie*, which refers to just the same period. The writer describes her novel's eponymous heroine as belonging to a significant group of Edinburgh women. "They went to lectures, tried living on honey and nuts, took lessons in German and then went walking in Germany; they bought caravans and went off with them into the hills among the lochs; they played the guitar, they supported all the new little theatre companies; they took lodgings in the slums and, distributing pots of paint, taught their neighbours the arts of simple interior decoration; they preached the inventions of Marie Stopes; they attended the meetings of the Oxford Group and put Spiritualism to their hawk-eyed test. Some assisted in the Scottish Nationalist Movement. . . ."

Whatever was lacking in the Orwell sketch of New Age history and geography is supplied in Spark. And betrayal is the implicit theme of Spark's novel. The author gives the word several meanings, but the primary reference is to the other main character's betrayal of Miss Brodie—which is also a betrayal by the author. Even thus narrowed down, the idea of treachery means a number of things; but one betrayal, I would suggest, is of Miss Brodie as an embodiment of New Age experiment and hope—the writer/ character's satirical repudiation of those hopes, and her/their entry into the Roman Catholic Church.

As a part of this general reaction, the brilliant journalism of the Edwardian/New Age was repudiated by Eliot, with his theory that contemporary poetry had to be obscure; by Yeats, with his nightmare vision of Shaw as an intellectual sewing machine; by Leavis, with his contempt for Wells when compared with James. Even Orage wanted a different, an eighteenth-century, taste, as we have seen. It is significant that he (and many others) obliterated the New Age by declaring that Victorianism was succeeded by Modernism. (When Edward VII died, in 1910, Orage said this marked the end of the Victorian age, Edward having been merely his mother's executor.) There were other tactics with the same effect—see Virginia Woolf's depiction of her father, Leslie Stephen, as a Victorian with Modernist children; and see Raymond Williams's theory of an interregnum at the end of the nineteenth century, which temporarily interrupted the development of many ideas that flourished in the Victorian age and then again in the modern. In many ways the memory of the New Age was obliterated as an embarrassment.

Such turning away from the New Age had consequences like lowering the intellectual status of journalism—making it the illegitimate, Ishmael form, or shadow-self, of literature. Journalism usually flourishes in New Ages, for the obvious reason that the truth is then something that happens—is news; it is not something always deferred or embalmed in the custody of intellectual system-makers. In our own New Age it was writers like Normal Mailer and Tom Wolfe and Frances Fitzgerald who had the most important things to say.

The Edwardian journalists seemed to many of their contemporaries the important writers of their age. And the generation of men and women of letters that followed them preserved some New Age loyalties. Edmund Wilson declared the triumph in literature of modernism and aestheticism in *Axel's Castle*, but remained himself a brilliant journalist. John Middleton Murry remained a New Ager in politics: Armytage's book on English communes takes Murry as its last major figure. F. R. Leavis—though stylistically the very opposite of a journalist—continued to follow a New Age line to some degree. His magazine, *Scrutiny*, was radically New Age in its idiosyncratic way in the cult of Lawrence and the antiideological stance in critical theory. *Scrutiny* was also fond of country-lore authors, like Richard Jefferies and George Sturt, and of the Arts and Crafts movement. There was also a strain of Puritanism (Nonconformity) in his taste that Tolstoy would have found congenial; this emerges in Leavis's self-alliance with George Eliot against Lord David Cecil and Bloomsbury. However, from many points of view, Leavis was conservative—for instance, in his severe treatment of Shelley.

SHELLEY

Some very striking cases of what happens in literature at the end and beginning of New Ages have to do with Shelley. He was himself a (belated) New Age poet. He had been only seven months old when *Political Justice* was published (Godwin, his spiritual father, was almost exactly the age of Shelley's biological father), and by the time he grew up, reaction had triumphed in England. But his temperament was rebellious, and he absorbed the ideas of the Revolution. When he met Southey the latter was amazed to see in this young boy a complete expression of his own past—of the half-forgotten spirit of 1793. As William St. Clair says, Shelley's debate with Godwin, which began in 1812, was in a sense a debate between the young and the old Godwin.

The older man did all he could to turn Shelley away from political action and toward literature—indeed, toward socially orthodox behavior. He had him prepare a volume of biblical extracts that should testify to his moral principles. When Shelley went to Ireland and engaged in political propaganda, Godwin wrote him several times in reproof, warning him in severe terms that, despite his personal feelings against violence, he was "preparing a scene of blood" for other people. (This is often the warning of the authoritarian against the New Ager; just so did Churchill warn against Gandhi when India approached independence.) Shelley acknowledged his error, and never again tried to change things by organized political action. Implicitly, he accepted Godwin's strategy of rerouting political conviction into literature.

Among literary scholars there is some consensus of approval for that strategy. William St. Clair seems to claim even moral success for it in the case of Godwin and Shelley. He says that the constant reprinting of, for instance, "Ode to the West Wind," in the popular anthologies, especially in those read in schools, led nineteenth-century readers back to Shelley's longer and politically heretical works, and so made a subversive cultural power out of literature.

An interesting agreement is to be found in H. N. Brailsford's *Shel-*

ley, Godwin, and Their Circle, which came out in the (very cheap) Home University Library in 1913. (It is no accident that Brailsford went on to write about Gandhi.) This is quite a brilliant essay in the best manner of the nineteenth-century New Age, except that the author does not have all the courage of his New Age convictions, especially in literary matters. He starts by saying that the history of the French Revolution in England begins with a sermon (Price's address) and ends with a poem, Shelley's "Hellas." Between the two stretch thirty-two years of the dawn, the clouding, and the unearthly sunset of hope. Shelley moved that hope from the factual realm into the ideal.

Brailsford frequently quotes Hazlitt's 1825 *The Spirit of the Age,* and seems to agree with its judgments. Both the nineteenth-century writer and the twentieth-century one grieve over the death of the New Age, the death of hope. Brailsford, for instance, quotes Holcroft, saying that men become what they are by means of their self-adjustments to society: "The generous feelings and higher propensities of the soul are, as it were, shrunk up, scarred, violently wrenched, and amputated, to fit us for our intercourse in the world, something in the manner that beggars maim and mutilate their children to make them fit for their future situation in life." This, clearly, is indignation against the reactionaries of Godwin's period. At the same time, Brailsford seems cowed by the force of Burke's arguments or the success of his prophecies—by the facts of the Terror. Thus he follows Burke in finding Richard Price a cold moralist who "despised the emotional aspects of human nature, and found no place for the affections in his scheme of the virtues." To say that is to distrust Reason, and to give the argument away.

Indeed, it seems to be without irony that Brailsford says, "Pantisocracy [meaning the failure thereof] was indeed a happy episode for English literature." If Coleridge had invested his energies in the New Age politics of pantisocracy, he would not have become a great poet. "One may doubt whether the 'Ancient Mariner' would have been written, had Coleridge travelled with Gerrald and Sinclair along the 'dark lane' that led to Botany Bay." Brailsford seems ready to endorse that sacrifice of political values in favor of literary ones.

His Chapter 8, which is entitled "Shelley," is enthusiastically reverent toward its subject, treating the poet's verses with the aesthetic mysticism Coleridge evolved. "Hellas" is "absolute" poetry, in the sense that Beethoven's *Eroica* Symphony is "absolute" music, beautiful beyond interpretation.

This mysticism is significantly unlike Victorian literary criticism at its best. Matthew Arnold, having renounced New Age hopes, logically went on to scorn Shelley and to offer that other great renouncer, Wordsworth, as literature's hero. Brailsford, on the other hand, quotes, but repudiates, Arnold's judgmental description of Shelley: "a beautiful but ineffectual angel, beating against the void his luminous wings in vain." Brailsford protests that to be beautiful *is* to escape futility, and to people a void with angels *is* to be effectual—is to be a poet.

Shelley and Godwin are Brailsford's heroes. He quotes Hazlitt saying: "The Spirit of the Age was never more fully shown than in its treatment of this writer [Godwin], first praising him so extravagantly, and then turning so savagely against him." That is reflected in Wordsworth's *Prelude*, where we read, after the lines about the Dawn:

> O Times,
> In which the meagre, stale, forbidding ways
> Of custom, law, and statute, took at once
> The attraction of a country in romance.

That was the point in history, as Hazlitt says, when "Mr. Godwin . . . carried with him all the most sanguine and fearless understandings of the time." Wordsworth's lines could be a description of the popularity of *Political Justice*. Then came the repression, and, in the Victorian Age, the relegation of New Age ideas to the status of, at best, "idealism." But Shelley's poetry compensates us for all these defeats, Brailsford feels.

Shelley certainly deserves the loyalty of New Agers for not turning conservative in his politics, as Wordsworth and Coleridge did, for staying radical. But he substituted aesthetic for political activity wholesale, as Godwin taught him to do. He turned his politics directly into emotion and literature, into rhetoric, which was a kind of aesthetic as well as political mystification.

At the beginning of the next New Age, in the 1880s, however, came the turn back toward Shelley. This was the movement of which Brailsford was a part. Matthew Arnold had given the law against Shelley, but Arnold was no longer a leader of thought. There was fairly generally a turn away from all the great Victorians in the 1880s, away from Arnold, Carlyle, and George Eliot. Shelley, on the other hand, was quoted by everyone of that generation; in "Two Cheers for Democracy," E. M. Forster names the ideal to which politics aspires: "Love, the Beloved Republic, That feeds upon freedom and sings." The New Age eclipsed the conservative consensus for thirty years or so.

At the end of that New Age came a turn away from Shelley and toward Keats—a turn that repeats the change of taste at the end of the eighteenth-century New Age. Among men of letters, both Eliot and Lawrence turn against Shelley; both Murry and Leavis turn toward Keats. Of those four, Eliot is the simplest case; he was not a son or even grandson of the New Age. D. H. Lawrence was the most complex and ambiguous case.

Lawrence had made a hero out of Shelley as a young man, but then turned against him. This must be understood partly in relation to Lawrence's private life, as I shall go on to argue. (He saw Otto Gross, who had had such a powerful influence on Frieda Lawrence, as another Shelley.) But we can also do perfect justice to this change by seeing it simply as a part of Lawrence's intellectual and literary development; his rejection of Shelley is a repression of his own New Age self—something he, like other writers at that point, had to repress. And because of the biographical connections, his case is a particularly interesting example of the general generational phenomenon.

LAWRENCE, GROSS, AND SHELLEY

Lawrence saw Gross as another Shelley, and made the two men's shared identity, the New Age idea incarnate, one of the polar principles in his world of thought. The two lives—Shelley's and Gross's—do in fact show a number of striking parallels. The two men lived a century apart and in different countries, and worked primarily in different fields, one in poetry and the other in psychoanalysis. But biographically as well as ideologically they exhibit the same developmental pattern. In childhood both were very precocious in their studies (both were gifted especially in science and philosophy) and also hypersensitive, morally and emotionally (both became vegetarians, in abhorrence of animal killing).

Both were important figures in the revolutionary movements of their times, as theoretical and practical anarchists. Each had a long and deadly quarrel with his father, who in both cases, at a climax in the quarrel, tried to legally appropriate his son's children—and went so far as to accuse his son legally of being crazy. Then they escaped from the conflict with their fathers by choosing a spiritual father— Godwin in Shelley's case, Freud in Gross's case—and then had to bear a weight of disapproval and persecution from that second father.

Both helped a number of young women to rebel against parental tyranny; the story of Harriet Westbrook in Shelley's life is paralleled by the story of Elisabeth Lang in Gross's. And both developed tragic relations with some of those female disciples, who fell desperately in love with their saviors and killed themselves in that despair. Both were "unmistakably noble" (Max Weber's phrase about Gross) and "finished gentlemen" (a phrase used about Shelley) but wounded others by treating them as "abstract ideas."

Both were absentminded, careless about appointments and meals, long-haired and untidy, youthfully slender and attractive: young men all their lives. Both were highly susceptible to women and hostile to marriage, both in practice and in theory. Shelley saw marriage as legalized prostitution; so did Gross. Each man's own marriage was lived in a semi-public whirl of discipular enthusiasm, with a tendency to become a libertarian commune; and Frieda Gross and Mary Shelley were in some sense handed over to their husbands' chief disciples, Ernst Frick and Thomas Jefferson Hogg.

Not only are there many such likenesses, but there is evidence that some people who thought about Gross saw those likenesses—notably Lawrence, who succeeded Gross as the lover of Frieda von Richthofen. Lawrence never explicitly compares the two men at length in any document that survives, but we can see that he did connect them, consciously as well as unconsciously, and he quite often talked about Shelley in ways that apply strikingly well to Gross, and vice versa.

He talks about Gross in the novel *Mr. Noon*, and the book of essays *Twilight in Italy*, which I shall come to in a minute. He alludes to him

in *Psychoanalysis and the Unconscious*, where he calls him "one of the
first and most brilliant of the analysts, a man now forgotten." That
book was published in 1921, and Gross had died, in tragic circumstances, in 1920; one might read "now forgotten" to mean that Gross
"now may be" forgotten. And in his poem "Ballad of a Wilful
Woman," about Frieda's previous love relationships, Lawrence associates Gross with St. John on Patmos, and describes him and Frieda
thus:

> They dwelt in a huge, hoarse sea-cave
> And looked far down the dark
> Where an archway torn and glittering
> Shone like a huge sea-spark.
>
> He said: "Do you see the spirits
> Crowding the bright doorway?"
> He said: "Do you hear them whispering?"
> He said: "Do you catch what they say?"

That archway was the New Age, and those spirits whispered New
Age promises. In this poem, as in life, Frieda turns away from Gross
toward Lawrence, but it is to Gross that the powers of prophecy are
attributed.

Lawrence's temperament would probably have struck us as considerably more conservative, or more timid, than Gross's, even if the two
had not been brought into confrontation. But the fact was that he had
to deal with Gross as a precursor in both the most personal and also
the most ideological sense. As far as the latter went, he had to develop
a theory of sexuality that would mark itself off from Gross's, and
would explain where Gross was wrong.

In the posthumously published and semi-autobiographical *Mr.
Noon*, for instance, Lawrence describes Johanna (Frieda) as having
been married to a "shame-faced sensualist" (Ernest Weekley in life,
Everard in the novel). She turned away from him toward a relationship with Eberhard (Gross), who belonged to an opposite type, which
Lawrence defines by associating it with "the non-sensual, quite spiritual poets like Shelley. . . . Now Johanna, after Everard, was aiming
in the Shelley direction, at the mid-heaven spiritual, which is still
sexual but quite spiritually so. Sex is open and as common and as

simple as any other human conversation. And this, we urge, is quite a logical conclusion of the whole spiritual programme." This spirituality was of the essence of Gross's New Age. But the program as a whole was wrong, Lawrence says, because sex, indeed life, cannot be wholly spiritualized.

The stress to which Lawrence was subjected by Frieda's comparing him with Gross is easy to imagine. (She *did* so compare him: when she eloped with Lawrence in 1912, Frieda wrote to friends in Ascona that her new man was "like Otto and Frick.") This is well conveyed in *Mr. Noon.* Johanna, the Frieda character, tells the Lawrence character that Gross was " a genius at love. He understood so much. And then he made one feel so free. . . . He made me believe in love—in the sacredness of love." Lawrence/Noon had to be inducted into the mysteries and disciplines of Ascona, including dance. Johanna "would dance in her glowing, full-bodied nudity round and round the flat, and she made him dance also, in his more intense, white and ruddy-haired nudity . . . with her arms spread on the air, she floated around in triumph."

It is easy to understand why, in the essays Lawrence wrote soon after his elopement with Frieda in 1912, he developed the idea of a set of antitheses, in which Shelley is an important example of a tendency, a direction, or what at other times Lawrence calls an "infinity." This particular infinity is what we have called the New Age idea, which needs, Lawrence says, to be balanced by some quite opposite tendency. These essays are to be found in *Twilight in Italy, The Crown,* and *A Study of Thomas Hardy*; they are some of Lawrence's most brilliant work and deserve more study than they have yet received.

Perhaps the most important of these antitheses is between Father and Son: the public allusion being to Christian theology, of course, but irresistibly suggestive of Hanns and Otto Gross, to all who knew anything of their story. Father and Son are also the antithetical poles of three antitheses: the Origin versus the Aim, and the Dark versus the Light, and the Self versus the Not-Self. Lawrence also includes two emblematic opposites, the Eagle and the Dove, and the Tiger and the Lamb. We can add that the Father, the Origin, the Dark, the Eagle, the Tiger—these are all to be found embodied in Hanns Gross. In Otto we see the Son, the Aim, the Light, the Not-Self, the Dove, the Lamb.

In *The Crown*, his set of essays of 1915, Lawrence associates the Father with the Law, with Darkness and Creation, with the Body and (at first sight paradoxically) with Woman. These are forces the Son denies. Historically speaking, the Father is associated with tyrants like Caesar and Saul; their opponents are virtuous sons like Brutus in Roman history, and David in the Bible.

The title phrase, "the Crown," derives from England's royal coat of arms, in which the Crown stands above the conflict between the Lion and the Unicorn (a parallel emblematic pair), sustained in its triumph, Lawrence says, *by* that conflict. Lawrence is trying to rise above and reconcile the conflict of Father and Son, Hanns and Otto, the authoritarian and the New Ager. Since he himself starts from Otto's position, and he is arguing himself into a different one, the stress of Lawrence's argument falls on Hanns's counter-truths.

In effect, therefore, these essays are a defense of the Father against the naïve mentality. The former propounds authoritarian truths we automatically deny but must learn to listen to. (This is disconcerting to anybody likely to be reading Lawrence, and that no doubt explains why these essays have been neglected.) According to Lawrence, our (New Age) reformers have gone against nature, saying, "Let no one suffer. . . . No mouse shall be caught by a cat." This is simply self-destructive; Shelley died because he wanted to be love triumphant.

In *A Study of Thomas Hardy*, we are told that the Jewish tradition worshiped a great physical God, the source of both maleness and femaleness. But when Christ came, he denied the Father, valuing not-being and pure love; and Northern Europe followed Christ, and other such prophets. Shelley, too, for instance, was oriented to the light and the not-me. Denying Darkness and the Woman, he was transcendently male. Lawrence saw the male as more prone than the female to transcendent enthusiasms.

In *Twilight in Italy* Lawrence tells us that in the Middle Ages Europe strove to achieve the "abstract" truths of Christ and Christianity—strove to turn away from primitive physical nature. But in the Renaissance, when pure mental Freedom became actually possible, Italy reversed its spiritual direction. Michelangelo then began to love the Father and the Body, and Botticelli painted Aphrodite. Meanwhile England, the North, Protestant Christianity went on as before, yearning toward Spirit and Abstraction; Shelley is again one of

Lawrence's examples. (One can say with certainty that he would have made Gandhi another such example, if asked.)

One of these antitheses pits Shelley against Shakespeare: Shelley is pure male—in the sense defined; Shakespeare is both male and female and therefore a better model to follow. Lawrence says that men should be internally well-balanced in their mixture of Father and Son; then they are happy, easy to mate, and so on. He saw himself as being more "mixed" than Gross was. Tolstoy, spiritual leader of the New Age, was for Lawrence the great betrayer; having known that happy temperamental balance, he then repudiated it (in the last thirty years of his life, when he became an ascetic New Ager).

The great opposition of the Son to the Father means the revolt of the spirit against the flesh, and of freedom against authority, and therefore of Shelley/Gross against all fathers and tyrants. The primary reference Lawrence offers is the distinction between God the Father and God the Son, the Old Testament and the New, the Law of Moses and the Sermon on the Mount. But in the year 1913, when Lawrence worked out these ideas, it is surely inconceivable that anyone living in the von Richthofen world could write of the conflict between Father and Son without thinking of Hanns Gross and Otto, for that was the year Hanns had his son arrested and locked up.

This was also the year Lawrence walked across the Alps and on at least one occasion took on Gross's identity, as he tells us in *Twilight in Italy*. He told someone he met that he was from Graz (Gross's birthplace), "that my father was a doctor in Graz, and that I was walking for my pleasure through the countries of Europe. I said this because I knew a doctor from Graz who was always wandering about, and because I did not want to be myself, an Englishman, to these two old ladies. I wanted to be someone else." Otto Gross was that other identity which at times he preferred to his usual one.

On this same trip he encountered Italian migrant workers who declared to him their militant faith in anarchism; part of their encounter is reported in the epigraph to this chapter. "What is this government?" asked their leader. "Who wants it? Only those who are unjust, and want to have advantage over somebody else." Lawrence comments, "I could feel a new spirit in him, something strange and pure and slightly frightening." "Pure" is one of Lawrence's code words for Shelley and Gross.

These anarchists had repudiated many of the safeguards of life, as Gross had done, and Lawrence was uncomfortably faced with his own conservatism. The essays just discussed are his self-justification, which is brilliant, but anxious and defensive. The Italians gave him a copy of a little anarchist newspaper they read, but Lawrence carried it around for some time without ever being able to read it. "I shrink involuntarily away. I do not know why this is so."

It is surely clear to *us* that Lawrence wanted to repudiate Gross, and Shelley, and all the kinds of New Age idealism he associated with them, in order to be free of the feeling of betrayal. This was a long-term project. In his essay "Reflections on the Death of a Porcupine," written in the last part of his life, he tells how he brought himself to kill an animal on his ranch in Taos. "Now never in my life had I shot at any live thing: I never wanted to. I always felt guns very repugnant: sinister, mean. [Lawrence tried to believe that other, more generous forms of violence—hitting with his fists, say—gave him no difficulty; but biographical anecdotes do not support his claim.] With difficulty I had fired once or twice at a target; but resented doing even so much. Other people could shoot if they wanted to. Myself, individually, it was repugnant to me even to try."

We note the word "resent"; this is a moral necessity he has convinced himself of, but cannot feel. He more than once asks Frieda if he should kill the porcupine, and she hesitates and is resentful but says yes. And he repeats, like an incantation, "Things like the porcupine, one must be able to shoot them, if they get in one's way. I, myself, must be able to shoot and to kill." This is authoritarian realism, which he is trying to live up to. His moral idea is—to use another essay's phrasing—"Blessed are the powerful, for they shall inherit the earth."

What is above all interesting for us in this is that he depicts himself and Frieda as temperamentally still New Agers—Shelleyans, like Gross—who have convinced themselves that they must change. They must be able to kill. They now believe in an infusion of the authoritarian temperament—of what Lawrence calls the Law in his "Study of Thomas Hardy"—to balance the naïve temperament and Love.

Lawrence is therefore often the spokesman for authoritarian realism. This conservatism comes to expression, for instance, in his essay, "A Propos of *Lady Chatterley's Lover*," where he presents his erotic theory as corroborated by the practice of the Catholic Church in the Mediterranean countries, and, beyond that, by paganism and the cycle of the seasons. At that point he is almost hand in hand with the T. S. Eliot of *Notes Towards the Definition of Culture*. (As a *novelist*, however, Lawrence is most often a spokesman for the New Age temperament.)

Thus it seems that Lawrence assimilated Gross's personal challenge to him in particular, which must have been a forceful one in 1912 and 1913 (such a brilliant mind, such a prophet of love, so important to Frieda, and such a dramatic fate) by blending him with Shelley, and by talking about him under the code name Shelley. In "A Study of Thomas Hardy" he wrote, "Shelley cannot properly be said ever to have lived. He transcended life. But we don't want to transcend life, since we are life." That use of "we" and that idea of "life" surely prompt us to think that Lawrence might have spoken those words to Frieda about Gross—or indeed Frieda might have spoken them to either man.

In "Introduction to These Paintings" Lawrence says that the northern nations have always been ashamed of their bodies, and in their art have demanded an escape from the body. For his example he turns to Shelley again. "Shelley is pure escape: the body is sublimated into divine gas."

On the other hand, Lawrence sometimes says Shelley is the greatest of English poets, and he seems to have had a more emotional and less stable relationship with him than with any other writer. (This is particularly true of the years immediately after his elopement with Frieda—the years of his indirect, anxious, concealed confrontation with Otto; see the number of references in that volume of his *Collected Letters*, so much more numerous than they are before or after.) It is moreover striking how many of Lawrence's friends make reference to Shelley in discussing Lawrence (Murry, Aldington, Ottoline Morell). Shelley's ideas, Shelley's phrases, Shelley's life story, the scandal surrounding them, even Shelley's hasty way of walking, are invoked as the closest analogies to Lawrence's.

And then Lawrence was a New Ager all his life in his recurrent dream of founding an anarchist community, in Florida, in Tahiti, in the Andes, in New Mexico. This is the dream often associated with the name Rananim. It was an Asconan aspiration—Gross, for instance, planned to found a free university in Ascona—a Utopian idealism such as Lawrence repeatedly made fun of, but could not finally renounce. The community dream was recurrent and was in a sense bequeathed to John Middleton Murry when Lawrence died; as Lawrence was to Gross, Murry was to Lawrence, and Frieda's relations with the three men—each of them in turn became her lover—confirm that equation.

Some of the fiercest of the quarrels between Lawrence and Frieda, we are told by Murry, were over Shelley. More exactly, Murry says that the recurrent pattern to their quarrels was that Frieda would provoke Lawrence by defending one of his "discarded prophets"—such as Nietzsche or Shelley. Yet she more than anyone, Murry says, had taught Lawrence to discard them.

Ostensibly these quarrels were over Frieda's praising Shelley's poetry, which Lawrence hated when he did not love it; but it seems likely that her praise (which Murry too thought insincere) irritated Lawrence so much because it relinked him to Shelley and Gross, while he was always determined to escape from that company, to be something quite different. Later in life, for instance, he liked to think that the Mexican peasants who stared at his beard called him "The Fox" to each other; he did *not* like to think that they called him "The Christ." He wanted an animal or at least a happily human identity. He did not want to be a Son on the Cross, a sacrificial savior.

Even more interesting for us, of course, is the question of what caused or explained the striking similarity between Gross and Shelley. Indeed, as I have implied, it seems almost a shared identity, of which the striking resemblances are only symptoms. My own answer to that question is that a world-conquering civilization like ours regularly—and especially in New Ages—throws off the seeds of revolt against itself. It produces stresses and strains that are felt by many individuals in the form of guilts and revolts; guilt for all the other races and classes subordinated to the ruling race and class; guilt for the other species sacrificed to the human race; guilt for the other genders (women and children and homosexuals) sacrificed to white male chauvinism. And revolt not only against the state and its laws, but also against the family, which is in many ways the building unit of the state, where the roles of husband and father are identified with that of master. In times of revolution, or any New Age, these stresses and strains are greater than at other times. And when those seeds fall into the fertile minds of young boys like Bysshe Shelley and Otto Gross, so gifted, so sensitive, so pushed and promoted, so fostered and stimulated by a proud and proprietary father, so insistently summoned to carry the father's name to new heights of social triumph—why, then you get this tragically destructive and nobly self-sacrificing identity that Gross and Shelley shared.

It is an identity that many other men have shared in other New Ages, perhaps most often men of religion. You find it in icons of the Saviour, the founder of Christianity, and in some of the saints of that religion. Frieda von Richthofen, despite her erotic ideology, was always looking for a contemporary Francis of Assisi. We know she saw traces of that identity in her father, and also in her second husband, D. H. Lawrence, though he resisted all beatification, as we have seen, just because that left him aligned with angelic Sons like the Saviour and Shelley (and Gross). It is no coincidence that in "The Crown," Lawrence links these names and speaks of "Shelley and St. Francis of Assisi" as two men who strikingly embodied "the white light of universal love." He does not mention Otto Gross there, but I would guess that it was in Gross that Frieda saw more traces of that identity than in any other man.

CHAPTER EIGHT

Prophetic Voices Again

> Art is play, and good when it is the play of normal, hard-
> working men, bad when it is the play of corrupt para-
> sites . . . The principal thing which I wanted to say about
> art is that it does not exist, in the sense of some great mani-
> festation of the human spirit.
>
> Tolstoy, in the 1890s

Although the nineteenth-century New Age, including Tolstoy and Gandhi, had, measured by ordinary standards, an expansive, exhilarated sense of reality, and though these two men are rightly seen as both figures of piety and the objects of piety, they were also highly skeptical minds and even abrasively cynical.

Such skepticism is characteristic of the ascetic New Ager in particular. These men were remarkable more for what they refused to believe in than for what they did believe in among our ordinary creeds and icons. This has been true of other men of religion: some early Christian teachers were sometimes confounded with the Greek Cynics because both groups were so hostile to and skeptical about the humanism of their day. Their sense of reality being different, they see as *maya*, illusion, what other people see as important facts.

I will therefore report here some part of what Tolstoy and Gandhi said about the issues of their day, especially the remarks that suggest what they might have said about some of our current predicaments and enthusiasms. Their topics and occasions for utterance derived from their own times and places—largely from inside their homelands, Russia and India—but included universal causes familiar to us like feminism and eroticism, and perennial issues like violence and nonviolence. Their thinking spread out in many directions, but I shall shape their criticism to converge again upon what they saw as a false sense of reality.

TOLSTOY ON POLITICS AND RELIGION

As early in the New Age as 1881–82, Tolstoy was writing his *Critique of Dogmatic Theology*, in which he rendered judgment on the Orthodox Church's Symbol of the Faith, on Filerat's "Catechism," on the "Epistle of the Eastern Patriarchate," and on Makari's (new) *Dogmatic Theology*, a selection of the state church's most important documents. These were systematizations of Christ's message, as any Christian theology must be—theorizations of the naïve truths of the Gospels. Tolstoy's judgment was that these works were in effect more blasphemous and faithless than anti-Christian books by Voltaire and Hume, because they adapted the Gospel message to give it meanings quite opposite to those originally intended and so perverted it, morally but also intellectually. Much of what concerned the Church seemed to him fundamentally unreal as well as wrong.

Christian dogmata, such as that God is both three and one, meant nothing to Tolstoy. He also dismissed the church sacraments as "savage customs" suited to an earlier phase of civilization. Reading official teachings of piety and moral theology would actually have made him an atheist, he said, if he had not independently found his way to faith—a naïve faith—in Christ's actual message. He described the experience of reading thus: "I had intended to go to God, and I found my way into a stinking bog, which evokes in me only those feelings of which I am most afraid; disgust, malice, and indignation." Despite himself, Tolstoy's rather terrible endowment of cynicism stirred to life, or rather—since it had always been alive—to active expression, when he read systematic Christianity.

We are likely to feel, as Tolstoy's contemporaries did, that what he is attacking is something specific to Czarist Russia's state church. Isabella Fyvie Mayo, however, reminds us that English Tolstoyans found his analysis perfectly appropriate to their country then—and on reflection who would dare declare that it is less applicable to our own?

As for Tolstoy's political views, in a short pamphlet of 1882 entitled

"Church and State" he declared the phrase "Christian State" to be as paradoxical and nonsensical as "hot ice"; either such a state is no state, or (more likely) its Christianity is no Christianity. Kings, after all, are simply anointed robbers. Christ's teaching is hostile to the state, and Christians, though not called on to destroy the state, are called on not to support it or to comply with many of its demands.

In this rewriting of Christianity and resistance to the Church Tolstoy cannot but remind us of our own New Agers like Matthew Fox and Father Thomas Berry (to be discussed later). But these men are directing our attention away from the narrowly social and human moral issues toward the ecological ones. That is their strength, and what gives them something new to say. But I think Tolstoy would have warned us against the exhilaration of allying ourselves with the forces of "Nature"—not because to do that is wrong, but because it may make us forget the ineluctability of the narrowly moral issues.

In 1884 Tolstoy finished *My Religion*, in which he described himself as having behind him five years of faith in Christ and thirty-five years of nihilism (faith in nothing). His life as novelist, husband, and father had been morally spurious. He presented himself to the reader as one of the robbers on the cross, come down to preach. (Gandhi also renounced his family heritage, and even described previous Gandhis as having been robbers of the poor.)

Tolstoy's conversion had occurred when he realized that Christ's declaration "Resist not Evil" (Matt. 5:39) meant what it said. This was a revelation to him because he had always been taught that Christ's laws were not practical, and so must be interpreted—in effect, silently circumvented.

In these arguments, Tolstoy treats Christianity as a New Age doctrine perverted by the authoritarian and systematic elements in culture. What he had been taught as being practical ethics was quite opposite in tendency—was authoritarian: "I was taught to judge and punish. Then I was taught to make war, that is, to resist evil men with murder, and the military caste, of which I was a member, was called the Christ-loving military, and their activity was sanctified by a Christian blessing." He was involved in this contradiction very early because he was born noble, but "nowadays," when military service and jury duty have been made universal, all men are involved in it.

Tolstoy's message was pacifism and of a kind more radical than most, because it was based on nonresistance to evil. We have today a peace movement, or a congeries of movements, quite comparable to the one Tolstoy knew. Tolstoy was skeptical and indeed hostile to all cries for peace that came from socially and politically established sources—the Hague Peace Conference sponsored by the Czar, and the newspaper and journal surveys of what prominent intellectuals had to say on the topic. He invested his hopes in the active and suffering individual, and small weak groups like the Dukhobors—in those at the base of society. He was skeptical about Gandhi's combination of political and religious values, although, if he had known as much as we about Gandhi's whole career, he would surely have realized how much he had to learn from him.

What Then Must We Do?, which was finished in 1886, described the Tolstoy family's recent move to Moscow, and the author's horror at the urban poverty he had to confront there. (Previously, living in the countryside, in the family home at Yasnaya Polyana, the little good he did "created around me an atmosphere of love and union with these people" in which he could calm his guilt). He described the Khitrov dosshouses, which he visited at the time of the Moscow census in which he was a volunteer worker, and then the five-course dinner and the white-gloved servants in the house he came home to after his visit. And when he spoke to friends of what he had seen, they assured him that it was only his extraordinary goodness which made it disturbing to him, thus corrupting his feelings about the problem.

The movement in defense of the homeless, led in Boston by Kip Tiernan, is a contemporary equivalent to Tolstoy's work of this kind. She is a sort of successor to Dorothy Day, the editor of the *Catholic Worker* who provided refuges for the homeless in New York in the middle of this century. It seems likely that Tolstoy would have admired these two women's work wholeheartedly. He and they were naïve rather than systematic in their work. His own style was often more declamatory, more bitter and denunciatory than theirs, but he, too, employed the criteria of practical effectiveness, examining the immediate and personal as well as the long-term or theoretical effect of an action.

In the last period of his life, 1894–1910, Tolstoy was leading the agitation about the Dukhobors. (His wife, Sonia Tolstoy, called the latter "arrogant revolutionaries," and said her children would soon be

unable to afford white bread as a result of their father's activities.)
The Dukhobor sect, as we know, refused to do military service for the
Russian state when the latter introduced general conscription in 1887.
More exactly, they at first submitted to the order, only telling their
young men not to actually fire a weapon. But when they were penalized, suffering reradicalized them, and in 1893–94 they renounced
tobacco, meat, and wine, redivided their property, and refused all
military service. In the summer of 1895 they burned their arms and
their conscripted young men refused further obedience. The Cos-
sacks were sent against them, and charged through their village twice,
raping the women. Three hundred men were imprisoned, four hundred families forced to sell up their farms.

Tolstoy wrote to the Dukhobors, giving them moral and political
support and advice, and wrote about them to the world. He made
them exemplary figures to all his disciples, the living embodiment of
his teaching, and the living proof that religious radicalism was not a
fashionable modern enthusiasm limited to intellectuals but a popular
and Christian tradition. The equivalent today is perhaps the American Indian cause and the cult of the memory of Wounded Knee. It is
not linked to pacifism in the same way, but the guilt and rage felt by
so many white Americans at their government's past and present
actions are similar. Those feelings are quite widespread and are discharged symbolically in the cult of American Indian life. The stores
devoted to Indian artifacts are like temples or the stores next to
temples where one buys what one needs to make an offering.

GANDHI ON WESTERN CIVILIZATIONS

Gandhi was never so much the controversialist as Tolstoy, but he
developed a critique of Western civilization as a whole at least as early
as 1897, long before he began *satyagraha*. He described it as being
unlike Eastern civilization because based on the law of might, which
he sets in opposition to the law of right. This theory sounds like
undiscriminating partisan hostility on his part (and it is easy to point
to the exercise of the law of might in the East), but Gandhi seems to
have offered this idea as something to which Western philosophers
and even the practical defenders of Western civilization might assent.

In fact he attributes these views to the philosophical General Jan

Smuts, and claims to have heard Smuts express them in their private conversations. Of course, white people in colonial situations did talk and seriously think in the terms of empire—which were quite unlike those of people at home. They did blaspheme against the liberal values enshrined in official discourse. The frontier was a social enclave where the authoritarian temperament expressed itself much more freely than elsewhere. Kipling was giving popular expression to such ideas, and was widely read in the colonies. Nietzsche, too, was being quoted to justify, or at least explain, imperialism.

What then can we imagine Smuts to have meant by such language? The law of might must have meant the frank espousal of the realities of war and peace as seen by the authoritarian or the systematic mind to whom all the New Age alternatives seemed a largely idealistic and wish-fulfillment philosophy of politics. Understood thus, we can understand the ideology Gandhi attributes to the West and the contrast he draws between it and the East as a complex idea. Though we are likely to be dismayed by his wholesale identification with the East, we can appreciate the vantage point it gives him for pointing to the gross destructiveness of the West. That destruction is after all a major fact of world history. We see it, for instance, in the West's cultural as well as military domination of other societies, whether those others are tribal or—as Hinduism was—imperial in their own way.

Patriotism and Death

If the two men agreed over one major political theme, the end of imperialism, they differed over the related theme of patriotism. Gandhi was a great nation-builder, even though his consecration as the father of the modern Indian state is ironic and inappropriate. He was indeed an Indian patriot, although of a very unusual kind, while one of Tolstoy's most Voltairean essays of this period is "On Patriotism," which begins with a satirical description of the patriotic, officially sponsored celebrations of the French fleet's visit to Kronstadt and the Russian fleet's visit to Toulon to celebrate the Franco-Russian Alliance of 1894.

Written very much in a tone that recalls current political satire and international alliance politics, NATO and Persian Gulf warmonger-

ing, and Star Wars, Tolstoy's writing of this kind is caustically enter-
taining.

Tolstoy flatly denied the "moral imperative" of nations and nation-
ality. Citizenship, he said, was in modern times so mixed an idea—
invoked by so many interest groups—and was so much the product of
manipulative propaganda, that "being French" or "being Russian"
could not mean any value worth living by. Patriotism and citizenship
he considered an ideology of slavery, fostered by governments and
facilitated by newspapers. But public opinion, which supported governments, could also destroy them. Let one man begin to speak the
truth, said Tolstoy, and all the opposition would melt away.

Even more aggressively, in the following year, 1896, he wrote "Patriotism or Peace?" about the oil war that had nearly broken out
between England and America over the Venezuelan frontier. This
was a situation like the one preceding our war in the Persian Gulf.
Nowadays, he said, patriotism could not be counted as a virtue. It had
been useful in the past to weld groups of men into states, but now
that work was done. He connected the theory of patriotism with the
practice of imperialism all over the world.

Tolstoy's essay "Patriotism and Christianity" declared the two ideologies incompatible. In 1895 a Pole had protested against this position. Tolstoy admitted that the patriotism of an enslaved nation (like
Poland then, India in Gandhi's time, our own contemporary equivalents) is more pardonable, although still an evil. And finally, in 1904,
he said that the feverish, insane excitement of patriotism that seized
the upper ranks of Russian society (in the war against Japan) was
merely a symptom of their criminal guilt.

In a variety of ways, therefore, Tolstoy was charging the landscape
of politics, and in a sense the front page of the newspapers, with the
fervor of religious feeling. The leaven of the spirit—what is called in
Christianity the Holy Spirit—was working, for his readers, in what is
normally a secular terrain.

A notable feature of these polemical essays is the rhetoric of his
own death that Tolstoy used to introduce and end several of them.
Thus, in his preface to "The Christian Teaching" (1898) he wrote,
"By my age and the state of my health I am standing with one foot in
the grave, and so human considerations for me have no importance.

Even if they had, I am well aware that this [what he is writing] could only disturb and grieve unbelievers who demand from me works of art and not discussions of faith, and also the believers who are perturbed by everything I write about religion and scold me for it."

The rhetoric of death, it will be seen, blends into a rhetoric of dharma, of duty, and on other occasions into a rhetoric of guilt and shame. Thus "There Are No Guilty People" (1909) begins, "Mine is a strange and wonderful lot." Although he has a long felt keenly the social oppression exerted by the rich; Tolstoy says: "I still live on amid the depravity and sins of rich society; and I cannot leave it, because I have neither the knowledge nor the strength to do so. I cannot. I do not know how to change my life so that my physical needs—food, sleep, clothing, my going to and fro—may be satisfied without a sense of shame and wrongdoing in the position which I fill. Now that I am over eighty and have become feeble, I have given up trying to free myself; and, strange to say, as my feebleness increases, I realize more and more strongly the wrongfulness of my position. . . . It has occurred to me that I do not occupy this position for nothing; that Providence intended that I should lay bare the truth of my feelings so that I might atone for all that causes my suffering, and might perhaps open the eyes of [others]." He will use his guilt and shame for the benefit of others.

But the central discourse is of death. "The Law of Love and the Law of Violence" (1908) begins: "The only reason I am writing this is because, knowing the one means of escape for Christian humanity, from its physical suffering as well as from the moral suffering in which it is sunk, I, who am on the edge of the grave, cannot be silent." He wanted to reintroduce death into our consciousness. A little later in that essay he says, "Throughout the centuries the best, that is the real people, always thought about *it*." That *it* means, How it will all end. This essay concludes, "This is what I have wanted to say to you, my brothers, before I died."

He employed a similar rhetoric in his fiction. In "Master and Man" (1895), Nikita dies at the end, but within the story had already *seemed* to die and recovered—a confusion of seeming and real death that has made the reader uneasy. Tolstoy's narrative stops with the sentence "Whether he is better off, or worse off, there in the place where he awoke after that real death, whether he was disappointed or found things there as he expected, is what we shall all of us soon learn."

The essay "I Cannot Be Silent" (1908) is similarly pervaded by images of death, and in particular of death by hanging. It begins by reporting a number of death sentences, then describes death by hanging, and gives anecdotes about hangmen. Tolstoy described the growth of violence in Russia in the recent past on the parts of both government and revolutionaries, condemning both, the government more severely.

"I cannot and will not any longer struggle against the feeling aroused in me by these crimes. . . . I hope my exposure of those men will in one way or another evoke the expulsion I desire . . . [expulsion from his caste privileges, which make him a participant in the crimes]. Nothing really would so fully satisfy me, or give me such real pleasure, as to be put in prison—in a real, good, stinking, cold, hungry prison. . . . It is impossible to live so! I at any rate cannot and will not live so. That is why I write this and will circulate it . . . that one of two things may happen: either that these human deeds may be stopped . . . or still better . . . that they may put on me, as on those twelve or twenty peasants, a shroud and a cap and may push me also off a bench, so that by my own weight I may tighten the well-soaped noose around my old throat." And he ended by addressing directly the hangmen and their administrators.

Gandhi, of course, did get into some real, cold, hungry, stinking prisons, and was indeed profoundly satisfied by the experience. We might also compare Tolstoy's discourse with that of Wendell Berry among today's New Agers.

> I am sickened by complicity in my race . . .
> I think I must put on
> a deathlier knowledge, and prepare to die
> rather than enter into the design of man's hate.

Or again,

> We sell the world to buy fire,
> our way lightened by burning men,
> and that has bent my mind
> and made me think of darkness
> and wish for the dumb life of roots.

In writing about his death in this context, Tolstoy performed something similar to Gandhi's political fasting. As the formalist critics say, both men "forwarded," brought to the front of their contemporaries' minds, the facts of individual dying. Each made his own death, and that of the reader, relevant to issues of public policy. The message was—Tolstoy said in *The Pathway of Life*—"Death, death, death, awaits you every instant." The meaning of that death is what you have to seek and seek relentlessly.

Tolstoy did not know two forms of death that hang over us: the threat of nuclear holocaust that would destroy our civilization, and the AIDS epidemic. Both of these forms of death have the effect of undermining the liberal and secular consensus of our time, and thus corroborating his (and Gandhi's) attitudes, which seemed then (and now, to many people) so retrograde and reactionary.

Gandhi was rebuked by Rabindranath Tagore over the Bihar massacre in the 1930s, because he interpreted it in religious terms as God's punishment of India. Tagore, a more modern mind, believed such an interpretation tended to retard the nation's development. He had complained before that the Gandhian movement was narrowing the freedom of Indian patriots, above all, their freedom of mind and imagination. India needed to expand its imagination, to rejoice in varieties of splendor. Gandhi's symbol of the spinning wheel was crowding out other images, and was itself an emblem of negation, poverty, and asceticism. Gandhi felt that the life of the mind proceeds as much by negation as by affirmation.

TOLSTOY AND GANDHI ON ART

Another way in which Tolstoy and Gandhi differed was in the amount of attention each devoted to aesthetics. In the first part of the New Age period Tolstoy was especially preoccupied with art, which had after all been his profession and in a sense his religion, while it had never been anything like that for Gandhi. Tolstoy was concerned especially with that new movement then called Symbolism or now called Modernism, a movement destined to clash with the Tolstoyan New Age everywhere, sooner or later.

Modernism began reaching Russia from France in the early 1890s. One of its sponsors was D. S. Merezhkovski, who in an essay of 1893 drew a contrast between Zola—politically a protester, but culturally respectable, and practically a member of the Academy—and Verlaine, a disreputable writer of obscure and decadent verses who lived in the cafés. It was the latter, Merezhkovski said, who represented the new in literature; the former, who represented the old truths, was the one comparable with Tolstoy in his political and moral activities.

In reaction against the new literature and its formalist theory, Tolstoy made a literary-critical criterion out of sincerity. In his introduction to S. Y. Semyonov's *Peasant Stories*, he contrasted that author with Flaubert, charging the latter with insincerity in his story of "Julien l'Hospitalier." "I feel that the author himself would not have done and would not even have wished to do what his hero does [lie with lepers] and therefore I myself did not wish to do it and do not experience any agitation at reading of this amazing exploit." How different is Semyonov's story: ". . . every time I read it I feel that the author would not only have wished to have, but certainly would have, acted in that way under similar circumstances; his feelings infect me and I feel pleased, and it seems to me that I should have done, or been ready to do, something good."

Gandhi teaches a similar naïve theory of literary values à propos Olive Schreiner, whom he admired for doing her own cooking, cleaning, and washing up. "She held that far from affecting it adversely, such useful physical labor stimulated her literary ability, and made for a sense of proportion and discrimination in thought and language." We shall find Gary Snyder saying similar things in our own day.

Moreover this whole contrast and conflict in literature is one we face today, between a literature embodied in the New Age authors of the West Coast, who are in some sense sincere/naïve, and the postmodern writers and theorists of academia, who are not. Sincerity is a name for the belief in the realizing of certain values; in a sense it is a belief in the possibility of being sincere, although the achievement of those values is another matter. Among those who aim at sincerity, some artists will succeed and others fail; but they will all differ from those who disbelieve in those values.

However, not all New Agers aim at sincerity in art. Some, for instance, are interested primarily in myth, and a psychology and philosophy based on myth that eludes the moral constraints of "Is this right or wrong?" For such people art as a whole is an alternative to moralism. The value attributed to art is a function of the value attributed to myth, and this tends to be very high. In our day, it is particularly the Jungians, like Joseph Campbell and Robert Bly, who press that claim, and they are undeniably New Agers, while Tolstoy and Gandhi stand for quite a different, an almost opposite tendency. (This mutual opposition is what was said before to divide the erotic from the ascetic New Age.)

This conflict became an issue for Gandhi in his encounter with the American Nilla Cram Cook, who attached herself to him in the 1930s. She was the daughter of George Cram Cook and grew up in avant-garde circles in places like Greenwich Village with a post-Nietzschean set of ideas, focused on the transcendent moral importance of art, myth, and love, values that seemed to her mutually dependent. She went to live in Gandhi's ashram while he was in jail, and they exchanged letters, in which she translated *satyagraha* into the terms of her philosophy. Soon he wrote to her, "I wish you will forget Pythagoras, Bacchus, and the Mahabharata. Why should you brood over the past when you have to reenact the Mahabharata at the Ashram?" He wanted her to move forward morally, but her imagination needed huge spaces of amoral freedom. Her letter, he writes, was "too imaginative and poetic for me. You have plenty of poetry in you. Your imagination knows no bounds. I want you to transmute these into an inexhaustible power for real service. We all have to aspire after being childlike." But for her, to transmute her imagination, especially in the direction of the childlike, was to deny it.

In *What Is Art?* (1898) Tolstoy criticized his contemporaries' reifying and mysticizing of art, a process like that which we saw in Godwin and Shelley at the time of defeat of their New Age. Tolstoy directly challenged the new aestheticism of his own day by criticizing contemporary work by the criterion of its usefulness and pleasurableness to peasants. The people, he said, have always had art of their own and know what art is for. Good art, he said, is that kind which promotes the key religious perception of its time, which "in our case" means the brotherhood of all men.

In the 1990s, in our case, we can surely say that key perception is the need to protect the environment. That is the locus of the feelings of spirituality which everyone today feels to a greater or lesser extent. Good art would then be that which promotes those feelings.

But our art, since the renaissance, Tolstoy says, has been a privileged caste's art, which means that it has functioned primarily to distract an idle class of aristocrats. (On February 4, 1897, he wrote in his diary, "The harm of art is principally this, that it takes up time, hiding people's idleness from them.") According to Tolstoy, art deprived of its proper (religious) subject matter becomes affected and obscure, artificial and insincere, and manifests erotic mania. (It is easy to imagine contemporaries like Wendell Berry and Wes Jackson saying very similar things about the equivalent art of our time.)

In fact, Tolstoy used the phrase "a military caste's art" because in Russia the aristo-military caste was still dominant in cultural matters. But what he had to say suited other European countries where the dominant class was different. Some of these thoughts Tolstoy developed further in his letter of October 4, 1887, to Romain Rolland in France. Rolland had written to Tolstoy as a student, conscious of a vocation to become an intellectual and troubled by Tolstoy's demand that everyone do bread labor. Tolstoy wrote him, "All the evil of the day comes from the fact that so-called civilized people, together with the scientists and artists, form a privileged caste, like so many priests; and this caste has the fault of all castes. It degrades and lowers the principle in virtue of which it was organized. We are born and we clamber upon the rungs of the ladder, and we find among the privileged the priests of civilization, of *Kultur*, as the Germans have it." For Tolstoy, the idea of the culture caste was inseparable from what I have been calling the systematic mind.

This is a particularly interesting exchange because Rolland more or less rejected Tolstoy's opinion but went on to become a spokesman for some aspects of the New Age in France (a leader of pacifism during the First World War) and the man who introduced Gandhi to a whole generation of Europeans. He remained an intellectual but was the only famous writer who profoundly attended to both Tolstoy and Gandhi (unless one counts the ambiguous case of the comedian Shaw).

THE SYSTEMATIC MIND DENOUNCED

Tolstoy saw a general triumph of the systematic mind in the twentieth century. He said we must distrust these "castes of the mind, which after having destroyed or subjugated the ancient ruling castes, the Church, the State, the Army, have installed themselves in the same place, and without wishing or being able to do anything useful for men, claim admiration and blind service from everyone."

In *Hind Swaraj*, Gandhi's equivalent for Paine's and Tolstoy's pamphlets, he, too, discusses the triumphs of the professions in Western civilization and to much the same effect. He finds the proud English institutions of Parliament and the daily press, too, merely expedient and insufficiently moral in their function. He attacks in turn the law courts, medicine, hospitals, railways, and textile factories. The whole modern system is a Upas tree, its root immorality, its branches the parasitic professions. Lawyers have enslaved India to English law and English eloquence. Doctors induce us to sin, because they suppress the punitive effect that overindulgence naturally has. And so on.

As is often the case, Gandhi's rhetoric is more simplistic than Tolstoy's, but his thought is similar. His countrymen's ancestors, Gandhi says, were wise to set a limit to their indulgences, intellectual as well as sensual, for (as a result of those limits) Indians are not trapped as the English are into life-corroding competition with each other. Our ancestors saw that the mind is a restless bird, Gandhi wrote, and their institutions caged it for its own good. (On other occasions, Gandhi called the mind a drunken monkey.) But modern civilization is a mere congregation of chattering birds and monkeys, since the need for limits have been forgotten or denied.

At the same time, we must note the respect both Tolstoy and Gandhi felt for the soldier, as surprising and challenging as this may be to our pacifist liberalism. They wanted their followers to develop a combative attitude, fighting energetically against the forces of state and society, and to fight in a disciplined way. This is particularly important to Gandhi, who was building up a political force. He often used the language of the castes to say he wanted Kshatriyas or warriors as his followers.

The attitude of both prophets to feminism, too, is not what New Agers expect. Though their message is antipatriarchal, it is not profeminist, and they set a high value on the qualities of meekness and submission that women developed as a result of the patriarchal distribution of gender roles. Tolstoy and Gandhi valued the experience, in some sense the culture, of weakness (not moral weakness, from their point of view, but much of what the world calls weakness). Thus some kinds of feminism, those which try above all to win for women the same freedoms and powers as men have had, were repugnant to Tolstoy and Gandhi.

The attitudes to life and to the divine source of life that we have discussed have what we might call a negative or contracted character, judged by the secularist standards that most of our ideologies observe, including those of the current New Age. One could call their sense of life "antitriumphalist."

If the greatest of New Agers, then, they were certainly not simply typical. But all of their values derive from their New Age realism, as validly as opposite values like erotic liberation do. Moreover, the dialectic between them and other New Agers is another way in which they are useful to us. They introduce into the New Age mentality a severity and force that we can feel to be valuable, but that might otherwise seem to be alien and to belong exclusively to the authoritarian temperament.

THE CALCUTTA MIRACLE

One of the remarkable achievements of the New Age Gandhian movement in India was Gandhi's stopping of the Calcutta massacre in 1947, in what was called the Calcutta Miracle. This phrasing was not inappropriate, for at its greatest, the New Age is always a postreligious cult of what is called in traditional religion "the spirit." And the events in Calcutta brought to birth some moments of vision—which are also moments of reality—that transcend and transform political facts.

The story begins in August 1947, the year of India's independence, when the focus of national attention had shifted away from Gandhi to the politicians who were to rule the new country. Gandhi was in Srinagar in Kashmir that month. It was his first visit to Kashmir, and—as Robert Payne tells it—for once he paid attention to the beauty of the landscape, finding no way to intervene in the politics. Since the Maharajah of Kashmir was Hindu, and the majority of the people were Muslims, and the dispute between India and Pakistan was already growing in violence, there was little Gandhi could do. He saw crowds shouting "Long live Gandhi" but also men waving black flags and shouting "Long live Pakistan."

The situation mirrored the larger one in India. Kashmir was disputed territory, and Gandhi was a stranger there, adrift among the warring tribes, with no hope of bringing the complex political problem to a solution. Visiting a refugee camp, he stood by the cots of women wounded in a racial riots. As he waved away the flies that settled on their wounds, he said, "You must not expect much of me."

To a deputation of workers from Jammu who asked him what would happen to Kashmir after India became independent, he answered only, "That should be decided by the will of the Kashmiris." He had not as yet found a context in which he could act—as he had failed to do ever since his imprisonment under the war regime, indeed ever since the Second World War had involved India.

He spoke of spending the rest of his days in Pakistan, perhaps in the Punjab or the Frontier Province. He knew there would be more violence there. In Lahore, which the Hindus were already evacuating, he shook his head and spoke the language of the soldier rather than the pacifist: "If the people in the Punjab were all to die, not as cowards but as brave men, I for one would not shed a tear."

He set off for the Ganges delta district of Noakhali because he expected the greatest bloodshed there. (In Noakhali, Muslims had lived side by side with Hindus, but in a majority and in hostility.) As his train went through Benares, he refused to show himself to the crowds on the platform because they were chanting political slogans. He was a living negation of their mood of triumph. At Patna he spoke against there being any celebrations on Independence Day. It should be a day for fasting, spinning, and praying. At a village station where crowds gathered he went to the window and shouted, "Why are you harassing an old man?" He feebly slapped one of the men who came hurrying up to see him.

He was indeed an old man, testy and enfeebled. When a guard on the train offered to move him from a leaky compartment to another, he said, "I will not make myself comfortable by causing discomfort to others." When the guard asked what he could do, Gandhi answered negatively and pedantically, "Do not harass people and do not accept bribes. You will serve me best by practicing these two requests of mine."

Since Direct Action Day in August 1946 Bengal had seen a series of riots, and now East Bengal was to be separated from the West. Lord

Louis Mountbatten, the last viceroy and the first governor general, knew that the worst trouble of all in India was to be expected in Calcutta, the capital of Bengal, an overcrowded city of three million people, including forty thousand lepers and four hundred thousand beggars and unemployables. It was a predominantly Hindu city set in a predominantly Muslim state, so the officials were Muslims but were distrusted by the masses. That was the reality behind the façade of the lush green Maidan and the Georgian mansions and office of the great trading companies along Chowringhee Road. Everyone felt that if ever trouble broke out in Calcutta's fetid, pullulating slums and congested bazaars, no number of troops would be able to control it. In late July, Mountbatten asked Gandhi to go there, saying that he had only one brigade of troops there and was not able to reinforce it. There were political gangs of hoodlums asserting every variety of ideology, armed with clubs, knives, pistols, and tigers' claws (vicious steel prongs to pluck out a man's eyes).

Gandhi, however, had decided to be in the delta villages of Noakhali for August 15, 1947, Independence Day, because of the severe risk of peasant rioting there. However, his way led him through Calcutta, where the authorities were also very nervous about what might happen.

First Lord Mountbatten and then Shaheed Suhrawardy, the Muslim mayor of the city, asked Gandhi to be there to prevent rioting. He at first agreed to stay there for just two extra days on his way to Noakhali at the prompting of Mohammad Usman, a former mayor. But then Suhrawardy flew in from Karachi and begged him to stay longer. The rule of law was breaking down and criminal elements were gaining control. Most of the Muslim officials were already seeking the comparative safety of East Bengal, but the ordinary householders and shopkeepers were trapped in the city.

The forty-seven-year-old Suhrawardy had some history of promoting Hindu-Muslim unity and was not entirely trusted by Mohammed Ali Jinnah, but was nevertheless a pillar of the latter's Muslim League. He is a leading figure in the story but we must rely on impressionistic and journalistic accounts of him. He is described in *Freedom at Midnight* as the prototype of the venal Indian politician. He had assured his continued position in power by using public funds to maintain a "private army" that clubbed his political rivals into silence. An opposite to Gandhi, he dressed in Western clothes, in silk suits and two-tone alligator shoes; his hair, trimmed every morning by a personal barber, was dressed with brilliantine. Payne describes Suhrawardy as a square-faced, heavily built man, a gourmand and a womanizer who represented everything that Hindus detested. He was a powerful orator with a decisive or overbearing manner, the embodiment of the authoritarian type.

A pillar of the Muslim League, Suhrawardy was an enemy of the Congress Party and Hinduism. He was rumored to have made a fortune in 1942 selling on the black market grain intended for the starving people of Bengal, and was said to have licensed the riots of Direct Action Day (Muslim aggression against Hindus) by telling his followers that the police would not interfere.

Gandhi agreed to stay a few days more, on two conditions: that the Muslims of Noakhali (and their masters in Calcutta) pledge safety to the Hindus there over the Independence Day period (if the promise was broken, Gandhi would fast to death), and that Suhrawardy come to live with him day and night in a Calcutta slum. This was one of Gandhi's habitual tactics, to induce representatives of mutually hostile groups to share their lives—a sort of practical New Age existentialism. He also told Suhrawardy to go home and consult his daughter (he had no wife, only one daughter). It was often Gandhi's way to approach other men via their wives or daughters. The implication was that, in these circumstances, the powerful politician in Suhrawardy would have give way to some alternative potentiality in his personality.

Driven in a dilapidated prewar Chevrolet, Gandhi arrived on August 13 at Hydari House, 151 Beliaghata Road, a decayed mansion on the edge of a canal. "There, rising over an open patch of dirt the monsoon rains had churned into a muddy slush, was a crumbling ruin, a decaying vision from a Tennessee Williams stage setting." Its broad terraces had Doric pillars and carved balustrades, but the house had long been abandoned to ants and cockroaches and the grounds to squatters. It was set in a Hindu district but on the edge of the Muslim slum of Miabagan, which had just been the scene of Hindu raids and a massacre by Hindus with homemade grenades and Sten guns. There was, Payne says, no one left alive in Miabagan.

The house stood on its own grounds, but open on all sides and surrounded by a sea of mud, damp and evil-smelling. Three rooms had been set aside for Gandhi. So much bleaching powder had been poured on the floors that everyone was in danger of asphyxiation. There was only one latrine to be used by the inhabitants, the police, the visitors, and the crowds.

A crowd greeted Gandhi with cries of traitor and a shower of bottles and stones. The Hindus accused him of defending only the Muslims. "You wish to do me ill and so I am coming to you," he said. And when Suhrawardy joined him there, there was a barrage of rocks thrown at the house. The house was in effect under siege. Those inside heard the breaking of glass mix with the shouts from outside. Some of the youths tried to climb in the window.

The forces of violence and nonviolence were in direct confrontation. There was, in rational terms, no new message for Gandhi to deliver, no arguments that his enemies had not heard a thousand times. Among the things they were enraged about was the message of peace itself—they were against Gandhi as well as the Muslims. It was up to him to somehow produce a shift in the precarious psychological balance in the city, beginning with the balance between himself and those who came to him, even though the latter came more than half intending to throw stones to cause his death, at least symbolically. If their minds shifted from violence to repentance, such a shift might then spread out to a larger group, and from them to enough more groups to provoke a mass movement. To make that happen, and immediately rather than gradually, was his only hope, implausible as it was.

When he received the rioters that first evening his declarations were negative: "You want to force me to leave this place. I never submit to force of any kind whatsoever! It is not in my nature. You can stop me doing my work, you can imprison me if you like, or kill me, I shall not call in the help of the military or pray to be spared!"

They accused him of being anti-Hindu, and he replied, "How can I, who am a Hindu by birth, a Hindu by deed, a Hindu of the Hindus in my way of living, be an enemy of the Hindus?" Of course there were plenty of answers to that; but there was a kind of power to it, too, when uttered by this man in this situation. When he was exhausted, they fell quiet, and eventually withdrew and dispersed; later one of the rioters said (or so we are told), "The old man is a wizard—everyone is won over by him."

Meanwhile, in Lahore in the Punjab, Hindus and Sikhs were isolated in the Old City and water supplies were cut off; women and children coming out with pails were butchered; geysers of sparks arose from blazes in six places. And in Amritsar, nearby, the Number Ten Down Express came in on Independence Day with nothing aboard but murdered bodies and the sign: "This is our Independence Day gift to Nehru and Patel." Calcutta should, by every calculation, have been worse, but by August 15 it was peaceful.

The day before, a procession of roughly five thousand Hindus and five thousand Muslims marched together through the city. There were after all plenty of people there who not only wanted peace but were willing to take risks to achieve it; it was Gandhi's task to ignite the lamp that would draw them out of hiding. Then a band of girls, both Muslim and Hindu, had walked through the city at night to come to Gandhi in the dawn to take darshan from him. That afternoon thirty thousand people attended his prayer meeting. The other side to the hysterical lust for violence in the air was terror at what they were themselves doing, and a readiness for grief and self-accusation. When Suhrawardy spoke to an angry Hindu crowd and admitted his responsibility for the Direct Action Day massacres, their mood reversed itself and they cheered him. He and Gandhi toured the city side by side in a car, and there were cries of "Gandhiji, you have saved us." Later crowds of up to a million assembled for his prayer meetings.

Knowing how unstable the situation was, he remained in the city, afraid to leave for fear of what might happen. And on August 31, Hindu Mashasabha youths brought him a bandaged man whom they claimed had been attacked by Muslims, and demanded from Gandhi the lives of all the Muslims in his house. (The story turned out to be a lie.) He was in effect alone. Suhrawardy, and his confidants, Pyarelal and Nirmal Bose, had left the house to make arrangements for Gandhi's continued journey to Noakhali. The youths forced their way inside. Then a large group gathered in the compound, shouting and jeering in a suicide gesture, himself among them. The atmosphere of violence was infecting him. Someone swung a lathi at him but missed;

a brick presumably aimed at him struck a Muslim standing next to him.

On September 1 there were more riots staged by the Hindu Mahasabha, the force that a few months later arranged to assassinate Gandhi in Delhi. Hindus led by RSS men (men of the Rashtra Swayamsevak Sangh, a branch of the Mahasabha party) attacked the Muslim slums, and a truckload of poor Muslims was blown up with grenades on Beliaghata Road. Gandhi arranged to get them to safety, and he went to the site minutes after the incident occurred. A crowd of Hindus offered to protect the Muslims, but with guns and bombs, because "we do not understand nonviolence." In what was surely a sign of his despair, Gandhi sent them a message that he was with them, for even he could not find an effective form of nonviolent action.

That night he decided to fast to death unless the communal leaders swore to prevent any more violence. He swallowed only water and bicarbonate of soda, and since he weighed only about 110 pounds to begin with, the effect of the fast was immediately drastic. The next morning he was missing one heartbeat in four, and his voice was reduced to a whisper. Almost immediately there was a political effect. A band of twenty-seven goondas (hoodlums) came to beg his forgiveness; then those responsible for the grenade attack brought him their weapons and asked for punishment. He sent them to live in a Muslim quarter, to take up its defense.

Amiya Chakravarty recounts the general feeling in Calcutta then in his *A Saint at Work*. He says that most Calcuttans' reaction to the fast was to find the idea remote, irrelevant or unreasonable. "[But] even while repudiating his method and its efficacy, the one question in people's minds would be, 'How is Gandhiji?' People would begin to feel uncomfortable: the grocer's boy, the rickshaw-puller, the office clerk, the school and college students would scan the new columns early in the morning and listen to the radio throughout the day and feel more and more personally *involved* in the situation." Chakravarty remembers how university students would come and ask to be excused from attending their classes because they felt disturbed and did not know what to do. And why?" "They would say that though they did not believe in such methods and in the philosophy behind it all, one thing struck them as curious; after all, if anybody had to suffer for the continued killing and betrayal in the city, it was not Gandhiji. He had taken no part in it. So, while others were engaged in crime, it was he who had to suffer like this. They felt awkward and some wanted to stop his suffering, and even gathered together weapons from streets and homes at great personal risk; they wanted to return them to Gandhiji." When men came home from work and were served their meal, they would find that the women had not eaten anything all day, lacking appetite. Restaurants and amusement centers did little business. So the feeling spread, and gradually took effect. A different kind of moral realism made itself felt.

The communal leaders worked out a joint declaration and on September 4 he broke his fast. Suhrawardy knelt at his feet, weeping, to offer him the first drink of lemon juice. They were all, for the moment, transported into another world—Gandhi's. This was New Age reality. And there was no more major violence in Calcutta.

Rajagopalachari said, "Gandhi has achieved many things, but there has been nothing, not even independence, which is so truly wonderful as his victory over evil in Calcutta." And Mountbatten wrote Gandhi, "In the Punjab we have 55,000 soldiers and large-scale rioting in our hands. In Bengal, our force consists of one, and there is no rioting. . . . [I] pay tribute to my One Man Boundary Force." Of course there was a profound difference between any literal Boundary Force and what Gandhi had done. But this is an example of not just Mountbatten, but history itself, making a pun on the idea of force—material and spiritual.

To call this a miracle is to use religious language, and thus—from the point of view of the systematic mind—legendary and childlike language. To both the authoritarian and the systematic mind it seems unrealistic. And, of course, those events could be described and analyzed in a different way that would secularize and desacralize them, and flatten out the New Age dimension. But the Calcutta Miracle was the sort of event that the New Age promises is possible.

CHAPTER NINE

Our Own New Age

> How do they recognize each other? Not always by beards,
> long hair, bare feet or beads. The signal is a bright and ten-
> der look; calmness and gentleness, freshness and ease of
> manner. Men, women, and children—all of whom together
> hope to follow the timeless path of love and wisdom, in af-
> fectionate company with the sky, winds, clouds, trees, wa-
> ters, animals and grasses—this is the tribe.
>
> Gary Snyder

Today the phrase "New Age" is one we are all familiar with, even
those of us who have never focused much attention on it. In novels,
on the screen, in newspaper articles and photographs, in conversations, serious and satirical, New Age is one of our categories of human
behavior.

Primarily, perhaps, we associate it with a kind of music, sixties
love-ins, long skirts and long, center-parted hair; with a low voice,
slow speech, and eyes that have known ecstasy; or with UFOs, psy-
chics bending metal bars, non-scientific medicine, gurus, ideas about
"self-realization," holistic food and holistic therapy; or simply with
stores that sell crystals, candles, incense, Tarot cards; perhaps above
all with "spirituality"—sometimes of a kind promoted by the established Christian churches, but much more often not.

In his "Why Tribe," Gary Snyder's is the voice of faith. Though
we owe it to the people of the "tribe" to listen to their best voice, we
owe it to ourselves to survey the phenomena more skeptically before
we make our own act of faith.

213

SHIRLEY MACLAINE

Perhaps the individual most widely though incongruously associated with this spirituality is the singer/dancer/comedian Shirley MacLaine because of her six very popular volumes of autobiography. These must have ensured that most readers at least know something about the range of ideas—supernatural, metaphysical, therapeutic, Orientalist, psychic—associated with the term "New Age." Her third volume, *Out on a Limb*, in 1983 lasted fifteen weeks on the *New York Times* best-seller list in its hardback edition, another ten in its paperback edition. Two million copies were sold and it was translated into thirteen languages. Later a TV mini-series based on that book put all of the volumes published up to then back on those lists again.

The fourth volume, *Dancing in the Light*, was on the hardcover best-seller list for thirty-one weeks in 1985. This installment took its epigraph from *The Dancing Wu-Li Masters*, Gary Zukav's attempt to link modern physics to Oriental philosophy, which represents another of the tendencies of New Age thinking. And following on the books, besides the mini-series mentioned, there were video presentations ("Shirley MacLaine's Inner Workout") and seminars.

The process by which MacLaine arrived at New Age spirituality was in many ways typical for her generation in America. Her youth was spent in show business and then her attention was attracted to politics in the 1960s. She played a prominent part in the McGovern campaign and made a trip to Communist China. And then, changing again—and making the same change as many other people—she began her exploration of "spirituality" that had its own elements of show business.

What, judging by the books, did this spirituality mean to her? It meant the practice of yoga, the chanting of mantras, the breathing of seawater, holistic medicine, crystals kept on all four corners of her bath. Trances and trance channelers, intimations of reincarnation and karma. Wisdom gained from spiritual entities and extraterrestrial beings—who were sometimes also available for sex. She learned that this is the Age of Aquarius, when the Yin, or female, energies emerge to displace those of the masculine Yang. She made journeys to the sources of Oriental and Native American mysticism—to the Himalayas and the Andes. She was told that she had been incarnated twice before as a man, and once before as a woman.

But this mysticism also managed to include a summary of Western science and philosophy, edited to become propaganda for supernaturalism. MacLaine's language in recounting her experience was often scientific, or quasi-scientific, referring to forces and vibrations and electromagnetism. Moreover, she traveled everywhere with a bagful of books—each one full of deep concepts and long words, including titles and authors of the best-accredited kind.

There is no point in my trying to report all this without striking any note of irony. That would be carrying decorum too far altogether. But my irony has no destructive intent. This philosophy is not the traditional balloon of hot air into which the pinprick of humor would let in some common sense. One of the key aspects of MacLaine's narrative is that it blends the implausible, the implicitly preposterous, with the most commonsense voice imaginable: "Look, these are the facts: how else ya gonna explain them?"

This is the voice of small-town Main Street America, of a plucky, spunky philistine averageness, dabbling, as Main Street America so often has dabbled, in the occult. It is the voice of the heroine in a 1950s musical—Little Annie Oakley, or Nurse Nellie Forbush in *South Pacific*. MacLaine is an excellent actor, and two of the traits she projects most forcibly are shrewdness and skepticism. Between the lines she writes about karma and metempsychosis she seems to be humming that she's as corny as Kansas in August—she's only a cockeyed optimist. Told what Einstein said about energy, or Kant said about morality, she replies, "Jesus, you mean *those* guys believed in this whaddya call it?" And between the bouts of spirituality come reassuring bouts of sex—with a Prominent Unnamed Politician—with MacLaine no doubt singing "I'm gonna wash that Karma outa my hair."

There may be reasons to be indignant about the huge amounts of money Miss MacLaine made out of these books, and about the power exerted by some New Age gurus over the credulous, and even about the political implications of the doctrine. The New Age in which she participates certainly is a very widespread commercial and educational enterprise, publishing many advertisement-stuffed quarterlies, some ordinarily priced, others given away free because they attract enough advertising revenue to support themselves, in food stores and Laundromats and incense-and-Tarot emporia. And every season there are innumerable courses, seminars, and international tours ("See Magical Britain") to take, on which quite a lot of money can be spent. The two-week tour of Magical Britain is advertised at $2,750 per person, double occupancy.

As for the political argument, in *Women of Power* Monica Sjoo has written a denunciation of this New Age, feeling she has been personally victimized by it: her attack focuses on one particular section of the movement in California, called Rebirthing, which she calls dangerous, mercenary, irresponsible, reactionary, and patriarchal. The New Age, she says, teaches that homosexuality is evil; takes no account of collective karma (political phenomena like imperialism); recommends money as another form of spiritual energy that one will naturally try to attract to oneself, and generally reinforces some of the worst features of contemporary white culture. The New Age speaks, for instance, of battles between the Light and the Dark, the good and the bad, while Sjoo espouses the dark and Africa, and declares that it is not sunlight of which we are starved but moonlight, which would feed our left brain. She herself belongs to the Goddess movement. As this suggests, there is much that Sjoo offers us as opposing the New Age that we ourselves might call New Age.

Similarly, Matthew Fox, in *The Coming of the Cosmic Christ*, attacks what he calls the New Age for its "pseudo-mysticism," for encouraging its believers to investigate their "past life experiences." But the Creation Theology he speaks for is a Catholic version of the New Age, and his sets of concepts and spiritual practices have, by orthodox criteria, a hectic "pseudomystical" temperature, a religious low fever.

There is an understandable tendency for the respectable leaders of the movement to repudiate the term. But some of them acknowledge it. John Todd (of New Alchemy Farm) describes an interesting alternative to property, an idea of "the stewardship of the land" as something to be found in many New Age communities." Indeed it is impossible to describe the contemporary scene without using the term, and to use it only pejoratively is to insult our own naïveté—which can be our best self, as I have shown.

Therefore it is my feeling that the movement should not repudiate the term because no other suits so many groups and assimilates them to each other; and because that multiplicity, and the implied mutual alliance, is most important to the movement. But the point is not purely tactical. New Age is a true name for the movement—true to its intentions and its character. Perhaps, like the Grail or the Flag or the Name of God, "the New Age" is too potent a symbol for its members either to invoke promiscuously or to repudiate.

OTHER NEW AGES

Clearly, however, we do need to distinguish the narrower meanings of the term today from the broader ones. In its narrower sense (the occultist and "spiritual") this New Age is not something I can take seriously, or can meet seriously on the terms on which it offers itself. So far I have felt my audience as people less sympathetic than I to the movement; here I must address myself to the opposite group who will be offended by my skepticism. I need (perhaps it is my limitation) to hear an unmistakably clear and serious voice. In in its broader sense, on the other hand, though the term's reference is strikingly multifarious and centrifugal, it *includes* exactly such a voice—the one I associate with Gary Snyder. Make that meaning central, and the concept of New Age could become a powerful and valuable cultural dynamism.

To take an example of another—opposite to occultist—edge of this amoebic phenomenon, the New Age's profile could be legitimately drawn in terms of Rachel Carson and those of her successors who have called attention to the poisoning of the planet—the ecology movement. Carson's studies of the sea are full of scientific analysis, and not at all occultist or obscurantist, but in some "lyrical" aspects of their form—like the line drawings with which the pages are decorated—they initiate an idiosyncratic form of discourse that we recognize as not mainstream.

This idiosyncrasy is developed further in, for instance, Brian Swimme's *The Universe Is a Green Dragon*, which is New Age in style, form, and format. (It was published by Bear, a New Age house in Santa Fe.) The cover photographs are of the Orion nebula, the type is large, and the margins are wide, as in books for children. The intellectual form is a dialogue, rather like Gandhi's *Hind Swaraj*, between "Youth" and "Thomas," a figure based on New Age spokesperson Father Thomas Berry. And the style is dominated by metaphors of fire, and dance, and splendor; enchantment, destiny, stars; even allurement and perdurance—a crossing, one might say (in a sour mood) of Arthurian fantasy and Tin Pan Alley.

We find drawings like Carson's again in John Hanson Mitchell's *Ceremonial Time*, an engaging account of—to cite his subtitle— "Fifteen Thousand Years on One Square Mile." Mitchell evokes the legendary, even the supernatural, and is bold in imagining the immense temporal perspectives of this new imaginative mode. "On summer nights in the lower fields near Beaver Brook, I can hear the intense energy of the Carboniferous period in the call of the katydids, cone-headed grasshoppers, and snowy tree crickets. I can hear the Jurassic in the caterwauling of the great horned owls; and in winter, in the darkline of hills beyond the icy marsh, in the spare spruce-dotted bogs, I can sense something of the lifeless, barren landscape of the glacial Pleistocene." By implication this ecological discourse speaks for both the Jungian and the scientific wings of the New Age.

The various ecology movements, practical and imaginary, give me my major clues to what I *can* take seriously in the modern New Age; I shall be giving that my best attention later. For the moment, however, I want to look at the rather shapeless form of the movement as a whole.

In order to add up to a powerful force, an alternative to the established authority it opposes, the movement has periodically made an effort to bring its different parts together. For instance, the famous Be-In at the San Francisco Golden Gate Park, on January 14, 1967, was advertised as bringing together Timothy Leary and Mario Savio (the prophet of drugs and the leader of political protest), Allen Ginsberg and Jack Weinberg—which mythically meant, the San Francisco *Oracle* suggested, to bring together Lao-Tzu and Spartacus.

It was a gathering of the tribes—meaning both the neighborhoods of San Francisco and all the world's tribal peoples. There were two posters, based on photographs, one of a Shaivite sadhu, with matted hair and beard and ashes, the other of a Plains Indian on horseback, his carbine replaced by a guitar.

Gary Snyder, who describes those posters as emblems of worldwide tribalism, believes in a Great Subculture which may go back as far as the late Paleolithic age—beginning with Paleo-Siberian shamanism and the first cave paintings, forming a tradition of shamans, yogis, and the great goddess. In opposition to this stand, as well as the armies of Philistia, those of High Culture, at least insofar as the latter are disciplined by the systematic and the authoritarian minds.

That opposition is covert though relentless, but an openly aggressive attack has been mounted by quite a different enemy, the born-again Christian Evangelicals. One example of this is Randall Baer's *Inside the New Age Nightmare*, published by Huntington House, in Lafayette, Louisiana. (Mr. Baer is a former adherent of the movement who was converted to Evangelical Christianity by Pat Robertson.) "Essentially, [the New Age] is a Satan-controlled, modern-day mass revival of occult-based philosophies and practices in both obvious and cleverly disguised forms. [He presents it as an acute moral and cultural danger.] . . . Over the last three decades, however, an enormous and unprecedented massive revival of occult-based practices has been taking place."

Baer quotes some striking statistics in support of his claim: for instance, that (according to a University of Chicago poll) 42 percent of Americans believe they have been in contact with the dead; that 23 percent believe in reincarnation; that forty million of them believe in astrology; that (according to *Forbes Magazine*) the New Age market does $3.43 billion in annual business; that New Age books alone sell for $1 billion a year; that fifty-two publishing houses have formed a New Age Publishing and Retail Alliance whose slogan is "A Consciousness Whose Time Has Come." Professor Carl Raschke of the University of Denver says the movement—a rejection of Judeo-Christian values—is the most powerful social force in the country.

This is not the place to counter Mr. Baer's charges, but it can be said that the New Age's occultism does not often seem "Satan-controlled," however uncomfortable one may be with it. One innocent example of what we might call occultism—or perhaps something parallel to it—would be the Orientalism already discussed.

Harvey Cox's *Turning East*, which gave us a narrative and autobiographical investigation of that, is an interpretation more to be trusted than Mr. Baer's. Cox has long been an ambassador between the New Age and traditional religion, moving from the latter toward the former and back. In a previous book, *The Seduction of the Spirit*, he described going to the Esalen Institution at Big Sur. The occasion was a coming together of Church Christianity and the Human Potential Movement. Cox went as a representative of orthodox, though liberal and experimental, Christianity. He and Bishop James Pike met Allen Ginsberg and Gary Snyder there. He joined in the group bathing in sulphur baths, which was a semi-scandalous feature of the liberation experience offered at Big Sur. Cox is an example of the second mentality confronting the New Age openly, whereas Baer seems to belong rather to the authoritarian type.

In his attack on the movement, Baer quotes with approval from his colleague Dave Hunt's *America: The Sorcerer's Apprentice*: "Even as the scientific and technological advancement which ushered in the space age is accelerating at an exponential rate, we are witnessing far and away the greatest occult explosion of all time." In this admonishment we find an infrequent coming together of the Evangelicals and the Old Left, for Hunt argues that the last such revival of occultism prepared the way for Hitler and the Nazi rise to power. But the Bible as much as German history warns us against the occult—"For false Christs and false prophets will arise. . . ." (Matt. 24:24)

Despite one's distrust of such allegations, however, the suspicion of evil does hang about some versions of the occultist New Age, like an ambiguous stain or a sulphurous smell. No account of the movement would be complete without an allusion to it. A more factual and mainstream press version of the charge is to be found in Steven Levy's book about Ira Einhorn, called *The Unicorn's Secret: Murder in the Age of Aquarius*, because the body of Einhorn's Texan girlfriend was found hidden in a trunk in his apartment. He was one of the circle that chanted a spell to levitate the Pentagon at the famous march in 1967—and like them wore his hair long, in a ponytail, with a thick beard, and a dashiki, long after most of his comrades had reverted to ordinary styles of dress.

Einhorn—who called himself the Unicorn—organized the Earth Week Be-In in Philadelphia in 1970. He was an organizer and presenter of New Age events, like Ginsberg, and like Cox he was a sort of messenger between two worlds, an ambassador from the hippie-world to the world of corporations, acting as a consultant on New Age phenomena both to Pennsylvania Bell Telephone and to the Congressional Clearing-House for the Future. He had survived the sixties

and seemed to prove, in the seventies, the essential moral respectability of the hippie phenomenon; which made the discovery of the
murdered woman's body even more disturbing to New Agers.

We have seen, therefore that as well as comedy there is controversy,
both over what the New Age is, and over whether to welcome or resist
it. This controversy is a feverish and even a large-scale current event,
and is conducted partly in books, although out of sight of most men
and women of letters. (The *non*book aspects of culture are a good deal
more obviously engaged on either one side or the other.) At the back
of Baer's book twenty-one other books like it are listed as attacks on
the New Age, while on the other hand, Bantam lists a series of
forty-one New Age "books to deal with the search for meaning,
growth, and change." And certain California presses, like North
Point, Sierra Club Books, and Harper and Row in San Francisco, have
published predominantly New Age literature. Indeed, as one walks
around bookstores one realizes what an important part of the American book industry this audience constitutes. No doubt the born-again
community supports a lot of publishing, too—though it is books of
the former kind that one is more likely to see around Harvard Square
or Telegraph Avenue.

There are crudities in the typography and the format of the Huntington House books, as well as their literary style, which suggest that
the Evangelicals' bookmakers are less in touch with the best in their
field (and vice versa) than the New Age bookmakers are. The work
of the latter often differs from "regular books" in other ways; they
often lack footnotes and even indexes, and include a list of names,
addresses, even phone numbers; but they are usually brightly colored
and handsomely printed and bound. The Evangelicals' books, on the
other hand, have a homemade look, a small-town sullenness. Between the two, in any case, they challenge the hegemony of "regular
books"; only in a university library is the book reader at all likely to
escape that challenge and sleep the sleep of Reason.

My interest, as I have said, is not to espouse either side of that
controversy, nor to attack the New Age from any other angle implying
either moral or intellectual superiority. The systematic and respectable mind, the critical-contemplative mind, should, more than its

rivals, acknowledge its own limitations and its lack of answers to most questions of crisis. Satisfying answers are unlikely to come from the respectable sources and the disreputable must not be turned away untried.

MARTHA QUEST

Shirley MacLaine with her basketful of highbrow books is after all very like Martha Quest (Doris Lessing's autobiographical character) in *The Four-Gated City*—itself a New Age book, incidentally, which announced Lessing's conversion to Sufi spirituality. And Martha Quest is the nearest thing we have had to a heroine representing the intellectuals of our time. The difference between her and what I called (thinking of myself) the critical-contemplative mind, is certainly to her advantage in many ways.

Yet she conducts her intellectual life rather like Shirley MacLaine. "Somewhere in Martha's life it had been instilled in her, or she knew by instinct, that one should never read anything until one wanted to, learn anything until one needed it. She was in for another of the short intensive periods of reading during which she extracted an essence, a pith, got necessary information, and no more." That could be Shirley MacLaine speaking. So, when Martha Quest feels the need for some new ideas, she puts on her coat and takes two large shopping baskets and goes off, not to the library but to the bookstores.

This clearly represents a deliberate intellectual naïveté in both, a courage and hope, which we have come to recognize as the essence of the New Age. Each hopes to understand all she needs to by using her own wits and running her own risks. One can put the same point negatively, of course—neither hopes to find out anything important by observing the intellectual decorum of the academy. But the positive use of the word "hope" is the important one for us to notice; and the example of the formidable Martha Quest will remind us that it is the *virtue* of hope that is in question, not an individual's natural endowment of sweetness and trust.

Martha Quest, like Shirley MacLaine, conducts her education by going to the stores (not to a library) and plucking off the shelf books that have no context for her—in the sense that academics give to context. That is, the two women don't approach their reading via the

regular scheme of subclassifications, within moral philosophy, physics, economic history, whatever, much less via the state of the art in
each discipline—the interpretations given to each idea by the best
recent critics. They refuse to employ that apparatus, and that refusal
helps make them recognizable as New Agers. Their approach is more
that of the supermarket than the academy. If a book makes a key use
of certain words, which seem to name concepts concerning the reader
at that moment, the latter pops it into her shopping bag, and almost
as quickly builds it into her rhetoric.

People like myself have to remind ourselves that this is not a cat-
egorically bad way to read. (Emerson said he read that way—of
course, the Transcendentalists had some New Age traits.) It is simply
very different from our own way. So, though I cannot disavow my
irony (the acutely felt difference between the two ways to read is part
of my identity), I can disclaim any triumphantist intent to spread it
around or to reinforce it in others.

NEW AGE LANDSCAPES

However, Shirley MacLaine's spirituality is only one, and after all
minor, aspect of the New Age today. Another, more sociological or
political way to locate the New Age is to think of the society or the
forms of social life that surround our great universities either in college towns or in city areas like Harvard Square or Telegraph Avenue,
Berkeley. I find the following evocation of the latter in a book of
1990, an evocation written simply to amuse, but good enough for my
purposes. "Many Berkeleyans had come to town as students. Caught
by political awareness, social concern, or artistic aspiration, combined
with disdain for material possessions, they had stayed. . . . [Some are
students, some are minor faculty—composition teachers, lab
assistants—but the majority have simply camped or squatted in the
groves of academe, claiming a space there as theirs. Their life-style
the author calls the Berkeley syndrome.] They worked twenty hours
a week to pay the rent, but they knew they were not insurance or real
estate agents; they were union organizers or metal sculptors. . . .

"Although it was Friday, on the Avenue it looked like a Saturday.
Street artists lined the three blocks between here and the Cal campus, a veritable convention of syndromees . . . displays of mushroom-

shaped candles, beaded earrings, or a table of T-shirts with maps of Ireland, the Tarot magician, the periodic table. . . . Tie-dyed T-shirts, dresses, shorts, tights, tablecloths. The entire length of the street could have been carpeted in the tie-dyed clothing hanging from the display-racks beside it."

This is a scene so familiar to me I scarcely notice it, much less think about it. But this is the background whence a New Age emerges; if you like, it is the New Age in its fallow phase, waiting to be activated. And campus people, even undergraduates, even those with right-wing opinions, tend to dress like New Agers. They set off across campus, from dorm to lab, booted and backpacked, as if across the Himalayas. And their manners imply that, coming from who knows whence and going who knows whither, they are hailing each other on some symbolic shore or mountain. Some of them in fact watch each other like hawks and know exactly how many points each has already scored in the career Olympics, but they talk like pioneers on some Appalachian trail. In such rituals and costumes the sources and re-sources of the New Age lie banked.

For an example of that background activated, emerged, or taking political form, one might look at Norman Mailer's description of the 1967 March on the Pentagon or at Doris Lessing's description of the 1960 Aldermaston March for peace and against nuclear power. In *The Four-Gated City*, "From above, television helicopters had seen in England's hedgy landscape a moving column of little people five miles long. . . . [They moved from Aldermaston, the nuclear power station, to Trafalgar Square in London, once every year.] Meanwhile the banners were those to be seen at any demonstration: C.N.D. . . . Peace . . . Labor . . . Trade Union . . . Youth . . . Young . . . Jewish . . . German . . . French . . . Trotskyite . . . Anarchist . . . And then the theatre groups, the bands, and the dancers and singers." It was, Lessing says, as if socialism had decided to have a carnival.

But she also describes—looking at the march from another angle—a girl wheeling a baby and carrying a placard with the legend "Caroline Says No"—no to nuclear war. We are ready to say, at least silently, "Who's Caroline? Who's going to care what *she* thinks?," but then we check ourselves. As Lessing points out, the March was a demonstra-tion of faith, many thousands strong, that the individual protest did matter: that, too, is New Age.

In *The Armies of the Night*, Mailer describes how a literal trumpet called the protestors to engage in symbolic battle at the Pentagon in 1967. There were people of many social kinds but among them were New Agers, whom he calls hippies. They were the ones with whom Mailer had most sympathy: "The hippies were there in great number, perambulating down the hill, many dressed like the legions of Sgt. Pepper's Band, some were gotten up like Arab sheikhs, or in Park Avenue doormen's greatcoats, others like Rogers and Clark of the West, Wyatt Earp, Kit Carson, Daniel Boone in buckskin, some had grown mustaches to look like *Have Gun, Will Travel*—Paladin's surrogate was here!—and wild Indians with feathers, a hippie gotten up like Batman, another like Claude Rains in *The Invisible Man*—his face wrapped in a turban of bandages and he wore a black satin top hat." Costume is nearly always the livery of the New Age (even Gandhi in his loincloth and Tolstoy in his peasant blouse), and in that carnival of revolution it was an important part of the action.

Shirley MacLaine, Telegraph Avenue, Harvey Cox at Esalen, *Silent Spring*, the Demonstration at the Pentagon; these are disparate phenomena but also aspects of the same thing. For many people, there was much that was absurd but also much that was hopeful in that thing.

Nor should we assign those hopes all to the sixties. In 1980 there was a conference called "Women and Life on Earth: Ecofeminism in the '80s," at the University of Massachusetts/Amherst, the opening statement of which was coauthored by Grace Paley and Ynestra King. In the same year Sun Bear held the first of his Medical Wheel gatherings near Mount Rainier; the half-Indian Sun Bear has founded a Bear Tribe Medicine Society with sweat lodge ceremonies. In 1982 the Church of the Earth Nation launched its publication, *Earth Nation Sunrise*, in Nashville, Tennessee, declaring that whole kingdoms already live in peace—the planted kingdom, the swimmers, the crawlers, the flyers—and that humans could do the same. And in 1984 Green politics was launched in this country at a conference at Macalester College in St. Paul, setting up Committees of Correspondence, like those of the eighteenth century New Age.

What concerns me is to redefine our New Age, to realign it with its historical precursors, and thereby to claim new contemporary representatives for it. It was not Shirley MacLaine, nor 1960s hippies, nor their gurus that drew me to the subject, but other, quite different figures, ideas, and modes of action that should be associated with that phrase. I have claimed that to rearrange our categories in that way could significantly energize our minds. It is, therefore, Gary Snyder's New Age that I must now argue is one for us to concentrate our attention on.

Gary Snyder's California

> I pledge allegiance to the soil
> of Turtle Island.
> One ecosystem
> in diversity
> under the sun.
> With joyful interpenetration for all.
>
> Gary Snyder

SNYDER HIMSELF

Wanting to put Snyder side by side visually with New Age figures of the past (the pictorial is always a help to concentration), we are lucky to find a kind of fictional snapshot of Snyder in the comic-and-serious description of him given by Jack Kerouac in *The Dharma Bums* back in 1958. The novel is a *roman à clef*, and Gary Snyder appears as Japhy Ryder, a sort of hero to the writer. (It is remarkable how many of Snyder's current circle of friends had read Kerouac's book before they met Snyder, and came looking for Japhy Ryder.)

Kerouac's narrator first sees the five-foot-seven Snyder "loping along in that curious long stride of the mountain climber, with a small knapsack on his back. . . . He wore a little goatee, strangely Oriental-looking with his somewhat slanted green eyes." He had on rough workingmen's clothes, bought secondhand from Goodwill, and a feathered green Alpine hat for climbing.

One of Snyder's boyhood friends remembers him dressing in just that style (Wobbly-stylish) in high school: lederhosen, moccasins, and a Robin Hood hat. As this informant says, that was pretty eccentric for an American high school in the 1940s.

Kerouac continues: "His face was a mask of woeful bone, but his eyes twinkled like the eyes of old giggling sages of China, over that little goatee, to offset the rough look of his handsome face." Ryder takes Kerouac and another man mountain-climbing.

He is the leader of the climbing group by natural right, and Snyder is presented explicitly—even then—as a hero. The Allen Ginsberg character in the novel calls him "a great new hero of American culture" and Kerouac says, "His voice was deep and resonant and some how brave, like the voice of oldtime American heroes and orators. Something earnest and strong and humanly helpful I liked about him." It seems clear that Kerouac and Ginsberg recognized the important thing in Snyder back in the early 1950s.

He was, of course, at that time one of the Zen lunatics, involved with Ginsberg and Kerouac in outraging the bourgeois with many kinds of extravagant and potentially self-destructive behavior. But he was also, we see, recognizably a spokesman for an old-fashioned and highly respectable American cultural style. As a boy he wrote letters to congressmen about preserving the environment.

Nowadays, in the commencement address I have already quoted from, he describes himself as a born-again Native American vernacular ecologist. Of the two challenges of our time, the end of the Cold War and the end of nature, the latter, he says, must be met with what he calls a trans-species erotics, which is based on a larger than human metaphysics. What is the world for? "For the marvelous seeing thinking human creature, but *also* and *equally* for the sleeping baby bat hanging in the eaves, or the hummingbird on a courtship dive." That is the heart of the doctrine he now teaches.

As I have mentioned, Snyder was born into the memory of the IWW movement, which was strong in the logging and mining parts of the Northwest. Deploring the impoverishment of our myth culture, he says his grandparents told him no stories but recommended he read Marx. Clearly, therefore, that heritage had its mythical or legendary side, but his parents did not know the trees and the rocks and the animal life they lived amongst.

After school in Portland, however, he went to the YMCA and to the Y mountain camp on Mount St. Helens in the summer. There was a moral and natural mysticism associated with those Y activities. One of his friends remembers when their leader asked the boys what they saw from a high point, and Snyder replied, "It's God, it's all God." The friend wonders now if this was only what Snyder knew the leaders wanted him to say, but if so, this shows even more clearly how much that nature mysticism was in the air. Two of the Y slogans were apparently "Body/Soul/Spirit" and "God first, others second, I third." At sixteen Snyder joined the Mazamas mountaineering club, in the clubhouse of which were pictures and books about mountain-climbing. And he was keen on bird-watching and all the associated wilderness activities.

We must see Snyder as a figure in a landscape. He belongs to the Northwest Coast and the North Pacific Rim. It is a landscape of mountains and forests, a climate of rain and mist, with a vegetable, animal, and geological life that is the main focus of his imaginative work.

Four Friends

Although Snyder is the central modern figure I compare with the representatives of earlier New Ages, I don't want to fit him out with any equivalent for the historical halo inevitably attaching to names like Paine and Gandhi. One's feelings about a contemporary (and more so if he is younger than oneself) are bound to be different. Such feelings, enhaloed, would have a tin-plate, Woolworth's look.

I honor Snyder as an unusually steady light burning among other lights on the North Pacific Rim—steady enough over enough time to make the faith they all share unusually clear and convincing. That is how he wishes to be seen. A recent book about him (*Gary Snyder: Dimensions of a Life*) contains contributions from about seventy-five members of his circle, and the editor tells us that Snyder wanted it to be a book for "the whole circle and period of time." He preferred it to present him as a part and not a leader of a movement.

Thus I want to first describe the group of like-minded contemporaries among whom I situate him. They do not use the term New Age about themselves. They apply it instead to others from whom they want to be distinguished. (Those others are both the occultists and the "cultural optimists," like Marilyn Ferguson and what she calls the Aquarian conspiracy.) I, however, must call them New Agers.

As I have done in discussing the first two New Ages, I shall compare

Snyder with two men and two women whose work to some degree runs parallel with and collaborates with Snyder's. (I then look for representative texts, and finally for his cultural allies, before dealing with him himself.) Pursuing that idea, I find Wendell Berry and Father Thomas Berry among the men, and Denise Levertov and Ursula Le Guin among the women. All four of them, like Snyder, celebrate a materialist religion that is both sensuous and spiritual—a passionate love of the basic materials and conditions of life on earth. In Snyder himself this takes the form of feeling for animals and for the animal in man.

Denise Levertov and Thomas Berry are particularly linked by their interest in Christian spirituality within the more general linkage of radical cultural politics. Levertov has been famous since the beginning of the Vietnam War for her participation in political protests, her antiwar readings, and her treatment of the same topics in her poetry. Berry has become a national name more recently as the concern about ecology has developed. Both are long-term opponents of the use of nuclear weapons, and of nuclear energy generally.

Ursula Le Guin and Wendell Berry stand in some ways closer to Snyder personally, Le Guin sharing with the latter the same landscape and timescape—the Northwest American coast from the immemorial past into the unimaginable future; Berry linked by a personal friendship and an aggressive alliance in defense of the soil. Both of them wrote for *Dimensions of a Life*, and Le Guin contributed a poem, "Naming Gary," which ends with the lines: "This man I call/Bear Walking the Watershed."

She describes him before as:

> a man who knows
> when to take his shoes off.
> He leaves two kinds of tracks
> and they are poems.

It is a sign of this group's heritage from earlier New Ages (from Ascona in particular) that Levertov and Le Guin are influenced by Jungian ideas, and the latter has taught at the San Francisco Jung Institute, together with Snyder. So have James Hillman and Robert Bly, who see culture in comparable terms of myth and nonrationalist mind, in the individual and the group. They are interested in rites and rituals, of the past and present.

It was not a mere accident that the annual Eranos Conferences, where Jungian ideas were developed in disciplines like philosophy, religion, and mythology, were held at Ascona. (It is also a meaningful coincidence that, at the beginning of this century, the California communes had relations with the Swiss ones.) Jung himself and Joseph Campbell were early influences on Snyder. And as the dancers of Ascona "danced the landscape"—that is, having absorbed the line rhythm of hill and slope and cloud and water, they translated that into movement—in just the same way Snyder sings (literally sings) the Panamint mountain range; gazing at it till the pattern of peaks and valleys translates into an up-and-down, to-and-fro rhythm and melody. This direct rooting of art in nature by artists is as distinctive as their rooting it in ritual.

Snyder's circle and idea descend, of course, from the erotic rather than the ascetic New Ages of the past. They do not mention Tolstoy, and though they honor Gandhi, they do not claim him as one of themselves. The sticking point is probably no more Gandhi's actual asceticism than his gentility—an antigenteel stress on rude and hearty physicality is important to Snyder. Gandhi's style was middle-class androgynous, Snyder's is working-class male. Of course, this is a matter of style, and in the substantial matter of nonviolent action, Snyder has aligned himself with the Mahatma more than once.

The four people mentioned represent a wide range of work and achievement, from Le Guin's science fiction, and pagan feel for the Northwest coastland, to Thomas Berry's Riverdale Center for Religious Research; from Levertov's interest in the great mystics of the Christian church to Wendell Berry's love of the farming community he grew up in.

Le Guin's parents, Alfred and Theodora Kroeber, are both names linked to the anthropological study of the California Indian cultures; and most poignantly to the figure of Ishi, the last survivor of the Yahi tribe, who became a personal friend of Alfred Kroeber at the beginning of this century. Their work, and the Indian culture it was devoted to, is reflected in many ways in their daughter's fiction, and Ishi also haunts the Northwest landscape of Snyder's imagination. His son, Kai, tells us that *Ishi, the Last of His Tribe* was one of the family's favorite bedtime reading books.

Levertov's family was equally remarkable in a different way. Her

father was a Russian Jew who became a Christian and then was ordained a priest of the Anglican church, where his special work was
concerned with reuniting Judaism with Christianity, and his intellectual interests were varied. Her mother was devoted to Nature, and
her older sister a fierce radical, so that the poet grew up breathing the
atmosphere of different kinds of radicalism. One parent was related to
a great Hasidic rabbi, the other was descended from a tailor-mystic
called "Angel" Jones.

The obvious connection between these four and Snyder is their
concern for the land, and their radicalized politics. But one can also
claim for all of them a strong loyalty to the best part of the past of
Western civilization.

It is not the same part of the West they embody in each case. I have
pointed to the Christian spiritual element in Levertov and Thomas
Berry, the anti-Christian element in Le Guin and Snyder: there is an
eighteenth-century squire aspect to Wendell Berry, a Wobbly radical
aspect to Snyder; and so on. And those who follow and praise them
tend (legitimately enough) to stress their feeling for *non*-Western
culture. But if one compares all these people with the general intellectual scene today, one finds them standing out as in some sense
traditionalists.

On the radical intellectual scene, many ideas now aggressively alive
are based on a repudiation of the main white or Western tradition,
which seems to many people fatally tainted with imperialism, capitalism or state capitalism, and the patriarchal mode. That tradition is
assumed to be intellectually and morally dead; it is no longer even
denounced, much less defended. Our contemporaries' energy goes
into quarrels between rival reversals of the past, and into witch hunts
within individual reversals, interrogating the various anxious claims to
have slipped the harness of the old. The four I have named are
therefore interesting for their attempts to combine the new with one
or other redeemed form of the traditional.

In Snyder's own case, for instance, it seems clear that despite his
desire for community evolving naturally, without a leader and a center
of authority, he has always been the leader. It also seems likely that
his authority has had a masculinist edge to it. Dale Pendell, one of the
contributors to *Dimensions of a Life*, says Snyder's style "tends towards
the samurai," and not everyone is comfortable with it. Some have said

that the Zen thing was for "Gary and his boys," and that to do it you had to be "tough." Pendell protests that that is unfair, but then concedes that there *was* a hint in the air that "dharma combat" might be decided by pugilism.

This does not make Snyder's preference for community insignificant—much less does it signify falsity—but it illustrates the variety of strengths he draws on, the combination of the old and the new.

TEXTS

Of the two texts I chose to represent the nineteenth-century New Age, by Carpenter and Tolstoy, the latter's *Kingdom of God Is Within You* perhaps finds its most striking modern parallels in the works of Wes Jackson and Wendell Berry.

Altars of Unhewn Stone, by the former, takes its title from Exodus 20:25: after Moses received the Ten Commandments, he was bidden to worship the Lord at altars untouched by human hand or tool. The author takes seriously both that biblical analogy and the whole Judaeo-Christian tradition. He declares that we live in a fallen world and have been given an enormous task: to redeem the evil work of our forefathers. One of his essays is entitled, "Hell Is Now Technologically Feasible."

In his earlier book, *New Roots for Agriculture,* Jackson examined four great historical failures to take heed of the dangers of what we call "development." The first of the four is the failure of prophets in history, and he cites Job, Plato, and Tecumseh as examples. They warned the men of their times about their destruction of the environment, but were ignored. Implicitly, he asked us to align ourselves with those patriarchal figures as their successors.

Jackson reminds us of Tolstoy by his own "prophetic stance," but he is quite different in his line of work. He is the director of the Land Institute in north Kansas, where agricultural research is conducted. The institute has two hundred acres, half of it tilled, the other half unplowed prairie. There are eight scientists there and eight agricultural interns, representing genetics, ecology, entomology, plant pathology, and the humanities. The students work a forty-three week year, and put together information from evolutionary biology, population biology, population genetics, and ecology.

234 PROPHETS OF A NEW AGE

But they believe "There is more to be discovered than invented."
Charles Lindbergh said we must combine the cleverness of science
with the wisdom of nature, but the Land Institute gives precedence
to the latter, and declares that both scientist and artist should subordinate themselves to the larger Creation.

Jackson reminds us of the grave consequences of not just modern
but all till agriculture. He begins his book by describing the Smoky
Hill River, which he sees from his workplace, on one quite ordinary
morning. There having been moderately heavy rain, and the fields
being plowed, the river carried a lot of sediment: good soil being
washed away. Jackson wants a world in which streams would mostly
run clear. He wants to develop a sustainable agriculture, on the model
of the prairie, with its polyculture of perennial grains and grasses.

With the plowing of the prairie, and the creation of the wheatfield,
comes soil erosion; and, in time, more dangerous consequences, like
pesticides, fertilizer, fossil fuel energy; above all, species specialization and impoverishment of the genetic pool. The prairie's economy
counts on species diversity, and genetic diversity within species, to
resist the epidemics periodically caused by insects and pathogens.

But what concerns us most is the moral and imaginative aspect of
this message. And it is no more Jackson's biblical piety than his frank
anger with humanity that aligns him strikingly with Tolstoy. In this
collection, he says that eleven of his essays originated in irrita-
tion, only three in joy. But he makes no apology, because "We all
live in a world of wounds." The gift of denial moreover allows us to
act positively and think creatively. It can supplement the affirmations in what amounts to a religious vocation—to restore this fallen
world.

A similar note of righteous anger is struck by Wendell Berry in
poetry and prose. In *The Country of Marriage* he says:

> And I declare myself free
> from ignorant love. You easy lovers
> and forgivers of mankind, stand back!
> I will love you at a distance,
> and not because you deserve it.
> My love must discriminate
> or fail to bear its weight.

And in "The Return," in *Openings*,

> Who has come and gone,
> leaving scattered here the litter
> that was all he meant?
> My neighbor and brother,
> a violent brainless man
> whom I must intelligently love
> though I do not, or become
> him, as he is.

Berry is our poet of responsibility, the responsibility to conserve our cultural heritage, which includes prominently our participation in nature. He tells us not to take that heritage for granted, or as something given us simply to be altered, by "modern" or "liberal" improvements. Not that he is hostile to everything liberal, but his stress falls on conserving and on tradition. His appreciation of traditional peasant work has been compared with Tolstoy's—what the latter showed, for instance, in his description of Levin's days in the harvest in *Anna Karenina*—and Berry names also personal and family traditions.

Americans have always been moving on, Berry says. They never stayed where they began, or fully intended to be where they were. The traditional communities, from the Indians on, have been America's designated victims of social change. We have lived in or toward the future; letting the old orders of domesticity, respect, deference, and humility fall away. The governing metaphor became the machine. We came to think work beneath human dignity. Among social groups, only the Amish have remained loyal to the values of work; and only they, with their distrust of machinery, have forborne to exert all the powers with which men found themselves endowed. Having the technology to do something has not been, for them, a sufficient reason for doing it. They have renounced the modern, have remained pacifists, have followed traditional agriculture and education, and so on.

Mainstream Americans, on the other hand, have been either exploiters or nurturers, or sometimes both together. Thus today's women's movement arouses Berry's distrust because it urges on men the dignity of nurturing, which is good, but it also urges that women seek equal access to the powers of exploitation.

Like Jackson, Berry talks much of morals and character, nineteenth-century concepts, which are needed to firm up twentieth-century ethics. He thinks in terms of health and disease. Health is rooted in organic wholeness: heal, whole, wholesome, hale, hallow, holy are concepts rooted in each other. Like an Old Testament prophet, he sees in towers (the Tower of Babel and the glass-and-steel skyscraper) danger and the risk of suicide. And he distrusts our passion for the future and for scientific technology. He is for instance opposed to mechanical birth control. He makes several quotations from *That Hideous Strength*, an antifuturist, antiscientist, anti–H. G. Wells novel, by C. S. Lewis, the Anglican conservative.

Berry (though not Snyder) often sounds much like those English conservatives who stayed at home, who grimly watched the emigrants sail west, and those settled settlers who watched the pioneer wagons drive on further west, seeing the recklessness that inspired such people and foreseeing the damage they would do. Such conservatism was a negative but strong force against imperialism. The title essay in Berry's collection goes back to Montaigne for an epigraph about imperialism: "the world is all topsy-turvied, ruined and defaced for the traffick of Pearls and Pepper."

Unsurprisingly, there is also a strong vein of the reactionary in Berry intellectually and aesthetically. He is no New Ager in literary matters. Shelley is an enemy for him; Pope (in the "Essay on Man") is a hero. Reading *Paradise Lost*, he sees Satan as clearly the villain of the story. His essay on "Unspecializing Poetry" finds Auden's poem on Yeats frivolous. It is the sterner poets like Dante and Milton who get things right.

Yet *Standing by Words* (1983) is dedicated to Snyder, and one can in fact see a basis for the two men's mutual respect and liking, even in literary matters, despite Snyder's being a radical experimentalist in many ways. In the essay "The Specialization of Poetry," Berry says that for a statement—such as a poem—to be complete, the speaker must be ready to act on it, to be accountable for it. (Tolstoy made this a literary criterion, it will be remembered.) In modern times, he says, poets have treated all language as arbitrary, in this way and others. Certainly it is the virtue of Berry's own writing, as of Snyder's, to be accountable; and clearly that is not the virtue of post-modernist writing.

If, instead of the pattern represented by Tolstoy's text, one asks for a modern equivalent to Carpenter's *Civilization: Its Cause and Cure* or *Love's Coming of Age*, one might turn to the writing of Native Americans like Paula Gunn Allen. Not that they are saying the same thing as Carpenter did, but their affirmation of the tribal is as central and important as his affirmation of the natural.

Each of these two mind-sets exerts a comparable authority within its congeries of ideas. Many New Age groups compete for the endorsement that it seems only the Native Americans can give. And the stores where you can buy American Indian artifacts, and books like Allen's, also stock some of the things you buy in a health food store. (Both those kinds of stores are vivid expressions of cultural guilt and nostalgia, adapted to the laws of practical commerce.)

In a 1976 issue of *Cross-Currents* entitled "The Good Red Road" we find an essay by Thomas Berry, "The Indian Future," next to an essay by Allen called "The Sacred Hoop." The latter reappears in her book of the same title, published in 1986.

In his essay, Berry says that the various primal peoples must call mainstream Americans back to a more authentic mode of being, and that American Indians have one of the most integral of all traditions of human intimacy with the earth.

Allen declares very sweepingly that there is a fundamental difference between the Native American tribal culture and anything European or Western. "I would caution readers and students of American Indian life and culture to remember that the Indian American does not in any sense function in the same ways or from the same assumptions as Western systems do." Indian tribal life-styles, for instance, are never patriarchal; indeed, they are usually gynocratic. They are thus charged with the dream that inspires many dissidents from the white culture; and though the latter must beware of simply imitating this other culture, they cannot but be fascinated by it. Being women-centered, the American Indians are sexually free, and often honor homosexuals. One often finds, in the tribes, nurturing, pacifist, and passive men and decisive, self-defining women.

Like Snyder, Allen believes in a worldwide "tribal subculture."

(The idea has somewhat different main features, for her.) The American Indians, she says, share features with tribes in Southeast Asia, Melanesia, Micronesia, Polynesia, and Africa. "We share in a world-wide culture that predates Western systems derived from the 'civilization' model." This world-historical scan is an equivalent for Bachofen's theory of a matriarchal and socially organic past, popular in Ascona, for its implicit promise of an innocent and gender-harmonious future. "The overwhelming message of belonging, of enwholement, that characterizes traditional American Indian literature, makes it and the tribes to which it belongs appealing to the American and European mind."

The tribal stories do not celebrate or even value emotion, in the individual sense. Instead they bring the private self into a group harmony with feelings of majesty and reverence. Consequently, Allen says in *Spider Woman's Granddaughters*, the Indian ethos is neither individualistic nor conflict-centered, as the Western ethos is. Thus Indian stories do not need a single hero or a single action. They need instead regularly recurring elements, and a coherence of common understanding. For Native Americans, humans exist in community with all living things, beginning with other humans. Ella Cara Deloria writes that the ultimate aim of Dakota life is to "obey kinship rules"— one must be a good relative. Singularity is antithetical to community. Every other consideration is secondary, including glory and having a good time. To be a good Dakotan is to be humanized, civilized.

This sort of analysis, and its implicit value scheme, is close to Asconan authors' analysis. The sense that American Indians were a cultural model for the West to learn from was developed by theorists in Ascona—a striking fact, since the two places were so far apart in the literal sense. Rudolf Laban has some striking pages on Indian dancing, in his *Ein Leben für Tanz*; and D. H. Lawrence, who counts as an honorary Asconan, has some brilliant essays also on their dance and their culture in general. (Mabel Dodge persuaded him to join her in Taos, New Mexico, because she foresaw he would share her passionate interest in the Pueblo Indians.) C. G. Jung, another Asconan visitor to Taos, was struck by how different Americans were from Europeans, and explained that by a mysterious Indianization of white settlers. Like Lawrence, he said that an alienation from the unconscious lay in wait for imperialists.

OTHER ALLIES

Of the very large number of groups or interests within the larger movement, I will briefly describe two, "sustainable development" and "animal rights," and then give more attention to "creation theology," a kind of ecological spirituality that is significantly like that of Snyder's group, while remaining—to my sense—significantly different.

The relation of the first group to the other two is explained to us by the editors of *In Context*. This journal describes itself as speaking for the Sustainability or Sustainable Development Movement, which seeks to develop sustainable systems, those which renew their own resources, in agriculture, in economics, and in culture at large. *In Context* distinguishes that idea from those of both the New Age Movement (understood in what I have called the narrow sense) and the Ecology Movement.

The crucial difference, according to the journal, is that Sustainability pays attention to systems of an economic kind, while the New Age is predominantly spiritual; and Sustainability concentrates upon *whole* systems, inclusive and reciprocal, while Ecology is interested more simply in the impact of human activities upon the environment. Of course, *In Context* admits, the three are closely connected, and most people would see them as one. By extension, most members of the Sustainability movement are "comfortable with" the idea of spirituality, of which the most favored form is "creation theology."

The word "sustainable" is a very potent one in New Age circles—as potent and as widely used as New Age itself. Charlene Spretnak, in *The Spiritual Dimensions of Green Politics*, asks, "What is sustainable religion?" But for the purposes of this inquiry it is best to restrict the word to its most empirical meaning.

The distinction from New Age, however, usefully points us to the dryer and more rational and empirical vocabulary of these others (which puts them into line with Tolstoy and Gandhi in the previous period). That last connection is generally, if loosely, acknowledged, at least as a heritage. The title of a book advertised in one of the movement magazines is *In the Footsteps of Gandhi*, by Catherine Ingram, which is composed of interviews with a dozen contemporary spiritual social activists; these include Gary Snyder, Archbishop Tutu,

Joan Baez, Joanne Macy, and the Dalai Lama. Moreover, one of the key phrases of that movement, "deep ecology," was coined by Arne Naess, as a contrast to "shallow environmentalism," and Naess is a Norwegian Gandhi scholar. (George Sessions, a student of these matters, says that Naess and Snyder are the two most influential exponents of deep ecology.)

A charismatic leader within the Sustainability movement is Hazel Henderson, who began her career as an activist in the 1960s, when she—then a New York housewife—organized support for a law against air pollution. She subsequently taught herself economics, and is now accepted as an authority in that field. Her book *The Politics of the Solar Age* has been taken as a major text, and was reissued, updated, in 1988. (A comparable figure is Lester Brown, of the Worldwatch Institute, which issues an annual *State of the World Report*. This is now published in twenty languages [*Reader's Digest* comes out in only fifteen].)

Part of Henderson's current work is devising new indicators of country development, to replace those employed in estimating gross national product; hers will include factors like literacy, health, environment quality, biodiversity, and income distribution. She is currently forming a service to supply her indicators in the form of a three-minute TV slot; they will appear first in *World Opinion*, which reaches a million people globally. A report that she and others recently drew up for President Perez of Venezuela was accepted by fifteen nonaligned countries at a conference in Belgrade.

As all this indicates, there are some reasons to regard this branch of the New Age as being already fully established as a powerful propaganda instrument, as much as the more spiritual branches described before, and with a more official audience. Sustainable Development is also established in the academic world as a branch of knowledge, with the advantages and the disadvantages (the imposition of an abstract jargon and elaborate conceptual schemes) that go with such establishment.

Animal rights is another important cause, characterizing our period and distinguishing it from earlier times. This is a classic example of the further extending and liberalizing of the public conscience; perhaps the equivalent in the nineteenth century (though Henry Salt gave animal rights itself some expression then) was the extension of public awareness to the tribal peoples. But animal rights also reflects a modern cult: people today want to come close to animals-in-the-wild—to be in their presence and imbibe something of their being: it is like what Hindus call "taking *darshan* of" a great man. One of the greatest movements of popular thought today is to reject our fathers' idea of nature being red in tooth and claw—replacing it with the idea of nature being green and procreative. We feel that movement as a daily pressure in innumerable television and movie films about animals. Daily, in front of their television sets, millions take *darshan* of animal life in its habitat.

Jane Goodall, one of the leading figures in this movement, published her autobiography in 1990: *Through a Window: My Thirty Years with the Chimpanzees of Gombé*. She is the best known of three women recruited by Louis Leakey, the famous archaeologist-anthropologist, to study the great apes some thirty years ago. He believed that their studies would provide clues to the behavior of the earliest human species, now extinct. Thus the animal rights movement is linked to the extension of our historical time scale and to a change in our ethics—a move to an ethics of species. We are being asked to think in thousands of years and in terms of species.

Goodall's studies of the chimpanzees of Tanzania have indeed taught us much about them, and about how close they are to the human, genetically and behaviorally. The use tools—for instance, wooden probes that attract and trap ants they like to eat. As our cousins, their fate attracts our nostalgia and our ecological guilt, so sensitive today. But she has also shown us that they are not, as had been thought, vegetarian. Indeed, on occasion they plan and carry out murderous wars of conquest—killing the other group's males and appropriating the females and their territory. They win out against baboons because of their "human" willingness to work together, and to share the meat.

These observations are, of course, disconcerting to those softer-hearted members of the New Age who want to see animals as better than ourselves. Goodall's work returns us in part toward the Darwinian image of conflict in nature. But she is primarily concerned with the endangerment of the species, and protests against the use of chimpanzees as laboratory animals. Thus she shares the essentials of the New Age vision. After describing a scene of a family of chimpan-

zees eating together in the forest, she writes, "Everywhere life entwined with life, uniting with death to perpetuate the forest home of
the chimpanzees. An endless cycle, ancient as the first trees. Old
patterns repeated in ways that would always be new. In such a lush
environment lived the chimpanzee-like creatures that became the
first men. Slowly then evolved. . . . Today striding the globe, humans clear the trees, lay waste the land. . . . We believe ourselves
all-powerful. But it is not so."

In this New Age discourse there is often dialectic. One example
was the conflict between Darwinian evolution and our gentler modern
idea. Another has to do with the hunting and killing of one species by
another. In Gary Snyder we find a love of animals that yet extends
into the hunter's feeling for his prey, and even into his sense of his
owing animals his death. He has said that he would like to die by
being killed and eaten by a bear. Clearly this would be merely silly if
it were not deeply felt, and backed up by a whole philosophy. But it
is: a philosophy of life exchange between species.

Several of Snyder's friends have stressed the importance of the
animal to him, and the interpretation of animal and human. Jerome
Rothenberg says that Snyder stares our animal nature in the eye as no
one else has done before. Will Staple says his achievement has been
to bring the nobility of the animal in humans to light. Snyder's sense
of animals can be compared with that, discussed before, found in
Rilke and Lawrence.

Somewhat further out, beyond the animals, are the various
groups—to be found all over the world now—who hug trees. The
symbolism is idealistic and impersonal. But an erotic dimension is
implicit in it as a possibility, as one can see in John Muir's ecstatic
letters about marrying a Sequoia and in D. H. Lawrence's naked
embrace of young fir trees: "The soft sharp boughs beat upon him, as
he moved in keen pangs against them." (This comes from Chapter 8
of *Women in Love*, and it is the Lawrence character, Birkin, who is so
described.) This plant-world eros, however, is probably still eccentric, even for New Agers.

Animal rights and sustainable development are just two of the range
of activities that are in some sense New Age, and potentially protestant and even revolutionary. It is an enormous range, difficult for us
to organize into a unity, but wrong for us to split up into separates.

Some are closely linked to each other. The poets, prophets, and storytellers who most concern me have a message in some ways very like, for instance, the Creation theologians Thomas Berry and Matthew Fox, who deserve some description here. The former's *The Dream of the Earth* was published by the Sierra Club in 1988. It is dedicated to the great red oak under which it was written.

Christianity as these men project it has much in common with the American Zen practiced by Snyder's circle on the San Juan Ridge, said to be Snyder's greatest achievement by some of the contributors to *Dimensions of a Life*. Both are experimental and eclectic religions, taking in religious ideas and forms from all over the globe, and from the past as well as the future. Both are sensual and imaginative celebrations of life.

But we should stress the experimental aspect of such religion, especially in Snyder's case. He has always had a feeling against most forms of Christianity; and some of his friends declare that he is even in Zen a skeptical humanist rather than a believer. As David Padwa puts it, there is a lot of Coyote in him.

The Dream of the Earth's main argument is that Christians need a new story, which means a new cosmology. Our present story is inadequate to our current survival demands. "It's all a question of story. We are in trouble just now because we do not have a good story. We are between stories."

Berry, who is a historian of culture by training, puts our situation into perspective by making a series of comparisons with historical precedents. For instance, St. Augustine wrote *The City of God* in response to the fall of Rome, as a strategy for cultural survival; and Berry is trying to write an equivalent for us today, though it must be significantly different from Augustine's.

A Passionist priest who now describes himself as a geo-logian or eco-theologian, Berry says that Christians must tell the story of Creation if they are to avoid Armageddon. The redemptive focus of Christianity, on individual sin and repentance, especially strong in Protestant Christianity, has done a lot of damage, and is no longer a valid message. It must be replaced or at least balanced by the focus of the New Story, which is about all life on earth, animal and vegetable, and before that, all matter. It is in fact a New Age story.

Berry was head of the Teilhard de Chardin Association before heading the Riverdale Center, and his thinking still bears traces of the concepts in which Teilhard blended Catholic Christianity with Hegel. (Snyder has reservations about Teilhard.) Two of his associates, former members of the Catholic Church now at odds with its authorities, are Matthew Fox, a Dominican, and Fritz Hull, of the Chinook Learning Center.

Berry's moral message is that we must learn to live lightly on the earth. This involves a series of changes in our values, even politically radical values. He calls our traditional economics pathological, and asks us to believe not in democracy but in biocracy. Democracy, he says, has been a conspiracy of men against the natural world; the U.S. Constitution has been a conspiracy against the North American continent. He wants to see bio-regions established, within or across countries, that will be politically self-governing and biologically self-sufficient. Berry argues that such bio-regions will allow for self-propagation, self-nourishment, self-education, self-governance, and so on.

He is respectful of and interested in science and technology in general, but points out kinds which have been or could be destructive. In the life sciences, therefore, biotechnology, for instance, must be counted bad, because each species' biological identity must be held sacred. The richness of our imagination depends on the diversity of species. The animal species awaken us to the deep mysteries of life.

Implicit here are two ethical principles that are importantly innovative. If we think in terms of forty thousand years of human life—and these writers think in even longer stretches—then the whole history of Christianity from its beginning is dwarfed; it begins and ends in the last month or so of the year of our development; some new and powerful ideas must be devised to maintain the plausibility of Christianity's claims to be universal. In the same way, if we now think in terms of species, we cannot give ultimate importance to individuals. The reverence we now feel for the salmon or the bear is not tightly focused upon the individual; "the salmon" does not mean one particular fish, and so neither does "the white man" or "the woman" mean an individual, as a focus of our moral sense. Our old ethics has to change; the life and death of the individual, and even its sufferings and experiences, must be subsumed in that of the group. Berry says we should think of ourselves as species, not as nations.

In what Berry calls normal, premodern, conditions, humans as they develop awaken to an awesome universe filled with mysterious power. For the last two hundred years we have been altering that, desacralizing (and desecrating) the earth, sacralizing instead our own machines and organizations. But now the psychic energies that so long sustained "the industrial illusion" are dissolving in our confrontation with eco-problems. Luckily, new energy is generated and expressed in the more than ten thousand eco-oriented groups in North America.

He quotes Paine's *Common Sense*: "We have it in our power to begin our life over again. . . . The birthday of a New World is at hand." Perhaps surprisingly, Berry seems to recognize a precursor in Paine, as well as in Blake. He proposed, as an organizing mechanism, Green Committees of Correspondence, like those of that earlier New Age—which have been set up.

Very closely aligned with Thomas Berry is Matthew Fox, who published a book called *Original Blessing*, a concept opposed to Original Sin (the modish shift from "negative" to "positive" values is typical) and then in 1981 an anthology called *Western Spirituality: Historical Roots and Ecumenical Routes* (the modish pun is also typical). In the Introduction to the latter he says the book's purpose is to put Westerners in touch with their biblical roots again; the Church has given too much weight to nonbiblical philosophies, like stoicism, gnosticism, and platonism or neo-platonism. The true source of Western spirituality is the Bible.

Fox criticizes Christianity for having changed, as it developed, from being a way of life to being a religion. (This was Tolstoy's criticism in *The Kingdom of God Is Within You*.) Theologians like St. Augustine and Bossuet gave too much power to the motifs of the fall and individual redemption. Alternative theologians like Pelagius, Scotus Erigena and Eckhart have been neglected. So has the whole female gender.

Fox is quite strikingly an ecclesiastical feminist. St. Hildegard of Bingen is one of the saints he most often cites, and he has written a commentary to her *Illuminations*. She was a twelfth-century mystic who recorded her visions in the form of what we now call mandalas.

He tells us she should be read in conjunction with Meister Eckhart, and in the place of Augustine and Aquinas. "I believe it is Hildegard rather than Aquinas who will accomplish this essential task for us [giving the twentieth century a cosmology]. For Hildegard is more steeped in women's wisdom than Aquinas. She gives us not just concepts but ways of healing psyche and cosmos. Art is the way; her mandalas as pictured in this book are ways; her drama, music, poetry, and her implicit invitation to make art our way of passing on a cosmic vision are all ways."

Fox enumerates several gifts that Hildegard offers us: from simply being a woman in patriarchal culture, to bringing together the holy trinity of art, science, and religion. She was prophet as well as mystic, and awakens us to a new, symbolic consciousness, with her mandalas, her poetry, and her music.

Hildegard's work, Fox claims, renders obsolete 99 percent of twentieth-century theological learning (returning us to what I called a naïve Christianity). She saw the world in terms we are only just now discovering—for instance, she invented the word "viriditas," the greening power. (There is now an annual Viriditas lecture at Berkeley, given by Snyder in 1986.) She saw the universe as lying in God's womb and as an egg—matriarchal and imagistic thinking. How unlike Augustine, whose introspective rationalism, and whose human chauvinism, has so dominated religion and culture in the West!

Fox's later book begins with his dream of a matricide, the killing of Mother Earth, and goes on to describe an awakening to mysticism. The connection of matricide and mysticism is both logical and Christian in the new sense. The paschal story of death and resurrection meaningful to *us* is not about the historical Jesus. It tells of the death of the earth, the resurrection of the human psyche, and the coming of the Cosmic Christ—who announces himself in the terms of astronomy and particle physics.

Discussing Hildegard, Fox says: "Today, cosmologist Brian Swimme teaches that the original fireball which began all of creation 20 billion years ago is literally present in our brains when photons go off, and in the process of photosynthesis. . . . In my opinion this synchronicity between a 12th century mystic and a 20th century physicist is one of the obvious examples of how Hildegard did not *know* all that she was saying."

This lavish rhetoric, which is to be found also in Thomas Berry, though somewhat more sober there, and in Brian Swimme himself, where it is even more excited, goes along with some sharp clear thinking. All of these men, and their colleagues, are truly impressive writers. But at times our ear detects the glibness of the seminary in their phrases, while in Gary Snyder we find a language and a thought that is stronger because it seems to be rooted in things and not words.

Praising his friend, the Japanese poet Nanao Sakaki, Snyder says, "His poems were not written by hand or head, but with the feet. These poems have been sat into existence, walked into existence, to be left here as traces of life lived for living—not for intellect or culture. And so the intellect is deep, the culture profound."

The poetic implicit there obviously applies to Snyder's own work; what I call glibness is an enemy he recognizes. In *The Real Work*, he says that his education at Reed College was very intense, and required a subsequent period of de-education (which did not mean a repudiation of what he had learned). After four years of such an intense experience, he says, one must spend another four years coming off it, getting in touch with people and one's body and dirt. Whatever one thinks of that as a general theory of education, in particular relation to him it seems to have worked.

SNYDER'S WORK

> Men who hire men to cut groves,
> Kill snakes, build cities, pave fields,
> Believe in god, but can't
> Believe their own senses
> Let alone Gautama. Let them lie.

Snyder remains the most striking individual case of our New Age, in whom we can see both the central strength of what he himself asserts and its connections to other things. His is a striking case also because we came to know him first in the context of the Beat Generation, which was an epitome of that romantic destructiveness and self-destructiveness on the part of Western artists that has lasted so long. Both in America and in Japan, Snyder seemed unpoetic, as a personality and as a literary voice, for the first years of his career. He was not the *poète maudit* of Symbolism, nor the Eliot/Stevens variant on that.

He was part biker, part working man, part Beatnik. But Snyder was able to survive the Beat phenomenon with a steady persistence, intellectual and moral, that makes him now seem quite unlike his former comrades.

Even if we compare Snyder with other New Age figures today, we shall again be struck by this reliability in him. Though he has reached out for culturally new, and radically exotic, things—for instance, in Zen Buddhism—he has combined that with the traditionally American. He has all the marks of a trained mind and a reading man, while being also a workman, and of the working-class man, using his lewd and laconic language.

Intellectually, he built the violently new into a continuity with the traditionally old from the first. He was able to see, for instance, Antonin Artaud as a trickster antihero, comparable with the trickster Coyote of the Indian stories—and to see William Burroughs, talking out of the side of his mouth, as half Coyote, half Dashiell Hammett. But he was never as self-destructive as either of those two. Though he read de Sade in the 1950s, he reacted strongly against him.

He has seen the need for a new economy and agriculture, a reversal of the frontier mind, but he has also spoken for the frontiersman, and even more *to* him. In *Dharma Bums* "Japhy Ryder" says, "Frontiersmen were always my real heroes and will always be." Perhaps it is most striking that, in the alien atmosphere of the New Age, Snyder has asserted the value of hunting. In fact, however, his way of looking at animal life is compatible with the species ethic mentioned before; as he kills the individual animal he affirms the life of the species.

Two of the central metaphors in his first book, *Myths and Texts* (1960), are logging and hunting, in both of which he was long engaged. The first he came to see as bad, but the second seemed good. "To hunt means to use your body and senses to the fullest." He recommends it as a spiritual discipline—as a form of meditation. To kill and eat what one has hunted is a sacred right, so long as it is done with grace and gratitude. We are ourselves to be consumed: we are part of an exchange of energy. Those who communed with nature, he says, often did so via a being they ate. The other animals we hunt are not our enemies therefore. They admire and love us; indeed that is fundamentally how we know we are beautiful.

Of course, Snyder reacted against much of that American working-class culture he came from, though his reaction was always accompanied by admiration. The usual literature of the American West, he says, is epic or heroic, full of feats of strength (i.e., forms of expansion and exploitation). It could just as well, he says, be an Icelandic or Aryan saga. But "Life in Nature," he says, "is familial and not heroic."

There are times, on the other hand, when he sounds like the Kipling of *The Law of the Jungle*, on the topics of animal life and its relation to our life—the jungle/wilderness has a law that is amoral when judged by purely human criteria, cruel to individuals. Coyote and Ground Squirrel, Snyder says, keep a compact that one is game, the other predator. Elegant forces (forces for us to admire) shape life and the world, and shape every line of our bodies. In "The Place, the Region, and the Commons" (in *The Practice of the Wild*) he describes shifting stream beds and some old men who follow their new courses, talking to them, talk which sounds just like stories in Kipling's *Puck of Pook's Hill*.

Like Jane Goodall and Annie Dillard, but unlike many New Agers devoted to nature, Snyder is ready to see its crueler side. In "Blue Mountains Constantly Walking," he says, "I like to imagine a 'depth ecology' that would go to the dark side of nature. . . . Wild systems . . . can be seen as irrational, moldy, cruel, parasitic. The other side of the 'sacred' is the sight of your beloved in the underworld, dripping with maggots." He distrusts the New Age reluctance to face such facts.

He believes in the value of work and craftsmanship, and his poems about work also sound more like Kipling than almost anyone who has written in between. He often recommends—for writers and for other people—the model of those traditional apprenticeships in which the beginner spent a long time just sharpening and taking care of the tools. This is what Zen was for him, but he also believes in the mastery of master mechanics, even in the literal case of garage workers. Americans have been living in the dream that we are going to get away from work, he says. He will even say that we must work without any hope of doing good—an ascetic note he rarely strikes.

Writing on this topic, he uses the word quality the way that Robert Pirsig does in *Zen and the Art of Motorcycle Maintenance*. "I think that I am second to none in my devotion to Quality; I throw myself at the lotus feet of Quality, and shiver at the least tremor of her crescent moon eyebrow." He says this against those he calls the mandarins of empire-culture. They profess to worry about a decline in intellectual and literary quality, but what they really fear is losing control over the setting of standards—a quite different thing. The concern for quality is one of the things that link Snyder to Wendell Berry.

If we compare Snyder as our representative with those of the past New Ages—for instance, with Paine and Gandhi—we surely find much to congratulate our own period on. Snyder has never played the leading role on a strictly political stage, as they did; we cannot think of him as the leader. But even negatively there is something to be glad of in that, in our escape from competition for the Leader position, while he also escapes the disqualification by human eccentricity or extremism from which Paine and Gandhi suffer to some degree.

All three are writers of manifestos; all three are reductive rationalists, but at the same time men of radical religion. Historically they differ, Paine being a spokesman for, and within, the European Enlightenment, Gandhi for the non-European countries' reaction against the Enlightenment's world spread, and Snyder for our current fear of that triumph's consequences. They have different personal identities: the poet, the mahatma, the revolutionary. And they have chosen different deaths: Snyder choosing the wilderness death, by the bear; Gandhi choosing (this was what he foresaw, from early on) assassination by a fanatic; Paine choosing (though it did not happen) the traitor's death, official execution, on the block or the guillotine.

Snyder's work has not been primarily political, but he *has* a politics. In one essay he says that it derives from the question of what Occidental and industrial civilization is doing to the earth. (The essay is called "The Politics of Ethno-Poetics.") He calls our attention to the unparalleled "waterfall of destruction" of the diversity of cultures and species around us. And on other occasions he will speak, semi-humorously in tone but seriously in substance, of *representing* the forests and the lakes politically.

Moreover, he has in fact taken on literal political-cultural responsibilities, attending regular committee meetings. During Jerry Brown's governorship of California, Snyder was chair of the state arts committee, and often consulted by the governor. He prides himself on showing that his anarchism does not mean a refusal to cooperate and co-work.

The collaboration with Jerry Brown must be symbolically evocative for us. (Snyder having no phone for some years after he went to live on the San Juan Ridge, the governor, when he wanted to consult with him, sent a state trooper on a motorbike up the ridge.) So too was the encounter with Daniel Ellsberg. The two met in Kyoto in 1960. Ellsberg had read *The Dharma Bums*, had but had more recently served in the Marine Corps, and was in Japan researching the mechanisms of official (secret) control over the use of nuclear weapons. Introduced to Gary Snyder, he said, "You're Japhy Ryder. You're the reason I'm in Kyoto." (It is worth noting that Snyder was sitting with a Hell's Angel when they met, in a beer hall.)

They spent the next day together, and argued about pacifism, Snyder for, Ellsberg against, without convincing each other. Ellsberg says Snyder was less than a year the older but he seemed much the senior; "to an extraordinary degree he was in charge of his life." Soon thereafter Ellsberg was sent to Vietnam, where he grew increasingly troubled by the work he was doing. He came to know two people, a woman called Janaki Tschannerl and a man called Randy Kehler, who were Gandhians, and who seemed "a lot like Gary in their way of being." They lent him books by Gandhi (and others) and he was converted to *satyagraha*.

By 1969 Ellsberg had begun copying those secret documents later known as the Pentagon Papers, having resolved to make them public and take the consequences (most likely life imprisonment). Being in California in 1970, he went to see Kehler (already in jail) and Snyder before flying east to face trial.

Such action is the stuff of modern legend, and if Snyder does not act the hero himself in these anecdotes, he does move among a company of heroes and makes their heroism possible.

The heroism, like the whole life-style, seems of a somewhat old-fashioned kind to us today if we have been influenced by current feminism. It seems clear that Snyder, and those most in sympathy with him, are assertively masculine, and that he cannot expect to win the votes of feminists. He has written poems sensitive to women, and he has been as acute as the feminists in his analysis of patriarchalism.

For instance, in "Dharma Queries" in *Earth House Hold*, he talks about the moment when tribes become nations; that, he says, is when the figure of God-in-Heaven comes into being, compounded out of the Pole Star, the War Chief, and the penis-as-weapon.

In important ways, however, his identity is rooted, as he acknowledges, in a phase of American culture that was masculinist and expansionist. For instance, he owns to curiosity as a major motive in his behavior—for instance, in his frequent traveling, to India, to Japan, to Alaska, to Australia. He is aware of the connection between that kind of anthropological curiosity and imperialism in its psychological manifestation. Such curiosity, he says, is a function of an expanding civilization. The opposite (in some sense better) is an uninquisitive respect for other cultures. We, he says, naturally find romantic the story of the 1902 encounter between Alfred Kroeber and the Mojave Indian who recited six full days of his people's narrative, which was thus preserved for anthropologists; but of these two heroes we should learn to focus our admiration on the Indian rather than the professor.

To sum up, Snyder has provided us with a treasury, an armory, of possibilities; of all kinds of work, literary, political, social; all kinds of interest, in agriculture, anthropology, geography, biology. All these things have been investigated for us by a man of intelligence, and the field is open on many sides to all those who can follow him. Whatever our own commitments, we can at least think of his friends and their work as a kind of ashram to which we repair recurrently. And they are the direct heirs of the last New Age.

For without, presumably, knowing anything about Ascona, Snyder is and has been in some sense an Asconan thinker. When he came back to San Francisco and the San Juan Ridge in 1968, he was like all those people who went to Munich and Ascona in, say, 1912. This was his New Age journey, to California. To say that is to reflect how much safer a messiah he has been than, say, Otto Gross. He has espoused some of the bolder thought experiments of his times, but without losing hold of common sense, and was able to pass over into different ideas in time. He has been a hero of the Odysseus kind, a hero of prudence and reason, clever at escaping and surviving, and at finding the golden mean between excesses—between Scylla and Charybdis. He traveled far from home as a young man, and lingered in strange places—like Circe's Island—but finally accomplished his great return, to reestablish himself in the place from which he started.

He has also acquired the sort of power he wants, by building up a community around him. In terms of his poetry, this means that he writes often to and about people and places on the San Juan Ridge. He writes for all his readers, in some sense he writes for the whole word, but more than other poets he writes first of all for his friends and neighbors. This gives his voice a different resonance, and saves it from the pathos of a lost cry in an enormous vacuum.

His Development

"The Revolution in the Revolution in the Revolution"
Among the most ruthlessly exploited classes:
Animals, trees, water, air, grasses.

We must pass through the stage of the
"Dictatorship of the Unconscious" before we can
Hope for the withering away of the states
And finally arrive at true Communionism.

To complete the parallel between our analysis of Snyder and that of Paine and Gandhi, let us follow him through his development, using the clues he has given us. His working-class political family could not help him to understand what was really happening around him, which was nature. The cities not far away from his home were only ghosts to him; it was the landscape that interested him.

He grew up on a small farm in Oregon, with only two acres of pasture, but his father did not know the names of more than fifteen kinds of trees. An old Salishan Indian who came selling salmon represented more of what the boy needed to know. At the age of eight or nine he went out to sleep alone in the woods, and at thirteen he went into the real wilderness.

That enthusiasm is, of course, traditional in American culture for boys; Snyder read Ernest Thompson Seton during his boyhood; and he was remarkable only in carrying that interest over into adult intellectual life. He read John Muir, the hero of preservation in California; indeed, he turned a passage of Muir's prose into verse. Via that line of study he was in touch with Thoreau and Transcendentalist thought.

During the First World War, his mother moved to Portland, into cheap housing built for shipworkers. His father lived in San Francisco, and his mother was a single parent from then on. She was apparently a strict disciplinarian who insisted that he do well at schoolwork.

He studied literature and anthropology at Reed College when he entered it at the age of seventeen in 1947. His honors thesis, on Native American myth, was later published. He lived very frugally, taking his own tea bags to the coffee house, and sleeping next to the furnace in a boarding-house basement. As later, he was the center of a group of admirers and followers.

He heard in college about the convergence of Mahayana Buddhism and Tao in Zen, and that that tradition was still alive in Japan, which he thereupon decided to visit. (At the age of eleven or twelve he had already seen Chinese paintings, which immediately meant much more to him than European art.) Again he was not unique among his friends in this interest in the East; one of his classmates, Philip Whalen, also went to Japan and actually became a Zen priest.

Snyder earned his living in a working-class way (and used a workingman's voice and vocabulary), logging and as a forest lookout. He was fired from the Forestry Service in 1954 for having Communist ideas. In 1955 he met Kerouac and Cassady, and the other Beatniks, and he and Kerouac lived together for a few months. He has described San Francisco in those days (ambivalently) as a small warm moist culture where those writers nourished each other.

He was in his youth an asserter of sensual freedom and a mocker of established middle-class morality. The disciplines of self-restraint seemed to him too easy, as well as self-destructive. Christians and Confucians get very roughly treated in is early poems, but so do even Buddhists.

Among his historical heroes then were the medieval Brotherhood of the Free Spirit, Edenists who met each other in the nude and were supported by the working weavers. Brought before the Church's Inquisition, they were charged with thinking man divine and with holding orgies of free love; that was true religion, as Snyder then conceived it. Nudity became and has remained a part of his own life-style. It has, of course, often been congenial to New Agers. One can think of Blake and Holcroft in the eighteenth century, and in the nineteenth century Gandhi—his self-exposure was of the ascetic and not the erotic kind, but it was a challenging nudity in the eyes of most of his contemporaries.

Snyder was a Orientalist as much as or more than other New Agers. In 1961 he traveled through India with Allen Ginsberg and Peter Orlovsky. He spent altogether about twelve years in the East, and his third wife was Japanese. This was the period of Snyder's life that corresponds to the South African period for Gandhi and the Philadelphia period for Paine. In Japan, besides the experience he had of Zen monastery life, he met a wandering poet who had a strong influence on him. Snyder says that in 1960s a subculture was emerging in Japan, as it was in America, best represented in this man, Nanao Sakaki, who had served in the Japanese navy in the Second World War (he saw on his radar screen the B-29 that carried the nuclear bomb to Nagasaki) and never afterwards "went home."

Sakaki lived under bridges in Tokyo, with beggars and prostitutes, for a few years. He also walked the length of Japan several times, teaching himself English and Greek and classical Chinese in libraries and teachers' houses. (This must remind us of Gusto Graeser in the years after he left Ascona.) Allen Ginsberg met him at the same time as Snyder did, and salutes him as "Brain washed by numerous mountain streams:. . . . Nanao Sakaki's hands are steady, axe and pen sharp as old stars."

Sakaki built junk sculpture on the riverbanks of Tokyo. Dropout students came to talk to him, and he set them disciplinary tasks, like walking and begging. His doctrine was austere. "Don't ever tell me you need anything," was a typical teaching, and "No need to survive." He and his disciples wanted to embrace all the marginal, non-"Japanese" life forms in Japan—from the Malayo-Polynesians in the south to the Gilyaks in the north. They called themselves *buzoku*, the tribe—taking the idea from America. They also applied to themselves Gandhi's name for the Untouchables of India, the Harijans. (Snyder dates his essay about this, "Suwa-no-se Island and the Banyan Ashram," 400067, making the first year that of the first cave paintings.)

Snyder and Sakaki and seven or eight others went to the island of Suwa-no-se, and cut back the bamboo and planted sweet potato here; that was where Snyder married Masa Uehara in 1967. Snyder estimates the group around Sakaki at about ten to twenty on the island, twenty to thirty in the Fujimi Mountain ashram, thirty to forty in Tokyo, and two hundred to three hundred in circulation. More recently, Sakaki has spent a lot of time in this country, and Snyder and he have gone together to Australia to visit aboriginal communities.

Snyder came home from Japan permanently when he saw the early stages of "the sixties" developing in America. Clearly he had always stayed in touch with America, and there were always things about Japan and the Zen monastery life that went against his temperament. He never could "sit" ten hours a day; and he regarded that as elitist even as an ideal—for many were working so that some could sit and meditate. He rode around Japan on his motorbike. And he went on writing poems, which was, according to orthodox Zen discipline, "inexcusable."

Moreover, Snyder believed that celibate monasteries function as a compromise with the state. If the monks had wives and children, they would be a tribe, and would work to transform society. As it is, the monastic orders draw in new men (cultural refugees) each generation. The world religions, he says, have all been complicit with empire. And the East was a lot slower than the West in discovering that history is arbitrary and that societies are only human.

In 1967, at the end of his time in Japan, Snyder had a recorded conversation with the English Benedictine monk Aelred Graham, who had written a book called *Zen Catholicism*, reconciling Zen and other features of youth culture it his own spiritual traditions. It is clear from the transcript that Snyder was suspicious of Dom Aelred's clerical blandness, and rather aggressively insisted on, for instance, the ineluctability of the drug experience (no one should talk about it who hasn't gone through it). He generally refused to reduce beat and hip experience to traditional humanist terms.

More important was his implicit disillusionment with Zen and with Buddhism—because of their political and sexual conservatism. It is clear that Snyder's attention was turning back to America and to what he could do there. The West, he said was now in a spiritual situation— everyone was having to makeup his/her own mind about everything. Asian Buddhists had had no such experience, and neither had old-style American Communists.

He thought that a new, anonymous religion might be coming to birth in America, and new cultural forms. People no longer published books or signed poems. The novel was a dying form. Music was supplanting literature. Religion was supplanting politics. The San Francisco *Oracle*, which sold fifty thousand copies an issue, mixed up every kind of religion, and everyone in that city talked about God, Christ, and Vishnu as interchangeable terms, loving all of them, and the legends and superstitions of those religions as much as their doctrines. The rationalist scruples about traditional theology of religious liberals like Bishop Pike (and Dom Aelred, implicitly) suddenly seemed out of date.

The only religious practice the hippie Americans balked at, Snyder told Dom Aelred, was celibacy. They were completely sexualized. The Japanese, on the other hand, he found asexual; basic sexual problems had not come to public consciousness there (in 1967); there were, for instance, no homosexuals in Japan (though, of course, there are homosexual acts). When Graham spoke of the bourgeois-puritanical strain in American culture, Snyder said that he never met such people: he had lived entirely inside the ten-to-fifteen-thousand-strong society of the turned-on.

"So my spiritual career has been half in the realm of peyote and shamanism, American Indian contacts, nature mysticism, animism, long hair and beads, and the other half concerned with the study of Sanskrit and Chinese and the traditional philosophies of the Orient." Indeed, Snyder has held on to both those halves all his life, though a different one of the two has been dominant at different periods.

As for Zen itself, in "The Zen of Humanity" he says that he has stayed with that religion because the discipline of sitting (doing *zazen*, meditation), boring though it is, is a primary one. It is as primary a human activity as taking naps is for wolves, and soaring in circles is for hawks. Fundamental to Buddhism are the three mysteries, of mind, speech, and body. You work on these by sitting, by singing, and by dancing (or doing yoga). He suggests that the long slow historical periods of peasant and tribal cultures, so uneventful to our minds, are like *zazen*.

He was asked why he had traveled to the East instead of looking for the spiritual nourishment he needed in the Native American traditions. (He has also been accused of the opposite—of exploiting Native American culture.) His reply was that Mahayana Buddhism had a cosmopolitan intellectual tradition that was liberated from tribal or national culture in the narrow sense, whereas to follow the Hopi Way you have to have been born a Hopi.

But like most New Agers, Snyder nevertheless acknowledges that he has learned from the example of the American Indians, who teach us, for instance, how we might survive here at rock bottom. The need to prepare ourselves to survive in minimal conditions is always implicit in what Snyder says. He is certainly not "in love with" the cultures of the Far East. India and China and Japan are as burdensome societies as any others.

He and his friends called themselves Dharma Bums in the 1950s, but more recently he has seen himself and his friends as White Indians—"many of us are again hunters and gatherers." Americans feel a need to be Indian, he says. The American Indian is the vengeful ghost lurking in the back of the troubled American mind. Eating at our hearts, like acid, is our knowledge of what we did to the continent and the American Indian. That need is no doubt another reason why he had to return to this country.

In the middle sixties, together with Allen Ginsberg and Richard Baker, Snyder bought a hundred acres near Nevada City in California, and in 1970 began to build—with the help of friends—the house he called Kitkitdizze, giving it the Maidu name for a low brushwood that grew there. This house has been an important part of his life. David Padwa has said that Snyder lives richly and elegantly, on very little, and that "to visit Kitkitdizze was to attend the home palace of a forest king."

Peter Coyote describes "its sense of unmistakable, timely gravity. The thick, orange clay roof tiles were supported by heavy, hand-hewn lintels and posts." The walls are adobe, the windows have small panes. There is a wood-fired range in the flagstoned kitchen. A central, rectangular room has a fire pit in the middle, and a water kettle hangs over it. Most of its design and accoutrements are therefore traditionally Japanese, but Coyote noted also a Winchester rifle, a bottle of Jack Daniel's, and a Macintosh computer. Snyder has never renounced property, or modern improvements.

Coyote used the past tense in his description because he wanted to describe the impact his first sight of it had on him. He knew of Snyder by repute as a Beat writer, while he himself had become a Digger, and felt that he and his friends had gone far beyond the Beats. They were planning networks of free food and clinics to supply free nomads like themselves, and junk yards to service their old cars, and crash-pads. (Peter Berg is another ex-Digger who has come over to Snyder's community.) But Coyote found what Snyder was building (in the literal sense, his house and later a zendo and a community school-house) persuasive of a different social strategy. On his first visit, the people at Kitkitdizze were naked, and he was struck by their brown skin and clear bright eyes and teeth; Coyote felt his own "grimy, hepatic pallor."

In some ways, obviously, Snyder has accommodated himself to America's householding ways, or always valued them. (Even in *The Dharma Bums*, Japhy Ryder looks forward to a house and family life.) This was true of his literary work, too. He won a Pulitzer Prize in 1970, and was soon thereafter one of the eight to ten American poets who could make a comfortable living by his publications and his public readings. *Turtle Island* (1974) sold seventy thousand copies, an extraordinary number for a book of poetry. At the level of poetry, or myth, what Snyder is saying is widely acceptable to America. He, of course, means it at more levels than "poetry" or "myth," but that is an ordinary difference between a prophet and his/her audience.

His poetic form has often been visionary and ecstatic, as well as humorous and commonsense, and so he has drawn on such precursors as Pound, Williams, and Whitman. (We are especially reminded of Pound by Snyder's eccentric spelling and comic slang.) He has long been at work on an "epic" called "Mountains and Rivers Without End." In *The Dharma Bums* Kerouac said this would be/already was full of information about soil conservation, the TVA, astrology, geol-ogy; those parts that have been published so far confirms this. (This testimony from the past reminds us both of how excellent a reporter Kerouac was and of how steady Snyder's development has been.)

His characteristic stresses in his early work were quite hostile to the ascetic line taken by Gandhi and the late Tolstoy. But Gandhian references do begin to appear during his time in Japan; references to Gandhi's village anarchism, and to nonviolence. And in recent years there are more signs of what might be called conservatism. He has made Wendell Berry into one of his principal allies. He has said he has taken more than his share of drugs, and does not think that it ever helped him to write. He has declared that fasting and solitude are universally parts of the Shaman tradition.

The earlier Snyder, was, of course, very different. Revolution was a word he frequently used to define the movement he belonged to; see "Buddhism and the Coming Revolution" in *Earth House Hold*. He distrusted Christ and self-sacrifice, preferring Buddha, the cynical and round-bellied, who was bisexual and "tried it all." But he has developed in a way that has included more, without becoming just inclusive. (Norman Mailer has also moved from revolutionary to conservative positions, without losing his intellectual honor; but Snyder's is surely the example with authority for us.)

In *The Old Ways*, a volume dedicated to the memory of Alan Watts, we hear the voice of the younger Snyder. His essay there, "The Yogin and the Philosopher" (contrasting those two options, with religion as a third way), describes the former as like the Pythagoreans and the ashram dwellers, with their special rules and diets. But the yogin, who is the option recommended to us, experiments. He speaks for the animals and the plants and all life.

Snyder's analyses of American culture are ruthless, but in some sense playful. The Americans are a nation of fossil-fuel junkies, though good-hearted and "the sweetest people on earth." Intellectually, Americans rely on a supermarket of adulterated ideas, like their adulterated foods. They have inadequate self-reliance and personal hardiness. A whole civilization of them is trying to get out of work. The one thing needful is to know how to flip over the growth energy of the West into a deep self-knowledge.

All his thought involves an enormous time frame: "I can't think about our situation in anything less than a forty-thousand-year time scale." The first arms race came with the development of bronze, or perhaps iron, weapons. And for hominid evolution we would have to work with a four-million-year scheme. His morality and philosophy are species-oriented, like those of other New Agers. Our race has a vertical axis of forty thousand years and a horizontal spread of three thousand languages and one thousand cultures.

He also has a New Age sense of space—for instance, what he calls biogeography. He belongs not to the United States, but to the San Juan Ridge country, and Nevada County, which he began to know by looking at the *Handbook of the California Indians* and the anthropological books of Kroeber. Biogeography means knowing the land with one's body, one's labor, one's walking. Maps, charts, and history are just the menu. Biogeography puts libraries and travel agencies out of business; it also destroys the pretensions of the nation-state.

SNYDER'S POETRY

Several of the contributors to *Dimensions of a Life* tell us what Snyder as a poet means to other poets. Alan Williamson places him in relation to the American landscape. He says that Snyder combined the coolness of Imagism and Objectivism with the traditions of Chinese poetry, and found therein the best way to describe the landscape of the American West, and so to achieve the sublime effects it calls for.

Scott McLean, on the other hand, says, "I had never heard a poetry that addressed the larger realms we awkwardly call 'nature' " with such precision, or with anything like this "absolute, hair-raising acceptance of its laws." McLean is an academic and was working on German idealist literature when he came across Snyder; so it was with German Romantic poets that he contrasted him. Nowadays, McLean sees human community as the other, equally important theme of Snyder's work. He ends his essay with a phrase that sums up the spirit of many contributions to *Dimensions of a Life*: "Nine bows, nine bows, dear Friend."

Jerome Rothenberg says that Snyder has made poetry an ecological survival tool—a vehicle to ease us into the future. This means that he is the poet for our postlapsarian or post-Marxist world—the world after our enchantment with Marxism ended. Brecht had taught us that to write of a tree is a sin in our time. But Snyder has shown that on the contrary, it is an exploration of matters central to survival.

Similarly, James Laughlin begins his essay, "There is no one alive whom I admire more than Gary." This is the keynote of the whole volume, because Snyder is the poet who has given us useful guidelines for what we can and must do. (This should remind us of Tolstoy's titles, like *What Then Must We Do?*)

However, this prophet's halo must not obscure the social fact that Snyder's primary identity is a verse-maker, and this has continued to be true despite all his changes and development. In this he is unlike

Gandhi and Paine—unlike even Tolstoy, since the latter found it necessary to renounce his art when he found his New Age faith. Being a poet and not a politician has made Snyder's social acceptance easier in some ways—made him less a target for assassination or execution.

Poetry has often been more variously and more intimately involved with New Age enthusiasm than fiction, and Snyder has found a way to combine his poetry with his teaching. It is a way the nature poets have known for centuries—Wordsworth is one of the great names in English—but it has features specific to our age that make it newly powerful.

All those who nightly take *darshan* of the animals on television, all those who look forward to the end of our civilization, who prepare their minds for catastrophe and for survival—all these are led in prayer and hymn, whether they know it or not, by the nature poets. And central among them stands Gary Snyder, all the more central for the traits of the rogue that blend with the solemnity of the priest.

His early essay "The Incredible Survival of Coyote," saying that the California Indians bequeathed modern poetry the coyote, announces Snyder's claim to be a rogue. The usual literature of the West, he said, was epic or heroic, serving expansion and exploitation, for the West ceased to be where a stabilized agriculture began. The literature he would write would be antiheroic, drawing on Indian and not white sources.

Thus the first thing about the Coyote tales that excited him was their Dada energy—they came leaping into a modern frame of reference, with no clear dualism of good and evil. "The trickster presents himself to us as an antihero." Coyote is the Old Man, but also the ancient Buddha. Without repudiating that idea, so far as I know, he has grown away from it. The friend of Wendell Berry is as much hero as antihero.

He has said that, after boyhood, he loved D. H. Lawrence first, as a poet, and then (a figure related to Lawrence) Robinson Jeffers. (Snyder was born in the year Lawrence died; there is a line of heritage there.) But T. S. Eliot also was a strong influence. Perhaps Snyder was thinking of Eliot when he compared poets with fungi, who can digest the symbol detritus of the culture, and thrive on what would poison others.

His 1974 collection, *Turtle Island*, makes us see ourselves more accurately on this continent of watersheds, plant zones, provinces, on which "the U.S.A." and its states and counties are inaccurate impositions. It contains some fine pieces of public poetry, like "Spel Against Demons," which says

> The release of Demonic Energies in the name of the People
> must cease
> Messing with blood sacrifice in the name of Nature
> must cease . . .

and pieces of imaginative history like "The Call of the Wild," which describes how

> The acid heads from the cities
> Converted to Guru or Swami,
> Do penance with shiny
> Dopey eyes, and quit eating meat.
> In the forests of North America
> The land of Coyote and Eagle
> They dream of India, of forever blissful sexless thighs.
> And sleep in oil-heated
> Geodesic domes, that
> Were stuck like warts
> In the woods.

Some of the most satisfying poems describe the dialectic between the old and the new America and his own position within it. No one, to my sense, dramatizes that dialectic so movingly. In "I Went into the Maverick Bar" he describes the bar in which he drinks double shots of bourbon, backed with beer, in some sense in disguise; his long hair tucked under his cap and his earring left in the car. He watches a couple dance, holding each other the way high school couples did in the 1950s. He talks to himself:

> That short-haired joy and roughness—America—and your stupidity:
> I could almost love you again.

But then,

> I came back to myself.
> To the real work, to "What is to be done."

He strikes the same note in "Dusty Braces":

> O you ancestors
> lumber schooners, big mustache
> long-handled underwear . . .
> you bastards
> my father
> and grandfathers, stiff-necked
> punchers, miners, dirt-farmers, railroad men . . .

These ancestors of his killed off the cougars and the grizzlies, and much of the life in California.

As a moral leader, Snyder is not much like Gandhi or Tolstoy, or Blake or Paine. His has been a more ordinary humanity, though transfused and transfigured. He has a greater share of that than any of his rivals for the role. He has also a more all-round intelligence. This is neither to his advantage or his disadvantage.

His path is smoothed, politically speaking, by his being a poet, and by his politics being ecological. But such smoothness is again not, for such a man, either to his advantage or to his discredit. It is in fact simply irrelevant. For us his achievement is to be there, in his ashram, an anomalous alternative, on the horizon, very much as Gandhi was for India.

onclusion

> Man is a skin-bound bundle of clutchings
> unborn and with no place to go
> balanced on the boundless compassion
> of diatoms, lava, and chipmunks.
>
> Gary Snyder

HOPE

What we have in our New Age is only a cleft in a mass of storm-clouds, through which a shaft of light gleams. It's the whole sky that is covered, and the clouds have that coppery gleam that means trouble—to put it mildly. The shaft of light is not much.

That is not a very brilliant metaphor, either; rather familiar and tired; but the weariness is part of its truth—any hope we have must be "against hope." We have already heard every promise, as well as every threat, and every possible analysis of our situation. So our sense of reality tells us to be realistic, to stop hoping. But that is because hope in itself belongs primarily to the naïve strains in our temperamental mix; it is restrained and restricted by the authoritarian and the systematic strains. Only by trusting to our naïveté, believing in the possibility of a New Age, can we recharge our energies.

To interpret the metaphor, this shaft of light is a shared sense of the holy, of spiritual value, a sense demonstrably living in us today, which has grown up around certain topics: the earth, the blue-green planet, the life on the earth, animal life, tribal life. Very strong feelings, charged with righteousness, have grown up around these concepts and their associated images, and pass from person to person, charging those personal relationships with the same righteousness. This is what we have, to set against our problems and against the strengths of earlier generations, and it is quite a valuable possession or state of being for those of us who have often in the past felt ourselves alienated from all holiness and righteousness.

Whether such a sense of the holy can develop into a religion—and whether such a religion can save us from the dangers we face— remains to be seen. But it is not impossible. That sense of the spirit acting in history that people feel during New Ages seems to be more poignant than ever in this one. We see around us so much behavior, good and bad, past and present, that defies normative comprehension, that exceeds prudent calculation and secular motivation. And we are trying to think about it.

For instance, spirituality is a word suddenly again in vogue today, as the reader may have already noticed. A book published in 1988, entitled *Spirituality and Society*, is one in a whole series of books promoting constructive postmodern thought, edited by David Gray Griffin. (Griffin's postmodernism is the world of thought that contrasts and conflicts with what he calls a modernism of thought dominant in Western civilization since the Renaissance; thus men like Locke and Adam Smith figure in Griffin's scheme as modernists.) His series promises constructive alternatives to other, deconstructive or eliminative, kinds of postmodernism to be found in, for instance, Wittgenstein, Heidegger, and Derrida. Two other volumes are called *The Reenchantment of Science* and *The Reenchantment of Art*.

The most recent volume in the same series, *Sacred Interconnections* (1990), says that this postmodern spirituality rejects both dualistic supernaturalism and atheistic nihilism. It goes with a new kind of religion. The book includes an essay by Richard Falk, who has often written powerfully about the nuclear danger. Falk uses the definition of modernism given above, and says, "In the late twentieth century, modernism retains control over political life, with a few relatively minor exceptions. But there is something new unfolding that challenges modernism from without and within." This loosening of the modernist grip on the political imagination Falk thinks of great significance. Perhaps we might also call it the loosening of the political grip on the general imagination. We have learned to expect challenge from politics and consolation from religion, but now we are getting the reverse.

The weakness of such thinking and hoping, so attractive in itself and so eloquently propounded all around us, is obvious enough—that it exists above all at the level of rhetoric and feeling. How can it get articulated with the action of our society, with its institutions, its powers? In fact, however, at the grass-roots level of *immediate* action, there are plenty of answers to that question. There are hundreds of organizations, and many of them seem to be thriving in every sense. The problem is only to decide which advice to follow, which group to join, which form of action to attempt. At a slightly more theoretical level, the question is more puzzling—the question of how to bring this spirituality together with traditional politics and traditional religion.

Some, of course, ask, Why should one need to reinvoke those old values? But surely most of us are not prepared to turn our backs on those agencies of truth, which still have immense potential. That we need not so renounce is what Snyder and his allies show us. Think of all "the Left" represents, and all it deserves in the way of support and criticism; think of all "the Church" represents, its treasuries of ritual, spirituality, the communion of saints. When the representatives of the New Age urge us to turn our backs on all that—as some do—we must surely say no.

But having turned toward those traditions, we have a number of choices to make, and everything depends on our making the right ones. The New Age in its narrower occultist and scientistic sense is a confluence of this new spirituality with traditional religion—but of the wrong kind, to put it crudely. The New Age in this other sense I have been defining is perhaps a confluence of this spirituality with traditional politics—and with a different kind of religion. At least that is what is suggested by a host of parallels and connections.

DIAGNOSIS

In the course of reading around this subject, I came accidentally upon more than one confirmation of the line of connections I was following. For instance, *Ecology in the Twentieth Century: a History*, Anna Bramwell's book of 1989, declares itself to be the first comprehensive treatment of the subject from a wider-than-one-nation perspective. It says that the three most important countries in that history have been Britain, Germany, and the United States—the three my argument has referred to. This is no mere coincidence, Bramwell suggests, because all three had large educated middle classes, with strong liberal and Protestant cultural traditions: the homeland of the Enlightenment and therefore a source of resistance to it. And thus many alternative ideas in medicine, such as sun worship, homeopathy, and vitamin therapy, originated in Germany.

Bramwell makes considerable reference to Ascona, surprisingly. Of course, though it has been ignored for over half a century, that place/idea must assume significance once historians investigate the ecological movement, which is what they now must do.

For, as Bramwell says, there is now an international political movement drawing on this tradition. The Green parties now poll between 7 percent and 11 percent of the national votes in Europe, and in the European Parliament there are (when Bramwell writes) more Green than Red deputies. In Britain three million people belong to ecological groups. The parties and constituencies emerge from a politically radicalized ecologism, an ecologism that had derived from the shift from mechanistic to vitalist thought at the end of the nineteenth century. But resource-scarcity economics has more recently given force and stringency to that old-fashioned holistic biology.

My own concern with the New Age is considerably broader than Bramwell's—I have admitted that it may seem amorphous. It is at least a very diverse phenomenon and concept. But the idea does remind us of a great congeries of people and activities that are potentially allied and potentially forceful. One comes across evidence of this in all sorts of places.

For instance, Catherine Albanese's *Nature Religion in America*, which came out in 1990, draws those same connections, though under the heading of "Nature Religion." Her subtitle is "From Algonkian Indians to the New Age," but she in fact begins with a mid-nineteenth-century singing group, the Hutchinson Family Singers, who between them exemplified many of these ideas. They began their life as New Hampshire Baptists—their parents having converted from Congregationalism—but became spiritualists. As singers they practiced "natural" music; as propagandists they sang for temperance and abolitionist gatherings, and at experimental communities like Brook Farm; they ate at Sylvester Graham's Vegetarian House in New York, and practiced botanic and herbal medicine and hydropathy; and as individuals, one renounced boots and shoes, another studied mesmerism and animal magnetism, and so on. The connectedness of their ideas is symbolized by one of their numbers, "Cold Water," which was sung in honor both of temperance and of the water cure. All these ideas, Albanese convincingly argues, are branches of natural religion. I would say they are all branches of a New Age movement.

Martin E. Marty contributes a foreword to *Nature Religion*; he is, in fact, the editor-in-chief of the Chicago History of Religions series, in which it appears. He says America has had two covenants: one biblical, and exemplified by Columbus and the Puritans; the other Enlightened, and exemplified by Washington and the Founding Fathers. They worship the God of Abraham and Isaac, and the god of Nature and Reason, respectively, and their covenants were grasped through churches and courthouses. Both were strikingly masculine, and marked by often obsessive concerns with contract and productivity, and by related stress diseases. However, Marty says, there has also been a counter-covenant, which is what we see in "nature religion," and which we associate with Native Americans, women, poets, healers, humorists, folksingers, and so on. This has significantly, savingly, softened the harshness of those primary covenants. Albanese and Marty are clearly pointing to the same phenomena of the New Age temperament as I am, though coming from a different angle.

Then in my reading I also met the phenomenon of Arthurianism, the interest in King Arthur and Camelot and Glastonbury, and in the historic and mythic roots of the legend. This popular interest has often been, in different periods, strangely suggestive of contemporary meanings, and remarkably persistent and recurrent in the realm of New Age activities. We have noted Blake's use of that myth. We also find, for instance, that George Bernard Shaw, G. K. Chesterton, and Laurence Housman supported a Glastonbury Festival in the 1920s. We know of the New Age connections between the first two and Gandhi, and Housman was another of Gandhi's warm admirers—but also an Arthurian revivalist.

On the whole, however, this seemed to be yet another mild and secondary version of New Age spirituality, and I decided not to devote any space to it. (It is perhaps worth saying that I have a full share of the systematizer's skepticism about things like Camelot: I am not well-disposed toward the fanciful and whimsical.) But then I read Geoffrey Ashe's *Camelot and the Vision of Albion*, in which I might have found much of my thinking done for me in advance.

Mr. Ashe's name was already familiar to me from my earlier work on Gandhi. His book *Gandhi* was one I made use of. What a strange coincidence, I thought, that he should also have written five books about Camelot—should have been, as I read on the book flap, the secretary of the 1966–71 project to excavate its site. But reading the book, I found that this was no accidental coincidence, and that his argument there, about Arthurian legends, returns to Gandhi, as its climax.

It begins by distinguishing Ashe's interest in the subject from that of the professional archaeologists, and by reflecting on the source of his and other people's nonprofessional interest. That interest, without any explicit ideology, was spiritually fervent, naïve as distinct from systematic. "The question which for me has hung over it all is: why? Where did so much enthusiasm spring from? Every allusion to the Cadbury project brought in inquiries, contributions, orders for literature, offers to help—dozens, hundreds of them, from both sides of the Atlantic. . . . Why do the authors of Arthurian books [as distinct from other authors] receive so many readers' letters?"

These letters were "personal," a word that has two faces. Being merely personal, such letters have no impact on the skeptical secularity of the systematic thinker (historian or archaeologist); but being profoundly personal, they are much more broadly significant than the latter's narrowly focused, impeccable research—his "contribution to the subject."

Ashe's own interest in Arthur and Camelot began when he read Chesterton's *Short History of England*, and then *The Battle for Britain in the Fifth Century*, by Trelawney Dayrell Reed. These books Ashe read in the 1940s. They are not, he says, authoritative on the subject in a scholarly way; but on the other hand, Ashe would never have been drawn to the subject by exact scholarship. (Clearly these words, scholarly and professional, are words that relate to our concept of the systematic, and are set in opposition to, and inferiority to, New Age naïveté.) "With all respect to exact scholars and professional archae-ologists, I think some of them know quite well that the Cadbury project would not have started when it did, if it had been left to them."

The subject first captured Ashe's mind, he thinks, by what it said about his country, England, which was then at war, though that sub-ject's implicit discourse was not in any ordinary way "patriotic" but almost the opposite. It tells how Arthur, having been king and made England great, was defeated and his kingdom ruined. And the story presents this ruin as right, although tragic. This was a mystical and politically subversive patriotism. He attributes the same motive to the fascination with the Arthurian felt by Chesterton, Charles Williams, and C. S. Lewis. "Behind [the story's] familiar surface I began to detect a mysterious offbeat quality, a transfiguring Otherness, far down in its almost hidden depths."

For instance, Chesterton began as a nineteenth-century New Ager, Ashe reminds us. He wrote a book on Blake, and admired Shelley, and was even more deeply influenced by Whitman, mainly as the voice of a direct, buoyant vision of reality. Like Blake he hated generalizations and was ardent for minute particulars. So he was hos-tile to the Fabians, and held that agnostic and atheist "free thought" was a prison cell of determinism (a kind of system). He thought older modes of thought (mythical and poetic) needed to be revived and preserved, and could not see the evolution of society in wholly pos-itive terms. Like Blake, he used myth to startle the reader into seeing freshly, free from the myopia of the conditioned response.

Chesterton's friend Hilaire Belloc also saw the Roman Catholic Church as the great representative of those older truths in the modern world. Belloc entered Parliament as a Liberal in 1906 but withdrew, embittered, in 1910, a progress that exactly paralleled Gandhi's se-quence of relations with the Parliament idea. Belloc and Cecil Chesterton wrote an attack on Parliament, *The Party System*. They saw Fabian ideas as dangerous because leading to bureaucracy, as they argued in *The Servile State*.

An article by Chesterton that strongly influenced Gandhi appeared in the *Illustrated London News* on September 18, 1909. Its New Age message will be clear from a couple of sentences about the Indian revolutionaries then in London (Gandhi's rivals for the leadership of the nationalist movement). "One of their papers is called *The Indian Sociologist*. Do the Indian youths want to pollute their ancient villages and poison their kindly homes by introducing Spencer's philosophy into them?" (Herbert Spencer was generally considered a classic case of the systematic mind.) Taking up his political work in India, soon after, Gandhi found his "true India," as Chesterton found his true England, far back in the legendary epoch of heroes and sages.

In fact, Ashe had become fascinated by Gandhi, and his anti-imperialism, long before he found the Arthurian subject. And it was only gradually that he realized the connection between them.

"A unifying phrase which seems helpful is 'collective mystique.' The Arthurian enchantment in all its forms can be so described. But so can other myths, hero-cults, and mass obsessions . . . such as Gandhi, a national hero who was the focus of a collective mystique in the twentieth century." Ashe admits the danger of cults that seem similar, like the "loathsome nationalist myths of the Hitler era." But he finds the risk worth taking: as he finds such truth as, for instance, Blake achieved worth the risk of nationalist mysticism.

I shall not follow Ashe as he develops his theory of the myth, fact, and legend of Arthur. What fascinates me is the way this clue led him in directions much the same as those I had followed. For instance, he says that the collective mystique of reinstatement is to be built into another modern nationalist program. "Arguably it has been the most successful programme in modern politics . . . I refer to Zionism, and the creation of the Republic of Israel. . . . Israel in its divinely appointed home is a psychological counterpart of the kingdom of Arthur." The kibbutzim succeeded because of the Zionist mystique of reinstatement, and the archaeological zeal of Israel is a proof of its mystical and mythical loyalties.

From this example, Ashe passes directly to that of Gandhism, in South Africa and then India. "The manifesto of his unique brand of nationalism was a pamphlet, *Hind Swaraj*," which Ashe then goes on to examine very much as an earlier chapter of this book does.

The next chapters, 9 and 10, begin Part III of Ashe's book, entitled "The Succession." It starts with Blake—"the only major British poet who has claimed to be a prophet in the Israelite style." Ashe finds that "Blake's serious thinking on revolutions—American, French, and otherwise—steadily approximates to the mystique as defined."

He quotes Blake's famous lines written against the rationalist philosophies of the eighteenth century, which are a very eloquent statement of the New Age faith.

> Mock on, Mock on Voltaire, Rousseau;
> Mock on, Mock on; 'tis all in vain!
> You throw the sand against the wind,
> And the wind blows it back again.
>
> And every sand becomes a Germ
> Reflected in the beams divine;
> Blown back they blind the mocking Eye,
> But still in Israel's path they shine.

Chapter 11 is entitled "The Dissentient Radicals," and deals with the
New Ages of the eighteenth and nineteenth centuries. Ashe begins
with "that laureate of the Left, Percy Bysshe Shelley." The latter's
major myth of regeneration, his counterpart to Blake's *Jerusalem*, is
the lyric drama *Prometheus Unbound*, composed in Italy in 1818–19.
Two of its last lines are

> To suffer woes which Hope thinks infinite;
> To forgive wrongs darker than death or night . . .

These are lines that Gandhi quoted to describe the spirit of his politics during his visit to England in 1930–31. This is a point worth
noting, for it was not Gandhi's wont to quote from the English poets.
Perhaps these lines were found for him by one of this secretaries; but
in any case they were an apt expression of what he wanted to say, and
that was because Shelley was a New Age poet.

In a letter to me, Ashe adds to the range of the topics and interests
so far listed as constituting Arthur's Return, the books recently written in service of the Goddess theory, notably the work of Monica Sjoo
and Marija Gimbutas, arguing for a matriarchal civilization and culture
that preceded the patriarchal one recorded in history.

Among other writers on the Arthurian material we find a member of
the Tolstoy family. Nikolai Tolstoy's Preface to *The Quest for Merlin*
ends with a quotation from the Russian mystical theologian Nikolai
Berdyaev. "History stands still and settles in the past. Only a prophetic vision of the past can set history in motion: and only a pro-

phetic vision of the future can bind the present and the past into a sort of interior and complete spiritual movement. Only a prophetic vision can re-animate the dead body of history and inform the lifeless static with the inner fire of spiritual movement."

This Tolstoy sees his subject in something of the archetypal terms employed by Mr. Ashe, rather than the moralistic terms used by his famous kinsman. Perhaps the latter would reproach him with Gandhi's words to Nilla Cram Cook, quoted before: "I wish you will forget Pythagoras, Bacchus, and the Mahabharata. Why should you brood over the past when you have to reenact the Mahabharata at the Ashram?" A prophetic vision, to be as grand a thing as Berdyaev claims, will surely have to combine some moral existentialism with the romantic splendor of the archetypes.

PROGNOSIS

On October 19, 1990, Boston Interface presented Matthew Fox, talking on "Action in the '90s," at the Watertown High School. Here one could see the New Age in action today. This was one of two hundred and fifty somewhat similar events that season presented by Interface, which is largely a volunteer organization, with two hundred part-time workers. Every seat in the hall was filled long before the event began, and everyone responded immediately to invitations by the speaker to, for instance, stand up and dance on the spot, to "breathe" together, to all whisper "here comes the image of God" (according to a rabbinic legend, in front of every human being as he/she walks forward come angels announcing him/her). These are familiar rituals of individual and small-group "Action in the '90s," and they are familiar to a movement with a large membership.

In front of the school, moreover, apparently quite unrelated, a bearded young man sat on the wall smiling and handing to everyone a leaflet entitled "An Open Letter to the Whole World," ornamented with flowers and illuminated capitals, and addressed "Dear Folks." He seemed to represent the New Age of the New Age—as far beyond the established Interface as Interface is beyond establishment liberalism.

His leaflet was an eminently sane and witty letter to the world—just mildly challenging to our suppositions about social conventions.

It read, in part: "Long ago I learned that the future is a legitimate room in our psychic mansion and we have at least as much right to hang out there as the bathroom, so I've been spending as much time as possible there for YEARS, learning everything I possibly could and struggling to put all my lessons together into a coherent form that addressed the urgency of our planetary situation.

"As it turns out, it seems I've been learning planetary midwifery. It seems humanity is ensconced in a prenatal condition. Humanity isn't born yet. The call went out for a midwife when the first nuclear bombs were detonated in 1945."

The letter ended with a name and address and an invitation to get in touch. "Art is prayer. The future and the past are eternity's lovers. The present is their embrace. Destiny is their child." This will remind us of earlier New Ages; some of us may think of Blake, others of Gusto Graeser (who wrote just such open letters to the whole world).

Inside the hall, meanwhile, we heard about new rituals of Action for larger groups—flower-pelting, snake-dancing on the beach—and how to overcome the two great obstacles to Action, which are fear (we must expand our hearts, take courage, take back from the Pentagon the idea of the warrior) and addiction (not only to drugs but to adultism, and all unequal relations, in which some have power and some do not). The Action of the nineties will include (as well as political radicalism) ecclesiagenesis, worshiping in circles, revisioning our bodies as rosaries or mandalas, and comedy-ecumenism—the weddings of churches.

Ideas, icons, myths, rituals—an endless proliferation of spiritual tools and weapons. All anyone has to do is take them and set to work.

POSTLUDE

It has of course occurred to me that not many people are likely to accept this invitation that I have been relaying. That is very understandable; the New Age is not even an ideology; and if one wants a full house at one's party—every chair occupied—one should devise some livelier entertainment than End-Time. However, the same thought was vividly present to those master spirits who, one might say, signed the little cards I have delivered, but that did not stop them. Apparently they had nothing better to do with their time.

One might say we get this invitation once a century. Of course it is being muttered all the time—in the muttering and stumbling of individual lives, if not in books. But all that is not generally audible. Those individual stumblings seem (to nearly all of us) to fit into a range between the brackets "comic to pathetic." Only rarely is the voice uplifted and our attention caught, so that we see the New Age truths as truths.

More than other periods, New Ages exist in our minds as promises, allures, and invitations. That is why those other periods have thus appropriated the counter-idea of reality. But in fact, of course, those promises have been kept sometimes, perhaps as often as other promises have been; and that allure, which gets embodied in art and in personal relations, is necessary to any eager or happy life. And if they should be unrealistic, how much of a condemnation is that? Our ordinary realism and our ordinary reality have been—how shall one put it?—deadly.

■ibliographical Notes

This is not an academic book: these notes are offered simply to help the reader find a source that is not fully identified in the text, when the information it offers is not generally available.

CHAPTER 1

The theory of temperaments, and the cultural psychology for an age of revolution, is developed in my *Cities of Light and Sons of the Morning*. My discussion of Tolstoy and Gandhi as New Agers began in *Tolstoy and Gandhi: Men of Peace*, and *The Origins of Nonviolence* and *The Challenge of the Mahatmas*. In fact this book takes up several themes and topics from earlier works of mine, or else develops the larger pattern into which they fit. For instance, *Mountain of Truth* presents a historical case of the naïve mentality asserting itself, while my discussions of adventure (in *Dreams of Adventure, Deeds of Empire* and *The Great American Adventure*, and other books) all have to do with the authoritarian mentality, concentrated upon confrontations of power. The present book is about the naïve mind and its quarrel with the systematic mind; the adventure books are about the third mentality.

Czeslaw Milosz's poem was published in the Spring-Autumn 1990 issue of *Antaeus*. *The Aquarian Conspiracy* is a book by Marilyn Ferguson that lists forms of New Age activity today in a fairly gleeful and triumphant mood.

Gandhi's autobiography, sometimes entitled *An Autobiography*, is sometimes to be found under the title *The Story of My Experiments with Truth*. Kipling's story "My Son's Wife" can be found in volume two of the Penguin edition of Kipling's short stories.

The comments on Wells by Sidney and Beatrice Webb can be found in *H. G. Wells: A Biography*, by Norman and Jeanne Mackenzie; and those on Morris by Hyndman and Engels in *William Morris: Romantic to Revolutionary*, by Edward P. Thompson.

CHAPTER 2

The story of Ascona is told in my *Mountain of Truth: The Counter-Culture Begins, Ascona 1900–1920*, though there is more material about Hanns and Otto Gross in *The Von Richthofen Sisters*. The main sources about Whiteway are Nellie Shaw's two books, *Whiteway, a Colony on the Cotswolds* and *A Czech Philosopher on the Cotswolds*. You can read about Chertkov's years in England in Alexander Fodor's *A Quest for a Non-violent Russia*.

The passages by Isabella Fyvie Mayo come from her notes to two of the Tolstoy pamphlets published by the Free Age Press: "The End of the Age" and "A Great Iniquity." The lines by Harold Monro come from his *Collected Poems*, with an introductory biography by F. S. Flint.

The book I mention by Geoffrey Ashe is *Camelot and the Vision of Albion*, which I return to in my last chapter. The autobiographical volume by Edward Carpenter is entitled *My Days and Dreams*. The main source for Thomas Davidson is *Memorials of Thomas Davidson*, edited by William Knight.

CHAPTER 3

The paragraph about Gandhi and the tactile sense comes from Bhikhu Parekh's *Colonialism, Tradition, and Reform* and Gandhi's own anecdotes come from his autobiography.

Israel Zangwill's remark about the ghetto is to be found in the article about him in the *Encyclopaedia Judaica*.

The quotation from F. S. Flint about Harold Monro comes from the latter's *Collected Poems*. Stephen Winsten's *Salt and His Circle*, with a preface by George Bernard Shaw, contains stories about Salt, Kate Joynes, and Shaw. The quotation from Michael Holroyd comes from his biography of Shaw.

CHAPTER 4

The 1912 pamphlet on Zionism quoted is by Israel Cohen, and is entitled *The Zionist Movement*. Martin Buber's 1930 essay on Gandhi can be found in his *Pointing the Way*; his *On Zion* has a useful introduction by Nathan Glatzer. Norman C. Bentwich's *For Zion's Sake* discusses Judah Magnes. The quotation from Conor Cruise O'Brien comes from his book *The Siege*.

The Walter Laqueur book is his *History of Zionism*; Maurice Samuel's book is *Harvest in the Desert*. The references to Gershom Scholem are to his autobiographical memoir, *From Berlin to Jerusalem*. The quotation from Samuel Goldreich can be found in Gideon Shimoni's *Jews and Zionism*.

I discuss Yeats and occultism in *Cities of Light and Sons of the Morning*. David S. Thatcher's *Nietzsche in England*, Tom Gibbons's *Rooms in the Darwin Hotel*, and Wallace Martin's *The New Age under Orage* are sources for A. R. Orage and Mitrinovic. Philip Mairet's *A. R. Orage: A Memoir* is the major primary source for Orage. The allusions to Alan Watts's ideas refer to his autobiography, *In My Own Way*.

Stanley Pierson's book is entitled *British Socialists*. The quotations attributed to Anna Kingsford and Edward Maitland are to their joint work, *The Perfect Way*. The major source for Robert Blatchford is Laurence Thompson's *Robert Blatchford: Portrait of an Englishman*.

Rudolf Laban (or von Laban) is discussed in *Mountain of Truth*.

CHAPTER 5

Edward P. Thompson's book is entitled *The Making of the English Working Class*. Burke's remark that this was an age of sophisters, economists, and calculators is quoted in D. F. Hawke's *Paine*. The quotations from Blake were taken from *The Portable Blake*, edited by

Alfred Kazin. Alexander Gilchrist's remark about Joseph Johnson is to be found in his *Life of William Blake*. The material about the lives of Paine, Coleridge, and the Wordsworths I took from recent biographies. The quotations of William St. Clair come from his book *The Godwins and the Shelleys*.

CHAPTER 6

The book about Blake entitled *Blake: Prophet Against Empire* is by David Erdman. Donald Worster's book about the history of ecology is entitled *Nature's Economy*. Henry Salt's autobiography is entitled *Seventy Years Among Savages*. Hazlitt's remarks about Owen were written for *The Examiner* in 1816; E. P. Thompson discusses them in *The Making of the English Working Class*

CHAPTER 7

D. H. Lawrence's "Study of Thomas Hardy" and "Introduction to These Paintings" are to be found in his posthumous volume, *Phoenix*; his "The Crown" and "Reflections on the Death of a Porcupine" are in *Phoenix II*. The accounts of Gary Snyder's early life and heritage are taken from *Gary Snyder: Dimensions of a Life*, edited by Jon Halper, and Snyder's *The Old Ways*. The first of those two includes Jerome Rothenberg's remarks on Snyder as a Wobbly Modernist, and Snyder's own comment that the Zen Buddhists of Japan have "got the message but not opened the envelope."

CHAPTER 8

Tolstoy's various reflections on the nature of art are summarized in my *Tolstoy and Gandhi: Men of Peace* and *The Origins of Nonviolence*. Gandhi describes his discussions with General Smuts, and reports Olive Schreiner's remarks about manual labor and writing, in his *Satyagraha in South Africa*. His letters to Nilla Cram Cook can be found in volume 54 of the *Collected Works of Mahatma Gandhi*. The two accounts I draw on of Calcutta in 1947 come from Robert Payne's *Life and Death of Mahatma Gandhi* and *Freedom at Midnight*, by Dominique Lapierre and Larry Collins. The context for the remarks by Rajagopalachari and Mountbatten is given in *Tolstoy and Gandhi: Men of Peace*.

CHAPTER 9

Gary Snyder's essay "Why Tribe?" can be found in his *Earth House Hold*. The mystery novel from which I took the description of the University of California campus is Susan Dunlap's *Diamond in the Buff*. John Todd's use of "New Age" occurs in his chapter in *Meeting the Expectations of the Land*, edited by Wes Jackson, Wendell Berry, and Bruce Colman.

CHAPTER 10

Aelred Graham's interview with Snyder is printed in his book *Conversations: Christian and Buddhist*.

Snyder's *The Old Ways* includes "The Yogin and the Philosopher," "The Politics of Ethnopoetics," "Rehabitation," and "The Incredible Survival of Coyote." The books that are named in what follows are also all by Snyder. The lines that begin "I pledge allegiance" are one of the "Little Songs for Gaia" in *Axe Handles*. "The Revolution in the Revolution in the Revolution" is from *Regarding Wave*. "Men who hire men" and "That silly ascetic Gautama" come from *Myths and Texts*. *Earth House Hold* includes "Buddhism and the Coming Revolution," which has some autobiographical remarks, and also "Passage to more than India" and "Suwa-no-se Island." There are several interesting interviews with Snyder in *The Real Work*; his remarks about quality are to be found there, and his comments on Americans as "fossil fuel junkies." *Turtle Island* includes the lines on the Maverick Bar, the "Spel Against Demons," "Dusty Braces," and "The Call of the Wild." *The Practice of the Wild* includes the remarks about the cruelty of nature.

Bibliography

Ashe, Geoffrey. *Camelot and the Vision of Albion*. New York: St. Martin's, 1971.

———. *Gandhi*. London: Heinemann, 1968.

Bentwich, Norman C. *For Zion's Sake*. Philadelphia: Jewish Publication Society of America, 1954.

Buber, Martin. *On Zion: The History of an Idea*. Introduction by Nathan Glatzer. New York: Schocken, 1973.

———. *Pointing the Way*. New York: Harper & Row, 1963.

Carpenter, Edward. *My Days and Dreams*. London: Allen and Unwin, 1916.

Cohen, Israel. *The Zionist Movement*. London: n.p., 1912.

Davidson, Thomas. *Memorials of Thomas Davidson*. Edited by William Knight. Boston: Ginn, 1907.

Dunlap, Susan. *Diamond in the Buff*. New York: St. Martin's, 1990.

Erdman, David. *Blake: Prophet Against Empire*. Princeton: Princeton University Press, 1969.

Ferguson, Marilyn. *The Aquarian Conspiracy*. Los Angeles: Jeremy P. Tarcher, 1981.

Fodor, Alexander. *A Quest for a Non-violent Russia*. Lanham, Md.: University Press of America, 1989.

Gandhi, Mohandas K. *An Autobiography*. Boston: Beacon, 1960.

————. *Collected Works of Mahatma Gandhi*, vol. 54. Ahmedabad: Navajivan, 1973.

————. *Satyagraha in South Africa*. Ahmedabad: Navajivan, 1928.

Gibbons, Tom. *Rooms in the Darwin Hotel*. Nedlands: University of Western Australia Press, 1973.

Gilchrist, Alexander. *The Life of William Blake*. London: Macmillan, 1863.

Graham, Aelred. *Conversations: Christian and Buddhist*. London: Collins, 1969

Green, Martin. *The Challenge of the Mahatmas*. New York: Basic Books, 1978.

————. *Cities of Light and Sons of the Morning*. Boston: Little Brown, 1972.

————. *Dreams of Adventure, Deeds of Empire*. New York: Basic Books, 1979.

————. *The Great American Adventure*. Boston: Beacon, 1984.

————. *Mountain of Truth: The Counter-Culture Begins, Ascona 1900– 1920*. Hanover, N.H.: University Press of New England, 1986.

————. *The Origins of Nonviolence*. University Park, Pa.: Pennsylvania State University Press, 1986.

————. *Tolstoy and Gandhi: Men of Peace*. New York: Basic Books, 1983.

————. *The Von Richthofen Sisters*. New York: Basic Books, 1974.

Halper, Jon, ed. *Gary Snyder: Dimensions of a Life*. San Francisco: Sierra Club Books, 1991.

Hawke, D. F. *Paine*. New York: Harper, 1974.

Holroyd, Michael. *Bernard Shaw*. Vol. 1: *The Search for Love*. New York: Random House, 1988.

Jackson, Wes, Wendell Berry, and Bruce Colman, eds. *Meeting the Expectations of the Land*. San Francisco: North Point, 1984.

Kazin, Alfred, ed. *The Portable Blake*. New York: Random House, 1946.

Kingsford, Anna, and Edward Maitland. *The Perfect Way*. London: Field & Tuer, 1890.

Lapierre, Dominique, and Larry Collins. *Freedom at Midnight*. Delhi: Vikas, 1976.

Laqueur, Walter. *A History of Zionism*. New York: Schocken, 1976.

Lawrence, D. H. *Phoenix: The Posthumous Papers of D. H. Lawrence*. Edited by Edward D. McDonald. New York: Viking, 1968.

―――. *Phoenix II*. Edited by Warren Roberts and Harry T. Moore. New York: Penguin, 1978.

Mackenzie, Norman, and Jeanne Mackenzie. *H. G. Wells: a Biography*. New York: Simon & Schuster, 1973.

Mairet, Philip. *A. R. Orage: A Memoir*, 2nd edition. New Hyde Park, N.Y.: University Books, 1966.

Martin, Wallace. *The New Age under Orage*. Manchester: Manchester University Press, 1967.

Mayo, Isabella Fyvie. Notes to Tolstoy's pamphlets, "The End of the Age" and "A Great Iniquity." Christchurch: Free Age Press, n.d.

Monro, Harold. *Collected Poems*. Introduction by F. S. Flint. London: Cobdan-Sanderson, 1933.

O'Brien, Conor Cruise. *The Siege: The Saga of Israel and Zionism*. New York: Simon & Schuster, 1986.

Parekh, Bhikhu. *Colonialism, Tradition, and Reform*. New Delhi: Sage, 1989.

Payne, Robert. *The Life and Death of Mahatma Gandhi*. London: Bodley Head, 1969.

Pierson, Stanley. *British Socialists*. Cambridge: Harvard University Press, 1979.

St. Clair, William. *The Godwins and the Shelleys*. New York: Norton, 1989.

Salt, Henry. *Seventy Years Among Savages*. New York: Seltzer, 1921.

Samuel, Maurice. *Harvest in the Desert*. Philadelphia: Jewish Publication Society of America, 1944.

Scholem, Gershom. *From Berlin to Jerusalem: Memories of My Youth*. Translated by Harry Zohn. New York: Schocken, 1988.

Shaw, Nellie. *A Czech Philosopher on the Cotswolds*. London: Daniel, 1940.

―――. *Whiteway, a Colony on the Cotsworlds*. London: Daniel, 1935.

Shimoni, Gideon. *Jews and Zionism*. Cape Town: Oxford University Press, 1980.

Showalter, Elaine. *A Literature of Their Own: British Women Novelists from Brontë to Lessing*. Princeton: Princeton University Press, 1976.

————. *Sexual Anarchy*. New York: Viking Penguin, 1990.

Snyder, Gary. *Axe Handles*. San Francisco: North Point, 1983.

————. *Earth House Hold*. New York: New Directions, 1969.

————. *Myths and Texts*. New York: Totem, 1960.

————. *The Old Ways*. San Francisco: City Lights, 1977.

————. *The Practice of the Wild*. San Francisco: North Point, 1990.

————. *The Real Work*. New York: New Directions, 1980.

————. *Regarding Wave*. New York: New Directions, 1970.

————. *Turtle Island*. New York: New Directions, 1974.

Thatcher, David S. *Nietzsche in England*. Toronto: Toronto University Press, 1970.

Thompson, Edward P. *The Making of the English Working Class*. Harmondsworth: Penguin, 1978.

————. *William Morris: Romantic to Revolutionary*. New York: Pantheon, 1977.

Thompson, Laurence. *Robert Blatchford: Portrait of an Englishman*. London: Gollancz, 1951.

Watts, Alan. *In My Own Way*. New York: Random House, 1972.

Winsten, Stephen. *Salt and His Circle*. New York: Hutchinson, 1951.

Worster, Donald. *Nature's Economy*. San Francisco: Sierra Club Books, 1977.

Index